First Edition

biography for beginners

Women Who Made a Difference

Laurie Lanzen Harris,
Editor

Favorable Impressions

P.O. Box 69015 • Pleasant Ridge, MI 48069

Laurie Lanzen Harris, *Editor*
Laurie Collier Hillstrom and Clarie A. Rewold, PhD, *Contributing Editors*
Dan R. Harris, *Senior Vice President, Operations*

Library of Congress Cataloging-in-Publication Data

Biography for beginners : women who made a difference / Laurie Lanzen
Harris, editor.—1st ed.
    p. cm.
    Includes bibliographical references and index.
    ISBN 978-1-931360-43-2 (alk. paper)
    1. Women—Biography—Juvenile literature. 2. Women heroes—Biography
—Juvenile literature. I. Harris, Laurie Lanzen. II. Title: Women who made a
difference.
    CT3207.B56 2011
    920.72—dc23
    [B]   2011017258

ISBN 978-1-931360-43-2

This book is printed on acid-free paper meeting the ANSI Z39.48 Standard.
The infinity symbol that appears above indicate that the paper in this book
meets that standard.

Printed in the United States
Manufactured by Thomson-Shore, Dexter, MI (USA); RMA574AJ392, May, 2011

Contents

Preface

Welcome to *Biography for Beginners: Women Who Made a Difference*. Since beginning the Biography for Beginners series in 1995, we have published six monographs in areas of high interest for young readers, including U.S. Presidents, world explorers, authors, inventors, African-American Leaders, and Colonial America and the Revolutionary War. Several years ago we surveyed librarians for additional areas of interest for young readers, and they suggested a volume on women of achievement.

The Plan of the Work

Like *Biography for Beginners: Presidents of the United States, World Explorers, and Inventors, African-American Leaders, and Colonial America and the Revolutionary War, Women Who Made a Difference* is written for early readers, ages 7 to 10. The volume is especially created for young students in a format they can read, understand, and use for assignments. The 60 entries are arranged alphabetically. Each entry begins with a heading listing the individual's name, birth and death dates, and a brief description of her importance to history. Boldfaced headings lead readers to information on birth, youth, growing up, education, marriage and family, and the nature of the individual's accomplishment.

Entries end with a list of World Wide Web sites. These sites have been reviewed for accuracy and suitability for use by young students. A bibliography of works used in the compilation of the entries is at the end of the Preface.

The entries also include portraits of the individual, as well as paintings, photos, and other illustrations to enhance the reader's understanding of the person's achievement.

Audience

This book is intended for young readers in grades two through five who are studying history for the first time. Most children will use this book to study one individual at a time, usually as part of a class assignment. Within the entries, the names of other individuals who appear in the volume are bold-faced, to act as a cross-reference. A Glossary of terms common to women's history appears at the end of the book. These Glossary terms appear in the text in bold-faced capitals.

Timeline of Women's Achievement

The volume contains a Timeline of Women's Achievement, to offer historical context to the biographical profiles.

Index

An Index covering names, occupations, and key words concludes the volume. The Index has been created with the young reader in mind, and therefore contains a limited number of terms that have been simplified for ease of research.

Our Advisors

Biography for Beginners: Women Who Made a Difference was reviewed by an Advisory Board that includes school librarians and public librarians. The thoughtful comments and suggestions of all the Board members have been invaluable in developing this publication. Any errors, however, are mine alone. I would like to list the members of the Advisory Board and to thank them again for their efforts.

Nancy Margolin   McDougle Elementary School
                  Chapel Hill, NC

Deb Rothaug   Pasadena Elementary
                  Pasadena, NY

Laurie Scott   Farmington Hills Community Library
                  Farmington Hills, MI

Joyce Siler   Westridge Elementary School
                  Kansas City, MO

Your Comments Are Welcome

Our goal is to provide accurate, accessible biographical information for early readers. Please write or call me with your comments.

Acknowledgments

I would like to thank the staffs of the many organizations who provided photos and illustrations for the volume, as well as the Library of Congress. Thank you to Dan Harris for outstanding design and layout.

Bibliography

This is a listing of works used in the compilation of the volume. Most of the works cited here are written at the high school level and are generally beyond the reading level of early elementary students. However, many librarians consider these reliable, objective points of departure for further research.

Columbia Encyclopedia, 2005 ed.

Compton's Encyclopedia, 2005 ed.

Encyclopedia Britannica, 2010 ed.

Laurie Harris, Editor and Publisher
Favorable Impressions

Introduction

The sixty women profiled in this volume come from all eras of history, and all areas of life. They have distinguished themselves in many areas of achievement, and in nearly every case, were the first of their gender to do so. Whether in politics and social reform, medicine and science, literature and the arts, or education and athletics, these women had courage, conviction, and the courage of their convictions to confront prejudice, discrimination, hatred, and even physical violence in the pursuit of equality, and the right to achieve in whatever field they chose. Along the way, they broke barriers for later generations of women, whose freedom to be educated, to vote, own propery, control their own money, as well as to pursue their dreams, owe much to these pioneers.

Leaders in Politics, Social Reform, and Human Rights

There is a great difference in the backgrounds of the women profiled here. Some were born to royalty, and were among the wealthiest women in history; some were born in slavery, and were desperately poor. The earliest entry is on the Egyptian leader **Hatshepsut**, the first important female ruler in history, and one of only three women in history to reign as Pharaoh. She is followed by the final Pharaoh of Egypt, **Cleopatra**, the most powerful female of her time. Nearly 1,500 years later, **Joan of Arc**, acting on what she claimed was the word of God, helped unite the French in battle. In the same century, **Isabella I** helped unite Spain, and paid for the voyages of Columbus, leading to the discovery of the New World. **Elizabeth I** of England was the most powerful woman of her era as well, and used her intelligence and determination to unite her country and establish a Golden Age of English history that now bears her name. **Catherine the Great** of Russia used her considerable powers to expand the boundaries of her country and consolidate the strength of the Russian monarchy.

In the United States, the ideals of freedom and equality motivated former slaves **Sojourner Truth** and **Harriet Tubman** to fight first for the cause of abolition and equal rights for African-Americans, then to join forces with other abolitionists to fight for a woman's right to vote. Three of the most important figures in women's history, **Lucretia Mott, Susan B. Anthony,** and **Elizabeth Cady Stanton**, were first active in the cause of abolition, then joined forces with Truth, Tubman, and others to mount the fight for women's suffrage. Through their political, organizational, and oratorical strengths, they created a powerful movement that, over the course of seventy-five years, led to the Constitutional amendment that guaranteed American women the right to vote. In Great Britain, **Emmeline Pankhurst** led the fight for women's suffrage, and faced harassment, arrest, and imprisonment in her quest.

Jane Addams, social reformer and champion of the settlement house movement, was also a staunch supporter of a woman's right to vote, and was among the first women of her era to defy societal convention and pursue a career, devoting her life to helping the poor of Chicago, and advocating for world peace, for which she won the Nobel Peace Prize. **Mary McLeod Bethune** worked to achieve equality for African-Americans in education, then devoted herself to the fight for Civil Rights. A champion of that movement, **Rosa Parks**, defied segregationist laws and forced the nation to confront racial bigotry in the South. **Coretta Scott King** worked tirelessly on behalf of Civil Rights for African-Americans, organizing the fight for equal rights for all. The rights of the disabled were transformed by **Helen Keller,** whose achievements and advocacy were the first steps in ending centuries of discrimination, ignorance, and indifference in the treatment of those with disabilities.

In the 1930s, First Lady **Eleanor Roosevelt** defied tradition to broaden the scope and responsibilities of the wife of the U.S. President. Because her husband, Franklin Delano Roosevelt, could not walk, she spent the twelve years of his administration traveling the country, listening to the people and devoting herself to helping them. After her husband's death, she became U.S. delegate to the United Nations, where she was the main force behind the Universal Declaration of Human Rights. In the 1940s, **Margaret Chase Smith** of Maine began a political career that broke more barriers for women, becoming the first woman elected to both the U.S. House and Senate, and the first to be nominated for the Presidency from a major party. **Sandra Day O'Connor** broke barriers of her own, in politics and the law. She was the first woman to be elected the majority leader of a state senate, and, in 1981, became the first woman to serve on the U.S. Supreme Court. **Condoleezza Rice's** career contains a number of "firsts," including first African-American woman to serve as U.S. Secretary of State. Another former First Lady, **Hillary Clinton**, established other notable firsts: she is the only First Lady ever elected to the Senate, the first woman to be elected statewide from the state of New York, and only the second woman to run for the presidential nomination for a major U.S. political party.

Women outside the U.S. have also continued to forge new paths for women in their own countries. In 1979, **Margaret Thatcher** became the first woman to serve as Prime Minister of Great Britain, as well as the first woman to lead a major world power in the modern era. In India, **Mother Teresa** devoted her life to bringing dignity to the poor and sick of Calcutta, which earned her the Nobel Peace Prize. In Burma, **Aung San Suu Kyi** continues her heroic efforts to bring democracy and peace to her beleaguered nation, for which she, too, was awarded the Nobel Peace Prize.

Pioneers of Science, Medicine, and Innovation

Many of the women in this volume have distinguished themselves in science, medicine, and innovation. **Elizabeth Blackwell** fought prejudice every step of her career to became the first woman to earn a medical degree from an American medical school, and to found the first medical school for women. **Florence Nightingale** fought prejudice to develop nursing as a profession, establish the first nursing school, and write medical manuals used around the world. As the founder of the American Red Cross, **Clara Barton** was both a health care provider and tireless advocate for those in need everywhere, whether victims of war or natural disaster. **Marie Curie** is one of the most important scientists in history: the first woman to receive a doctoral degree in France, and the first person to win two Nobel Prizes, while developing radiation therapy as a major medical tool. As scientists and inventors, **Rachel Fuller Brown** and **Elizabeth Lee Hazen** collaborated on the creation of the first anti-fungal antibiotic. **Gertrude Elion**, also a scientist and inventor, created life-saving drugs to treat cancer and other diseases, for which she won the Nobel Prize. Another Nobel

Prize winner, **Barbara McClintock,** is one of the most important geneticists of the 20th century, who broke barriers in research and academics to achieve scientific breakthroughs still important today.

Rachel Carson's research into DDT and other pesticides helped spark the development of the modern environmental movement. **Margaret Mead's** studies into the cultures of the peoples of the South Pacific islands introduced Americans to the field of anthropology, and to a better understanding of themselves as well. **Jane Goodall's** 50-year study of the chimpanzees of Africa has led to a greater understanding of the plight of animals and environments threatened by pollution or human intervention.

The twentieth century has been a time of great innovation and exploration for women, beginning with **Amelia Earhart**, whose courage and expertise led her to become one of the finest aviators of her time. As the Space Race between the U.S. and Soviet Union escalated, **Valentina Tereshkova** became the first woman to journey into space. It took nearly 20 years for the U.S. to bridge that gender gap, but in 1983, when **Sally Ride** became the first American woman to soar into space, she inspired the aspirations and dreams of a generation of girls. In 1994, **Mae Jemison** became the first African-American woman to fly in space. And it isn't only the skies that witnessed the continued achievements of women. Marine biologist and oceanographer **Sylvia Earle** has championed the importance of the oceans, especially their health and the dangers of pollution, to the people of the world.

Authors, Artists, and Musicians

The authors covered in this volume also represent a number of "firsts" for women. Poet **Anne Bradstreet** was the first American woman to publish a book; she was followed by **Phillis Wheatley**, who was the first African-American to publish a book in the U.S. **Louisa May Alcott** was the first author of realistic fiction for young readers, whose *Little Women* has influenced generations of female writers. **Harriet Beecher Stowe's** *Uncle Tom's Cabin* introduced Americans, and the world, to the horrors of slavery, becoming one of the most influential books of the 19th century. Though her works would prove just as influential, **Emily Dickinson** preferred the most private of lives; unbeknownst to anyone, she created poetry of depth and astonishing creativity that has made her one of the finest poets of the modern era. At the end of the 19th century, **Nellie Bly** became one of the first female journalists in the nation, writing articles that brought to light the horrors of slums, mental asylums, and political corruption. In the 20th century, **Pearl S. Buck** became a world-renowned author, whose books on China won her the Nobel Prize in Literature, the first American woman to be so honored. Later in the century **Toni Morrison** became the first African-American woman to win the Nobel in Literature, and her novel *Beloved* was named the best book of the last 25 years.

Clara Schumann was a gifted composer and virtuoso pianist before her marriage to Robert Schumann, whose reputation overshadowed her own. In recent decades, music historians have restored her reputation as one of the greatest musicians of her era. **Mary Cassatt** became one of the first major painters of the Impressionist school, breaking barriers for women by choosing to have a career as an artist, and accomplishing that goal in a male-dominated profession. **Georgia O'Keeffe** is considered one of the most important artists of the 20ᵗʰ century and one of the most successful women artists of all time. **Marian Anderson** broke racial barriers to become the first African-American to perform with the Metropolitan Opera, and, when denied the right to perform at Constitution Hall in Washington D.C. because of her race, performed a legendary concert on the steps of the Lincoln Memorial. After creating the Vietnam War Memorial in Washington D.C. as a college student, **Maya Lin** has gone on to build a career as one of the most important artists of the current era.

In the field of athletics, the career of **Babe Zaharias Didrikson** is astonishing. An outstanding athlete in many sports, she was also an Olympic champion and one of the finest golfers, male or female, who every played the sport. **Wilma Rudolph** overcame both polio and racial bigotry to win three Olympic gold medals and become one of the finest track stars in history. **Jackie Joyner Kersee** inspired a generation of young girls with her outstanding achievements in track and field, winning six Olympic medals in a career that has gained her the reputation as the finest female athlete of the 20ᵗʰ century.

In these life stories, one is struck, and humbled, by the incredible courage of each of these women, who faced, at the very least, prejudice and scorn, and at the very worst, threats to their own personal safety in pursuit of their goals. This volume is dedicated to that courage, and to women of achievment everywhere, who inspire each new generation in the aspirations so eloquently outlined by Elizabeth Blackwell 100 years ago:

"I do not wish to give women first place, still less a second one—but the most complete freedom to take their true *place, whatever it may be."*

Laurie Lanzen Harris, Editor & Publisher
Favorable Impressions

Women Who Made a Difference

Abigail Adams

1744–1818

American Patriot and Wife of President John Adams

ABIGAIL ADAMS WAS BORN on November 11, 1744, in Weymouth, Massachusetts. Her name at birth was Abigail Smith. When she was born, Massachusetts was one of 13 American colonies that were ruled by the king of England. Abigail's father, the Reverend William Smith, was a minister and community leader. Her mother, Elizabeth Quincy Smith, was a homemaker. Abigail had an older sister, Mary. She also had a younger brother, William, and a younger sister, Elizabeth.

The first home of John and Abigail Adams, in Quincy, Massachusetts, is on the right. John Adams was born in the house on the left.

ABIGAIL ADAMS GREW UP in a rural area. Poor health kept her from being very active as a girl. She spent much of her time reading and writing letters to family and friends.

ABIGAIL ADAMS WENT TO SCHOOL at home. Like most other girls of her time, she did not have a formal education. Girls were expected to become wives and mothers. Abigail mostly learned cooking, sewing, and other skills she would need in these roles. But she was very bright and curious about the world. She read many books in her father's library to expand her knowledge. Later in her life, she became a big supporter of equal education for women.

MARRIES JOHN ADAMS: On October 25, 1764, Abigail Smith married John Adams. John was a well-educated young lawyer. He hoped to get involved in politics. They bought a farm in Braintree (later renamed Quincy), Massachusetts. Abigail gave birth to five children over the next ten years: daughters Abigail ("Nabby") and Susanna, and sons John Quincy, Charles, and Thomas. Sadly, Susanna died before reaching the age of two.

During the early years of their marriage, John often lived and worked in the city of Boston. While he was away, Abigail took care of the children and ran the farm. It was unusual for women to conduct business in those days. But Abigail bought and sold land and livestock, hired farm employees, and supervised the planting and harvesting of crops. She felt proud of her role in supporting the family. "I hope in time to have the reputation of being as good a Farmess as my partner has of being a good Statesman," she wrote.

SUPPORTS WOMEN'S RIGHTS: Whenever they were apart, Abigail and John wrote long letters to each other. Many of these letters discussed the growing tensions between the American colonies and England. Beginning in 1764, English leaders had tried to put the colonies under tighter control. They charged high taxes on products that people in America needed, like sugar, paper, and tea. Many colonists felt that it was not fair for England to charge them taxes without giving them a say in government.

Some colonists, known as Loyalists, wanted to work out their differences and remain part of England. But many others, known as Patriots, wanted to break away from England and form a new country. In 1774, leaders of the 13 colonies got together in Philadelphia, Pennsylvania, to decide what to do. John Adams was chosen to represent Massachusetts at this meeting of the Continental Congress.

Abigail wrote letters to John during his time in Philadelphia.

This is the kitchen at the Adams' house in Quincy.

In one famous letter, she asked her husband to expand legal rights for women. Abigail argued that women should be allowed to own property and get a good education. "In the new code of laws which I suppose it will be necessary for you to make, I desire you would remember the ladies and be more generous and favorable to them than your ancestors," she wrote. "Do not put such unlimited power into the hands of husbands. Remember, all men would be tyrants if they could."

THE REVOLUTIONARY WAR: The tensions between England and the American colonies eventually exploded into war. The fighting started in Lexington, Massachusetts, on April 19, 1775. Although the war did not threaten the Adams farm, Abigail found even distant battles upsetting. "The constant roar of the cannon is so distressing that we cannot eat, drink, or sleep," she noted. Abigail also struggled to deal with shortages of goods and epidemics of disease during this time.

On July 4, 1776, John Adams and other members of the Continental Congress decided to separate from England and form a new nation. They issued the Declaration Of Independence to inform the king of their plans. General George Washington led the Continental Army into battle against British troops.

In 1778 John Adams traveled to France. He helped convince the French government to give the Americans money and supplies to fight England. Abigail missed her husband terribly during his time in France. They continued writing letters, but it took months for mail to go across the ocean.

With assistance from France, the Americans finally managed to win the war. On September 3, 1783, John Adams and other Americans signed a peace agreement with England. The Treaty Of Paris recognized the United States as an independent nation. The new country stretched from the Atlantic Ocean west to the Mississippi River, and from the Canadian border south to Florida.

In 1784, Abigail and the children joined John in Europe. By this time, Abigail and her husband had not seen each other in five years. The Adams family lived in France for a while, then moved to England. Abigail served as an advisor to her husband and as a hostess of official gatherings during this time.

BECOMES FIRST LADY: The Adams family returned to the United States in 1788. The new country created a Constitution and formed its own government. George Washington was elected as the first president of the United States. John Adams served as Washington's vice president from 1789 to 1797.

After Washington decided to retire, John Adams was elected the second president of the United States in 1797. As First Lady, Abigail hosted social and political gatherings and advised her husband on important issues. Many people knew how much President Adams counted on the First Lady's advice and support. They often went to Abigail when they wanted something from the President. Political opponents sometimes called Abigail "Mrs. President" because she held so much influence.

During John Adams's term as President, the nation's capital moved from Philadelphia to Washington, D.C. The area around Washington was mostly wilderness at this time. Adams was the first President to live in the White House. Abigail had to entertain official guests when the building was not even finished yet.

REMEMBERED IN LETTERS: John Adams lost the election of 1801 to Thomas Jefferson. Abigail and her husband retired to their Massachusetts farm. They spent the next 17 years there together. Abigail suffered from poor health for much of this time. She died at home on October 28, 1818.

Abigail's friends and family saved many of the letters that she wrote during her lifetime. In 1848, one of her grandsons published a book of these letters. It was the first book ever published about a First Lady.

ABIGAIL ADAMS'S HOME AND FAMILY: Abigail lived in Quincy, Massachusetts, until her death in 1818. Six years later, her eldest son, John Quincy Adams, was elected President of the United States. Abigail thus became the first American woman ever to be the wife of one president and the mother of another. She was the only woman to hold this distinction until Barbara Bush in 2000.

HER LEGACY: Abigail Adams is admired for commitment to her family, and the cause of the Revolution. Her letters reveal that she was a bright and capable woman. She was ahead of her time in many ways. For example, she considered herself equal to her husband and freely advised him on many topics. She also argued in favor of women's rights and ending slavery. Her letters provide a vivid picture of the politics and personalities of the Revolutionary War era.

WORLD WIDE WEB SITES

http://www.whitehouse.gov/history/firstladies/aa2.html

http://www.firstladies.org/biographies/firstladies.aspx?biography=2

Jane Addams

1860-1935

American Social Reformer and Activist

Founder of Hull House Who Helped Create the Settlement House Movement
First American Woman to Win the Nobel Peace Prize

JANE ADDAMS WAS BORN on September 6, 1860, in Cedarville, Illinois. Her full name was Laura Jane Addams, but she was always called Jane. Her father, John Huy Addams, was a successful business-man and state senator. Her mother, Sarah Weber Addams, died when Jane was two years old. Jane was the youngest of five children.

JANE ADDAMS GREW UP in Cedarville. She was very close to her father, and shared his beliefs in **ABOLITION**—ending slavery. From a very young age, she felt a great compassion for poor people, and wanted to devote her life to improving their lives. Jane also suffered from tuberculosis of the spine. It was a very painful condition and left her with a curved back.

JANE ADDAMS WENT TO SCHOOL at the local schools. She attended Rockford College in Illinois, and was an excellent student. After she graduated from college in 1881, she went to medical school briefly. But she suffered terrible back pain from her earlier illness. She decided to have back surgery, and then spent many months recovering.

By 1883, she was better, and went on a trip to Europe with friends. She enjoyed hiking, seeing the countryside, and visiting museums. But the poverty of the people in the large cities overwhelmed her. She returned to the U.S. and thought about what she had seen, and what she could do.

Addams faced another problem, too. At that time, women were supposed to become wives and mothers. She wanted much more: she wanted to become a social reformer, to change society and help poor people.

Addams returned to Europe in 1887 with her good friend Ellen Gates Starr. They visited Toynbee Hall, the world's first "settlement

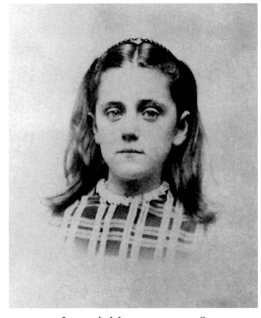

Jane Addams at age 8.

9

house" in London. Settlement houses were places where the poor could find help with food, housing, education, and other social services.

FOUNDING HULL HOUSE: Addams and Starr returned to the U.S. determined to begin a settlement house. Addams bought a shabby mansion in one of the poorest sections of Chicago, which was home to a large immigrant population.

Addams called it Hull House, for its former owner, Charles Hull. It opened in 1889, and soon became the most famous and successful settlement house in the world.

Addams and her staff lived in the house, to truly share in the lives of the people they served. She set to work creating programs to help the poor of the neighborhood in many ways. She provided food, health care, and help with housing.

Addams had a special interest in the health and well being of children. In many families, both parents worked all day, and there was no one to care for their children. Addams created a nursery school and kindergarten so that the young children could be cared for. She developed after school programs so that older children had somewhere to go, and something to do. She offered job training to all, and gave special care to immigrant families, offering courses in English and applying for U.S. citizenship. She provided a library, plays, and concerts.

Addams did important work throughout the community. She helped people find work, and she fought for decent working conditions. She took on the owners of "sweatshops." Those are factories where men, women, and children worked under terrible conditions. Addams forced them to improve. She also helped pass the first

Hull House circa 1909.

laws in the state that determined how factories should be run. She even became a garbage inspector so that streets were cleaner, and healthier, for the residents. And she helped establish public parks and the very first public playground in Chicago.

Addams's interests expanded to include the public schools, and in 1905 she was named to the Chicago Board of Education. Soon, she was chair of the School Management Committee. She was named the first president of the national Conference of Charities and Corrections.

Addams and her staff also helped people when they had problems with the police or the law. She saw first-hand how poor people, especially children, were often denied justice. At that time, there were no separate laws or courts for children. When children were charged with crimes, they were tried in court as adults. To fight that,

Children standing on the grounds of Hull House, 1908.

Addams helped create the very first juvenile court in the world.

Hull House was a tremendous success. In its first year alone, its programs helped 50,000 people. In its second year, that number doubled, as Hull House hosted 2,000 people each week. To raise money, Addams gave speeches in Chicago and around the country. Soon, cities nationwide were creating settlement houses based on her ideas. People from other countries came to Chicago to study Hull House so they could develop programs of their own. Addams became a famous and beloved figure all over the world.

OTHER POLITICAL ACTIVITIES: In the early 20th century, Addams became involved in other social and political activities. She fought for women's right to vote, and for the establishment of unions to help workers gain decent pay and working conditions. She was also one of the first members of the NAACP, the National Association for the Advancement of Colored People. That is an organization devoted to equal rights for African-Americans.

The cause most important to Addams was world peace. She was an outspoken supporter for peace, and when World War I began in 1914, she spoke out against it. She did not want the U.S. to become involved in the war. She argued that the nations of Europe should stop fighting and find a peaceful solution.

When the U.S. entered the war in 1917, Addams was harshly

Addams with other delegates of the Women's Peace Party in 1915. She is seated in the front row, second from the left.

criticized for her views. The once-beloved figure faced the charge that she was not a loyal American.

Addams held fast to her beliefs. She became president of the Women's International League for Peace and Freedom. She spoke out against war all over the world. After Germany surrendered and World War I ended, many of the country's children were starving. Addams spoke out again, arguing that the U.S. should help starving children, wherever they are. Once again, she was condemned by some for her views.

After the war, some Americans were denounced for their political beliefs. Addams defended them. Again, she was attacked for her views, and even called a traitor. She was wounded by the criticism, but did not change her mind. She traveled to Europe, where she was still a honored figure.

WINNING THE NOBEL PEACE PRIZE: In 1931, Jane Addams was awarded the Nobel Peace Prize. That is one of the most important awards in the world. It is given each year to an individual, or individuals, who work for peace. She was the first American woman ever to receive the award.

LATER YEARS: Addams managed Hull House for 46 years. Under her direction, it expanded to cover an entire block in Chicago. In the mid-1930s, her health began to fail. Jane Addams died in Chicago on May 21, 1935, of heart disease and cancer. She was mourned around the world. Thousands came to her funeral in Chicago.

Jane Addams at a "Votes for Women" demonstration in Chicago, 1912.

JANE ADDAMS HOME AND FAMILY: Addams never married or had children. She lived most of her adult life at Hull House, which was, in most respects, her true home.

HER LEGACY: Jane Addams is remembered for her devotion to the poor of the world, for establishing the settlement house movement, and for her tireless work on behalf of world peace and of the right of all citizens, male and female, rich and poor, to live in peace and dignity. At a time in history when women's roles were limited by society, she blazed a new path. She showed how women could create new roles for themselves and how they could outline and achieve what they wished, based on their own vision and determination.

WORLD WIDE WEB SITES

http://www.swarthmore.edu/Library/peace/Exhibits/janeaddams/

http:// nobelprize.org/nobel_prizes/peace/laureates/.../addams-bio. html

http://www.lkwdpl.org.wihohio/adda-jan.htm

Louisa May Alcott

1832-1888
American Author and Creator of *Little Women*

LOUISA MAY ALCOTT WAS BORN on November 29, 1832, in Germantown, Pennsylvania. Her parents were Bronson and Abigail Alcott. Bronson was a philosopher and teacher and Abigail was a homemaker. Louisa was the second of four girls. Her sisters were named Anna, Elizabeth, and May. The family moved to Boston, Massachusetts when Louisa was a baby.

LOUISA MAY ALCOTT GREW UP in a loving family that valued education, hard work, and close family ties. Louisa and her sisters were very close to their parents and their parents' friends. Her parents were firm believers in several social reforms of their time, and their daughters were raised in those beliefs. They were fervent **ABOLITIONISTS**, believing that slavery was morally wrong. They also believed in **WOMEN'S SUFFRAGE,** a woman's right to vote.

Bronson Alcott belonged to a group of philosophers called "Transcendentalists." Among the Alcott's family friends were famed American philosophers Ralph Waldo Emerson and Henry David Thoreau. As a young girl, Louisa read the books in Emerson's library, and tutored his daughter, Ellen. She went on long nature walks with Thoreau, learning about the natural world around her.

Louisa's mother, called "Marmee," was one of the most important influences in her life. Marmee encouraged Louisa's early talent in writing, and each of the sisters wrote regularly in a journal. Her mother told Louisa "to make observations about our conversations and your own thoughts. It helps you to express them and to understand yourself." Louisa kept her journal throughout her life. She also began to write plays that were performed by her sisters, as well as poems and stories.

When Alcott was growing up, women's roles were largely limited to wife and mother. But Marmee told her girls they could do much more. She encouraged them to become educated, and to choose their own path in life. Perhaps most importantly, Louisa's parents taught their children the value of self-reliance and charity toward others.

Like Jo in *Little Women,* Louisa was a tomboy. She loved to climb trees, run, climb fences, and be outside. "No boy could be my friend till I had beaten him in a race," she said.

The Alcott family lived in many different places while Louisa was growing up. They moved 22 times in 30 years, mostly between Boston and nearby Concord, Massachusetts. The family lived for awhile as part of a community called Fruitlands, but when that failed, they moved again. Finally, in 1857, Bronson Alcott bought a home in Concord, Orchard House, where they lived until 1877.

LOUISA MAY ALCOTT WENT TO SCHOOL at home, educated by her father. He believed that knowledge came from within each individual. For him, the teacher's role was to nurture the love of learning in each student.

Louisa wrote of him, "My father taught in the wise way which unfolds what lies in the child's nature, as a flower blooms, rather

"Orchard House," Louisa May Alcott's home, Concord, Mass.

than crammed it, like a Strasbourg goose, with more than it could digest."

Unfortunately, Bronson Alcott's theories of education were not widely accepted. He wasn't able to make enough money as a teacher, and the family was often quite poor.

GOING TO WORK: Louisa and her sisters began to work as teenagers, to help out the family. "I will do something by and by," she claimed. "Don't care what, teach, sew, act, write, anything to help the family. And I'll be rich and famous before I die, see if I won't!"

From the age of 15, Louisa took many different jobs, working as a teacher, seamstress, servant, and other jobs. She continued to write, too, and began to sell her poetry and short stories to magazines.

MAKING A LIVING AS A WRITER: Soon, Louisa's income as a writer was enough to support her family. In 1854, her first book, *Flower Fables,* was published.

In 1858, tragedy struck the Alcott family. Louisa's sister Elizabeth died, and the family mourned her loss deeply. Three years later, in 1861, the Civil War began. Louisa wanted to help, so she moved to Washington, D.C. and became a nurse. She wrote letters home to her family about her experiences. These were published as a book, called *Hospital Sketches.* While treating soldiers during the war, Alcott came down with typhoid fever. It left her weakened for the rest of her life.

After the war was over in 1865, Alcott became the editor of a children's magazine, *Merry's Museum.* In 1867, her publisher asked her to write "a book for girls." Alcott wasn't sure about the assignment. "I plod away, though I don't enjoy this sort of thing," she wrote in her journal. "Never liked girls or knew many, other than my sisters. But our queer plays and experiences might be interesting, though I doubt it."

LITTLE WOMEN: Alcott wrote *Little Women* in just three months. When it was published, in 1868, it was a sensation. Readers everywhere, young and old, thrilled to the story of the March girls. Alcott based the lives of her characters on her own family. She was the model for Jo, Anna appeared as Meg, Elizabeth was Beth, and May was Amy. Bronson and Abigail appear as Mr. March and Marmee.

Much to Alcott's surprise, the world took the March family to their hearts. Readers loved the way each character was created as a distinct individual, with warmth and realism. The character of Jo especially was praised as believable in every way. Alcott won acclaim as the first writer to create realistic fiction for young readers. Her eager readers clamored for more.

MORE BOOKS ABOUT THE MARCH FAMILY: Alcott wrote eight more books about the Marches. Known as the *Little Women* series, they include *Little Women, or, Meg, Jo, Beth and Amy, Part Second, An Old-Fashioned Girl, Little Men, Eight Cousins, Rose in Bloom, Under the Lilacs, Jack and Jill,* and *Jo's Boys and How They Turned Out.* These books follow the March girls as they grow up and have families of their own.

The Little Women books made Alcott a famous author. Her books sold so well that her family, at last, no longer had to worry about money. She wrote more books, for children and adults, but none were ever as popular as the Little Women series.

Throughout her life, Alcott devoted herself to social reforms, especially to women's rights and women's suffrage. She wrote about

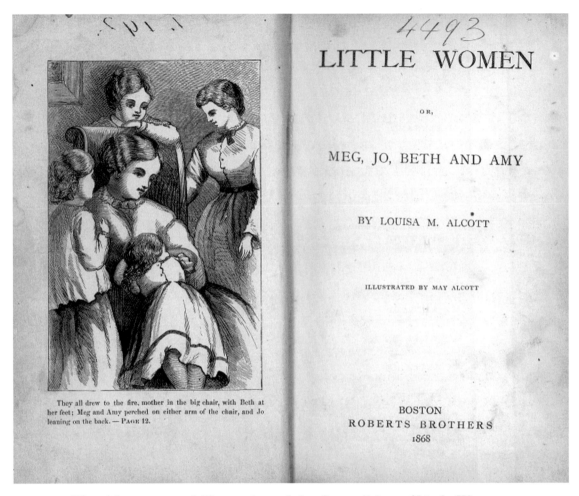

The title page and illustration of the first edition of Little Women.

the topic in newspapers and magazines, and was part of efforts to register to vote. She herself became the first woman in Concord to register to vote, for a local school election, in 1879.

LOUISA MAY ALCOTT'S HOME AND FAMILY: Alcott never married, and lived her entire life with her family. Though she had no children of her own, she raised two of her sisters' children. After May died in 1879, she became the guardian of May's daughter Louisa. She also adopted Anna's son John.

Alcott moved her family to Boston in the 1880s. There, she lived with her father and her sisters' children. But her health was failing, and she died in Boston on March 6, 1888, at the age of 56.

HER LEGACY: Alcott is remembered as the first author to write realistic fiction for young people. Her work has influenced writers, especially women writers, for generations. In the March family, she created some of the most believable and beloved characters in all American literature. They are as alive and lively today as they were when she first created them, nearly 150 years ago.

WORLD WIDE WEB SITES

http://www.lkwdpl.org/wihohio/alco_lou.htm

http://www.louisamayalcott.org/index.html

Marian Anderson

1897 – 1993

**African-American Classical, Opera, and Spiritual Singer
First African-American to Perform with
the Metropolitan Opera**

MARIAN ANDERSON WAS BORN on February 17, 1897, in
Philadelphia, Pennsylvania. Her parents were John and Anna
Anderson. John sold ice and coal. Anna was a teacher before she
had children. Marian was the oldest of three girls. Her two younger
sisters were named Alyce and Ethel.

MARIAN ANDERSON GREW UP in a loving, nurturing home. She
grew up loving music, and started to sing at three. She remembered

"beating out some sort of rhythm with my hands and feet and la-la-la-ing a vocal accompaniment. Some people might say that these were the first signs of music in me. I would only say that I felt cozy and happy."

Marian's family attended the Union Baptist Church in Philadelphia. She began to sing in the church choir at age six. When she was eight, she earned her first fee. She was paid 50 cents to sing at church. Flyers circulated in the neighborhood, saying: "Come and hear the baby contralto."

"Contralto" refers to a particular range in the signing voice. There are four parts in traditional vocal music. They are soprano, alto, tenor, and bass. In her career, Marian sang as a contralto, which is between alto and tenor.

Yet, even as a child, Anderson could sing higher and lower than the traditional contralto range. She could sing an incredible three full octaves. That's 24 notes in sequence, from lowest to highest pitch. By the time she was 13, she was singing in the adult choir. If any of the soloists in any voice part couldn't perform, Marian would sing the part.

She played instruments, too. She studied piano, and, after scrubbing steps for five cents, she saved enough to buy a violin for $3.98. She played it until it fell apart.

A FAMILY TRAGEDY: When Marian was just 12 years old, her beloved father died of a brain tumor. The family had to move in with her father's parents. It was a difficult time. Anderson recalled feeling that "tragedy had moved into our house." Her grandmother was strong-willed and domineering. She was "used to being the boss of her own house and the people in it," Anderson wrote later.

Her mother went to work as a domestic laborer, and also took in laundry. Marian and her sisters helped out any way they could. Anderson was devoted to her mother. She credited her mother with giving her the strength to face all the challenges of life.

MARIAN ANDERSON WENT TO SCHOOL at the local public schools in Philadelphia. She did well in school, and remembered liking spelling bees and speech classes. She started high school at William Penn High, a commercial high school. She took typing and shorthand, courses designed to help her find an office job.

But the focus of her schooling soon changed. She sang a solo at a school concert, and an important community member heard her. He thought a young woman of Marian's talent should be taking college preparatory courses. He also thought she should be studying music. Anderson transferred to South Philadelphia High School. There, she began taking more challenging courses and studying music.

FACING RACISM: When she was 15, Anderson first faced the racist attitudes that frequently threatened her career. She tried to apply to a music school, but was rejected. "We don't take colored," the school clerk told her.

The words stung. "It was my first contact with the blunt, brutal words. This school of music was the last place I expected to hear them. True enough, my skin was different, but not my feelings." As she would do throughout her career, Anderson refused to let the bigoted views of others define her.

SERIOUS TRAINING: Anderson first began to study music seriously at 15. A well-known singer and teacher named Mary Patterson accepted her as a student, and her vocal training began in earnest.

*Anderson performing on the steps of the
Lincoln Memorial, April 9, 1939.*

Serious vocal training begins with developing technique. Anderson learned how to breathe properly. She did scale studies and other exercises to develop the strength and flexibility of her voice. She studied the correct pronunciations of words from several languages—English, German, French, and Latin.

Anderson loved the training, and worked hard. She knew she needed the foundation of solid technique. "The purpose of all the exercises and labors was to give you a thoroughly reliable foundation and to make sure you could do your job under any circumstances. There is no shortcut," she said.

STARTING A CAREER IN MUSIC: Anderson began performing in the Philadelphia area while she was still in high school. When she got paid, she'd give most of the money to her mother. She also began to study with a well-known teacher named Giuseppe Boghetti. He helped her develop the songs and sound that made her an international star.

Anderson began to study the *lieder* (LEE-der), or songs, of great composers like Franz Schubert and Johannes Brahms. They require outstanding technique, but also emotional power. They often tell a story, and are set to folktales or poems. Anderson brought out the sensitivity and beauty at the heart of these great songs. She also performed famous arias from operas by composers like Mozart and Verdi.

She was also known for her beautiful performances of spirituals. In songs like "My Lord, What a Morning" she brought to life, and celebrated, an African-American art form.

Anderson began to tour the country. She earned enough to buy a house for her mother and sisters. In 1923, she won a vocal competition in Philadelphia. She was the first African-American ever to win the contest. In 1925, she won a national competition. Her prize was the chance to perform with the great New York Philharmonic Orchestra. Her concert was a tremendous hit.

SINGING IN EUROPE: Anderson decided to travel to Europe to study and perform. She was a sensation. While touring Finland, she met the famous classical composer Sibelius. She visited him at his home, where she sang one of his pieces. "My roof is too low for you," he exclaimed.

In Austria, the great conductor Arturo Toscanini heard her sing. "Yours is a voice such as one hears once in a hundred years!" he told her.

Anderson returned to the U.S. in triumph. She began a national tour in New York City. Her schedule was hectic: she gave up to 100 concerts each year. She became a true national treasure. She was adored for her beautiful voice and artistry, and her humble, dignified manner.

SINGING AT THE WHITE HOUSE: In 1936, First Lady **Eleanor Roosevelt** invited Anderson to sing at the White House. She was the first African-American to sing at the President's home.

CONSTITUTION HALL AND THE D.A.R.: In 1939, Anderson became the unlikely center of a controversy. Her manager wanted to book her at Washington D.C.'s Constitution Hall. The Hall is run by the D.A.R. (Daughters of the American Revolution). It is a conservative women's group that, in 1939, would not allow African-Americans to perform.

First Lady Eleanor Roosevelt, a member of the D.A.R., was outraged. She quit the organization. Harold Ickes, then Interior Secretary, arranged to have Anderson perform at the Lincoln Memorial. It was one of the most memorable concerts ever heard in the nation's capitol.

THE LINCOLN MEMORIAL CONCERT: On Easter Sunday, April 9, 1939, Anderson stood on the steps of the Lincoln Memorial and sang to a crowd of 75,000. Among the listeners were Supreme Court justices, members of Congress, and Civil Rights and religious leaders.

Anderson walked to the platform, closed her eyes, and began to sing "America." She sang Schubert lieder, opera arias, and closed with spirituals. A hush fell over the audience. It was, in the words of one spectator, "a silence instinctive, natural, and intense, so that you were afraid to breathe."

Anderson posing with African-American serviceman at the
January 1943 dedication of the mural depicting her 1939 concert.

"What were my own feelings?" Anderson wrote later about the controversy. "I was saddened and ashamed. I was sorry for the people who had precipitated the affair. I felt that their behavior stemmed from a lack of understanding. They were not persecuting me personally or as a representative of my people so much as they were doing something that was neither sensible nor good."

FIGHTING PREJUDICE IN THE CONCERT HALL: Anderson was a private woman. "I was not designed for hand-to-hand combat," she said. But she continued to confront and overcome prejudice wherever she could. While touring the South, she came face to face with the racism that limited the lives of African-Americans. It was the time of Jim Crow laws. Businesses—hotels, restaurants, concert halls—could legally discriminate against black people.

But when Anderson performed in the South, she refused to allow the segregated seating that was legal under Jim Crow. At that time, African-Americans could be forced to sit in segregated, inferior areas. She insisted instead that African-Americans be able to sit in every section of a performance hall.

SINGING AT THE METROPOLITAN OPERA: Anderson broke another racial barrier in the 1950s. On January 7, 1955, she became the first African-American to perform with the Metropolitan Opera, one of the most important opera companies in the world. When she appeared on stage, the audience gave her a standing ovation, before she sang a single note.

Anderson sang at the inauguration of President Dwight D. Eisenhower in 1957. President Eisenhower asked her to become a musical ambassador for the U.S.

Anderson performs at the January 1943 dedication of the mural depicting her 1939 concert.

Anderson traveled the world, singing and bringing the beauty and dignity of her music to thousands. Eisenhower also named her to the United Nations Human Rights Committee.

In 1961, Anderson sang at another presidential inauguration, this time for John F. Kennedy. In 1964, she began her farewell tour. She started at Constitution Hall, and finished in New York's Carnegie Hall. After she retired, she frequently appeared at charity fund raisers for organizations like the NAACP.

Anderson also founded a scholarship given each year to a young singer. It has helped launch the careers of such great African-American singers as Grace Bumbry.

MARIAN ANDERSON'S HOME AND FAMILY: Anderson married Orpheus Fisher in 1943. They had no children. They lived on a 100-acre farm in rural Connecticut. Fisher died in 1986. Anderson developed heart disease and moved to Portland, Oregon, to live with her nephew. She died in Portland on April 8, 1993.

HER LEGACY: Marian Anderson was one of the greatest musical artists of the 20th century. She was also a courageous figure in the struggle for equal opportunity for African-Americans. At the time of her death, the opera star Jesseye Norman paid tribute to her. "Marian Anderson was the personification of all that is wonderful, simple, pure, and majestic in the human spirit. She wore the glorious crown of her voice with the grace of an empress."

WORLD WIDE WEB SITES
http://www.library.upenn.edu/exhibits/rbm/anderson/index.html
http://www.lkwdpl.org/wihohio/ande-mar.htm
http://www.mariananderson.org/legacy/

Susan B. Anthony

1820-1906

American Activist and Champion of Women's Rights
Led the Movement for Women's Suffrage

SUSAN B. ANTHONY WAS BORN on February 15, 1820, in Adams, Massachusetts. Her parents were Daniel and Lucy Anthony. Daniel was a cotton manufacturer and Lucy was a homemaker. Susan was the second of eight children.

SUSAN B. ANTHONY GREW UP in a family that belonged to the Quaker faith. They believed in the natural equality of all people, male and female, black and white. Susan grew up to share her parents' passion for the **ABOLITIONIST** cause, the ending of slavery, and other social reforms. Susan and her siblings were also raised to value education, self-discipline, and self-respect.

SUSAN B. ANTHONY WENT TO SCHOOL first at home, where she learned to read and write at the age of three. When she was six, her parents moved to Battensville, New York. There, Susan went to a district school. But her male teacher refused to teach her long division. He thought that girls had no need of education.

Susan's parents took her out of the school. For the next several years, she was educated at home, at a school created by her parents. Her teacher was a woman named Mary Perkins. Susan was then sent to a boarding school in Pennsylvania.

FIRST JOB: After she graduated, Anthony became a teacher at a Quaker boarding school. It was an all-girls' school, and she taught there from 1846 to 1849. In 1849, Anthony moved to Rochester, New York, where her family lived.

A LIFE DEVOTED TO SOCIAL REFORM: Anthony was actively involved in several of the major reform movements of the 19th century. Her first efforts were on behalf of the **TEMPERANCE** movement.

TEMPERANCE: The temperance movement was devoted to the prohibition of alcohol in the United States. It was based on the belief that alcohol was a dangerous drug, and that alcoholic men abused their wives and children. Many Quakers were members of the temperance movement, and Anthony helped found the Women's State Temperance Society of New York. Her first public speech, which she gave in 1849, was on behalf of temperance.

ABOLITION: Many people who supported temperance were also involved in the fight for **ABOLITION.** Anthony's family had long believed in the cause. At her parent's home she met such famous abolitionists as Frederick Douglass and William Lloyd Garrison.

Anthony became active in the anti-slavery campaign, working for the American Anti-Slavery Society. From the 1850s to the outbreak of the Civil War in 1861, she traveled, gave speeches, and wrote on behalf of abolition. She sometimes faced hostility, even threats, when she spoke.

While working for abolition, she met **Elizabeth Cady Stanton**. Stanton shared Anthony's fervent beliefs in temperance, abolition, and, especially, women's rights. The two worked together for the next 50 years in the fight to gain women equal rights, including the right to vote.

WOMEN'S RIGHTS: It is hard for young readers of the 21st century to understand the condition of women in the 19th century. At that time, American women had none of the rights they have today. They did not have the right to an education or employment. They could not own property or control their own money. Married women had no rights; in cases of divorce, only men could get custody of children. If a woman made money in a job, the money was not hers. It belonged, by law, to her husband, or her father. Also, women made a fraction of a man's salary for the same job. Women were also not free to speak in public.

Most important, for Anthony, was the fact that women could not vote. They had no voice in electing the government or making the laws that controlled them. For her, the campaign for a woman's right to vote was crucial to equal rights. "There never will be complete equality until women themselves help to make laws and elect lawmakers," she said.

Susan B. Anthony with Elizabeth Cady Stanton.

WOMEN'S SUFFRAGE: Anthony led the fight for women's suffrage—for the right of American women to vote. She began her campaign in 1852, when she was not allowed to speak at a New York temperance convention. After being told that "ladies were invited to listen and learn" only, she promptly formed her own female temperance society. From that point forward, she worked tirelessly for women's rights in every category.

PROPERTY RIGHTS: In 1854, Anthony began to circulate petitions to allow married women to have the right to own property and all women to vote. That same year, she was again refused permission to speak. She had traveled to Washington D.C. to speak at the U.S. Capitol and the Smithsonian, but was forbidden to do so. She did not let it stop her. Instead, she traveled to New York and continued to campaign for women's rights.

She saw results in 1860, when the New York State Married Women's Property Bill became law. For the first time, it allowed married women to own property, keep their own wages, and have custody of their children in divorce cases.

EQUAL RIGHTS IN EDUCATION: In Anthony's era, women were not allowed to go to college. In some states, girls could not go to school with boys. In 1857, she spoke at the New York State Teachers' Convention, campaigning for equal education for women, and for African-Americans.

In 1863, during the Civil War, Anthony and Stanton organized the Women's National Loyal League. They fully supported the Thirteenth Amendment to the U.S. Constitution, which outlawed slavery. They also campaigned for the Fourteenth and Fifteenth Amendments, which granted African-American men citizenship and

Susan B. Anthony's house, Rochester, New York.

the right to vote. They wanted those same rights given to women, too. They wanted to amend the Constitution, making women's right to vote the law of the land.

When the Civil War ended in 1865, Anthony, Stanton, and other women's rights activists, redoubled their campaign. Anthony and Stanton started a newspaper, "The Revolution," calling for equal rights. Its goal was: "Men their rights, and nothing more; women, their rights, and nothing less."

EQUAL RIGHTS IN WORK: Anthony also campaigned for women in the workforce. At that time, women made a fraction of men's salaries for the same work. She claimed that women and men should make the same wage for the same job. Women were also banned from labor unions, which worked on behalf of male workers only.

She encouraged women to form their own union, and helped establish the Workingwomen's Central Association.

CHALLENGING THE VOTING LAWS: In 1869, Wyoming became the first territory to allow women to vote. But Anthony wanted voting rights for all women, in every state in the country.

In 1872, she tested the voting laws in New York. She led a group of women to the polls in Rochester, where she voted in the Presidential election. She was arrested and, while waiting for her trial, continued to lecture on behalf of women's right to vote. She was convicted of violating voting laws, and fined $100. She refused to pay, claiming "taxation without representation is tyranny."

Anthony continued to campaign for women's rights. She wrote and published a history of the women's suffrage movement. Between 1869 and 1906, she appeared before every Congress to plead for a suffrage amendment. She began to take her campaign to other countries, too. In 1888, Anthony organized the International Council of Women. In 1904 she helped found the International Woman Suffrage Alliance.

Her hard work continued to pay off. In 1900, the University of Rochester agreed to admit women for the first time. To help finance the changes, Anthony pledged the value of her own life insurance policy.

In 1905, Anthony met with President Theodore Roosevelt to promote the cause of women's suffrage. She wanted him to sponsor an amendment to the Constitution granting women the right to vote.

On February 15, 1906, Susan B. Anthony's 86th birthday was celebrated in Washington, D.C. There, she gave another stirring speech in support of women's suffrage, in which she said "Failure is impossible" in the quest for the vote. She died a month later, on March 13, 1906. She was mourned all over the world as a pioneer in women's rights.

Marble statue of Elizabeth Cady Stanton, Susan B. Anthony, and Lucrecia Mott in the U.S. Capitol, Washington D.C.

SUSAN B. ANTHONY'S HOME AND FAMILY: Anthony never married or had children. She lived with her parents for most of her life. In 1866, her mother, Lucy Read Anthony, bought a house in Rochester that eventually became her home and the headquarters of the National Woman's Suffrage Association. It is a national land-mark today.

HER LEGACY: Susan B. Anthony is one of the most important woman in the history of women's rights. She was fearless and tire-less in her pursuit of the right for women to vote, to be educated, to enter any profession, to own property, and to hold public office. Thanks largely to her efforts, American women today enjoy rights denied to women for centuries.

Although Anthony died before its passage, the **NINETEENTH AMENDMENT** to the Constitution, which guaranteed a woman's right to vote, was finally passed on June 4, 1919, and ratified on August 18, 1920. It was known as the "Susan B. Anthony" Amendment, a just and fitting legacy of a woman who had devoted her life to its principles.

WORLD WIDE WEB SITES

http://www.rochester.edu/sba/suffrage_sba_ecs.html
http://susanbanthonyhouse.org/

Aung San Suu Kyi

1945-
Burmese Political Leader and Human Rights Activist
Winner of the Nobel Peace Prize

AUNG SAN SUU KYI WAS BORN on June 19, 1945, in Rangoon, Burma. Her name is pronounced "Ong San Soo Chee." Her father was Aung San, who led the movement for independence in Burma. Her mother was Ma Khin Kyi, a nurse. Aung San Suu Kyi was the youngest of three children.

When Aung San Suu Kyi was born, she was named Suu Kyi. In Burma, there is not a formal family-naming tradition. Instead, parents give each child a personal name. Also, Burmese women do not take their husband's name when they marry. So each individual has a very individual name. Suu Kyi added her father's name, Aung San, to her own, to honor him.

AUNG SAN SUU KYI GREW UP in Burma, a nation in Asia that is about the size of Texas. It is bordered by the countries of Thailand, China, Tibet, and India. When Suu Kyi was born, Burma was a British colony. Her father, a general in the Burmese army, led the fight for independence from Britain.

In 1947, Burma became an independent nation. Suu Kyi's father was among a group of leaders who were elected to lead the new country. But tragically, her father and several of the new leaders were assassinated in July 1947. She was just two years old.

AUNG SAN SUU KYI WENT TO SCHOOL in Burma for elementary school. When she was 15, her mother was named Burma's ambassador to India. Suu Kyi moved to India with her mother, and went to high school in New Delhi. She was an excellent student.

Suu Kyi went to college at St. Hugh's College, which is part of Oxford University, in England. She studied economics, politics, and philosophy. While in college, she met her future husband, Michael Aris.

FIRST JOBS: In 1969, Suu Kyi moved to the United States, where she worked for the United Nations for two years. In 1972, she returned to England, where she and Aris married. They moved to Bhutan, a country in Asia, where Michael was a tutor for the royal family. Suu Kyi worked for the Ministry of Foreign Affairs.

The couple returned to England, where their sons, Alexander and Kim, were born. Suu Kyi continued her work as a scholar.

RETURNING TO BURMA: The lives of Suu Kyi and her family changed forever in April, 1988. She received a call from Burma that her mother had had a stroke. She returned home to care for her, at a time when her country was in turmoil.

When Suu Kyi arrived, the Burmese people were protesting against the rule of the current head of government, General Ne Win. His government was run by the military. It restricted people's freedoms and took away their rights. After months of demonstrations, the general stepped down as the leader of his political party.

The people of Burma wanted Suu Kyi to become the leader of a new movement for democracy. "As my father's daughter, I felt I had a duty to get involved," she said. She spoke to huge crowds of

Aung San Suu Kyi with a crowd of school children in Burma, June 2002.

people, and called for a democratic government.

But the military party responded with brutal force. There were violent demonstrations in which thousands of people were killed. Suu Kyi and her supporters would not give up. They founded a new party, the National League for Democracy, to give voice to their beliefs.

Suu Kyi traveled all over Burma. She spoke to millions of people and called for peaceful, nonviolent reform and free elections.

UNDER HOUSE ARREST: In July 1989, the government placed Soo Kyi under "house arrest." She no longer had the freedom to leave her own home. Yet she continued to write and to speak on behalf of democracy.

In May 1990, elections were held in Burma. Even though Soo Kyi was still under house arrest, her National League for Democracy won in a landslide. But the government refused to recognize the election results. Soo Kyi remained detained in her home. She was not charged with any crime, nor was she allowed a trial.

Despite the government's efforts, Suu Kyi remained a beloved leader of the Burmese people. And the story of her struggle spread around the world. The world's leaders spoke out against her continued arrest. They called for the Burmese government to release her.

THE NOBEL PEACE PRIZE: In 1991, Suu Kyi was awarded the Nobel Peace Prize. That is one of the most important honors in the world. It is given each year to an individual who works for peace.

Suu Kyi continued to be held under house arrest. Her husband and sons were allowed to visit, but only for brief periods. In 1995,

Aung San Suu Kyi at a rally in Mogok in May 2003.

Suu Kyi was allowed to leave her home, but the military government restricted where she could go. When she tried to leave the country by train in 1996, she was not allowed to cross the border.

A FAMILY TRAGEDY: In 1999, Suu Kyi's husband Michael Aris learned he had cancer. He tried to visit his wife, but the military government wouldn't let him in the country. Suu Kyi knew that if she left, she would not be allowed to return to her country. Tragically, Michael Aris died of cancer in March 1999.

In 2000, the military party again placed Suu Kyi under house arrest. For ten years, she was only briefly been allowed to leave her home. In 2003, she was imprisoned following a skirmish involving her supporters. The military party in control of Burma (which they call Myanmar) would not let her travel freely or promote democracy. Yet she remained a beloved leader in her country. She continued to speak out against the current government and promote democracy.

Aung San Suu Kyi on the day she was released, November 13, 2010.

Finally, on November 13, 2010, Suu Kyi was released from house arrest. She greeted her many supporters with hope and relief. "Thank you for welcoming me like this," she said. "We haven't seen each other for so long, I have so much to tell you." Whether she will be allowed to travel freely in her own country remains to be seen. But for her loyal supporters, in Burma and around the world, her release was welcomed as a step toward change in her besieged country.

AUNG SAN SUU KYI'S HOME AND FAMILY: Suu Kyi married Michael Aris in 1972. They had two sons, Alexander and Kim. Michael died in 1999. After not seeing his mother for 10 years, Kim was finally allowed to visit her in November, 2010. Alexander also hopes to be reunited with her soon.

46

HER LEGACY: Aung San Suu Kyi has become a symbol for peace and freedom all over the world. Her determination to bring democracy to her people through peaceful means has made her a hero to millions.

WORLD WIDE WEB SITES

http://newsvote.bbc.co.uk/mpapps/pagetools/print/news.bbc.
  co.uk/2/hi/asia-pacific/1950505.stm?ad=1

http://nobelprize.org/nobel_prizes/peace/laureates/1991/kyi-bio.
  html

Clara Barton

1821-1912

American Nurse and Founder of
the American Red Cross

CLARA BARTON WAS BORN on December 25, 1821, in Oxford, Massachusetts. Her full name was Clarissa Harlowe Barton, but she always wanted to be called Clara. Her parents were Sara and Stephen Barton. Sara was a homemaker and Stephen was a farmer and state representative. Clara was the youngest of five children, with two brothers and two sisters.

CLARA BARTON GREW UP in a large family who taught her to read and write by the age of four. She was a shy child, but showed strength and determination, too. When her brother David hurt himself in a farming accident, Clara, at the age of 11, nursed him back to health.

CLARA BARTON WENT TO SCHOOL at the local schools in Massachusetts. She was an excellent student, and at the age of 16, got her first job as a teacher.

TEACHER: Barton began teaching in a one-room schoolhouse in 1837, at a time when most teachers were men. In 1850, she moved to Bordentown, New Jersey. There, she started a free public school, which she ran herself. It was hugely successful: by the end of the first year, she had 200 students. Soon, there were 600 students at the school.

The local community noticed the success of Barton's school. They decided to build a larger school, and when it came time to hire a principal, they hired a man, not Barton. They also paid him twice what she had been paid. Barton was furious. She resigned.

PATENT OFFICE: Barton moved to Washington, D.C. She got in touch with her congressman, Alexander De Witt. He recommended her for a job with the U.S. Patent Office. That is the department that takes applications for inventors and inventions.

Barton did an excellent job at the Patent Office. Her boss, a man named Charles Mason, also made sure she was paid what the male employees were paid. But when Mason left for several months, Barton's new boss refused to pay her. She was asked to leave her job.

Barton eventually got her job back, but then lost it again when a new President was elected. Barton moved home to Massachusetts for a few years. She was rehired by the Patent Office in 1860, when Abraham Lincoln was elected President.

THE CIVIL WAR: In 1861, Civil War broke out between the Union and the Confederacy. Thousands of Union soldiers poured into Washington, D.C. Some were wounded. All needed basic supplies: clothes, food, shelter, and nursing assistance.

Barton could see that the Union forces were unprepared for all the needs of the soldiers. She set to work, using her organizational skills to provide what they needed. She collected clothing, food, and medical supplies and organized their distribution to the men. She raised money from the public on behalf of the soldiers.

Barton helped the soldiers out in other important ways, too. She wrote letters for them, listened to their problems, and read to them. But she knew the greatest need was on the battlefields.

"ANGEL OF THE BATTLEFIELD": Barton asked to be put near the scenes of battles, so that she could treat wounded soldiers. Her request was granted, and over the course of the war, she treated wounded soldiers in Virginia, South Carolina, and Maryland.

In 1864, Barton became head of the field nurses for the Union. Her work was dangerous and difficult. But she did it with courage. "I may be compelled to face danger, but never fear it," she said. "And while our soldiers can stand and fight, I can stand and feed and nurse them." For all of her efforts, she became known as the "Angel of the Battlefield."

Barton took on another difficult task: she helped families find their wounded and missing soldiers. President Abraham Lincoln

Portrait of Clara Barton by Civil War era photographer Matthew Brady, c. 1865.

appointed her to head the Office of the Search for Missing Men. He wrote, "To the Friends of Missing Persons: Miss Clara Barton has kindly offered to search for the mission's prisoners of war. Please address her, giving her the name, regiment, and company of any missing prisoner."

Barton and her assistants received 63,000 letters from the families of the missing. Through their efforts, 22,000 missing soldiers were eventually identified.

THE RED CROSS: In 1869, Barton took a trip to Europe to rest after all of her work on behalf of American soldiers. But soon she was once again involved in war relief efforts. She went to Geneva, Switzerland, the home of the International Red Cross. It had been founded by a man named Henry Durant in 1859. It was devoted to helping victims of war, both soldiers and civilians. It did not take sides in wars. Its services were available to all victims, regardless of a country's military or political stance.

At the Geneva Convention in 1864, many European nations had signed a treaty outlining the treatment of victims of war. It allowed for the treatment of the sick and wounded during wartime, without respect to nationality. The U.S. had not signed the treaty.

In 1869, while Barton was in Europe, the Franco-Prussian War began. She immediately began to help the wounded as a volunteer with the International Red Cross. She made a red cross, the symbol of the organization, out of a piece of red ribbon, and wore it proudly.

When she returned to the U.S., Barton met with President Rutherford B. Hayes. She wanted the U.S. to join the International Red Cross. But Hayes didn't want to sign the treaty. Barton kept campaigning for the U.S. to join. Finally, in 1882, President Chester

A. Arthur signed the treaty. The U.S. was finally part of the Red Cross.

Barton formed the American Association of the Red Cross in Washington, D.C. in 1881. In 1893, the organization was renamed the American National Red Cross.

Barton was head of the American Red Cross for its first 23 years. Under her guidance, it developed into one of the most important relief organizations in the world. She organized relief efforts for victims of forest fires, floods, earthquakes, and epidemics. She reached across international borders, bringing food aid to countries ravaged by natural disaster.

Clara Barton's house in Glen Echo, Maryland.

Barton became an honored and beloved citizen of the world. She received the Iron Cross from Germany, the Silver Cross from Russia, and the International Red Cross Medal.

LATER YEARS: Barton retired from the Red Cross in 1904, at the age of 83. Despite the demands of her job, she was also involved in other major social reforms of the time. She was a fervent supporter of **WOMEN'S SUFFRAGE,** and knew and supported the efforts of **Susan B. Anthony** and others who fought for women's rights.

In her 80s, Barton established a new relief organization, the National First Aid Association. It offered instruction in first aid and emergency preparedness. It eventually became part of the Red Cross.

Barton was also a prolific writer and speaker. She continued to speak and publish books into her 90s.

CLARA BARTON'S HOME AND FAMILY: Barton never married or had children. She devoted her life to helping others until her death, on April 12, 1912, at her home in Glen Echo, Maryland. Her home is now an historic site, run by the National Park Service.

HER LEGACY: Clara Barton was a tireless advocate for those in need everywhere, whether victims of war or natural disaster. Her legacy is the organization she founded, the American Red Cross. Its thousands of employees and volunteers serve the nation and the world, reflecting her spirit of courage and compassion.

WORLD WIDE WEB SITES
http://www.redcross.org/museum/history/claraBarton.asp
http://www.nps.gov/clba/

Mary McLeod Bethune

1875 – 1955
African-American Educator and Civil Rights Activist

MARY BETHUNE WAS BORN on July 10, 1875, in Mayesville, South Carolina. Bethune became her last name when she married. Her name when she was born was Mary Jane McLeod. (Her last name is pronounced "muh-CLOUD.") Her parents were Samuel McLeod and Patsy McIntosh. They had been slaves on a cotton plantation until 1865. That year, when the Civil War ended, they became free.

After the war, the McLeods continued to work for their former owners, as tenant farmers. They saved their earnings and bought five acres of farmland near Mayesville. They built a log cabin that they named "The Homestead."

Mary Jane was her parents' 15th child, and the first to be born free. Most of her older brothers and sisters had been sold into slavery as infants. After the war, those brothers and sisters came home. The family was finally reunited.

MARY BETHUNE GREW UP in a family that knew hard times even after they were freed. All the children worked hard in the fields. They grew food to eat and cotton to sell. Mary was a hard worker. It was said that by the time she was nine years old she could pick 250 pounds of cotton in a day.

The McLeods were a religious family. The children were taught that God rewards those who have a strong faith and work hard to help others. The Homestead became a welcome gathering place for friends and neighbors. As a child, Mary saw her parents share what little they had with others.

A SEGREGATED WORLD: One day Mary went with her mother to deliver laundry to her former owner. She was invited to play with the women's white grandchildren. Among the bright, shiny new toys was something that caught Mary's eye. It was a book. When she reached out to pick it up one of the white children told her, "Put that down. *You* can't read."

The experience with the book changed Mary forever. She promised herself that she would learn to read one day. In later years, Bethune said that the white girl's words made her see the importance of education. She began to wonder if the reason white people had better houses and a better way of life was because they knew how to read and write.

EARLY SCHOOLING: Mary finally got her chance to go to school. A Presbyterian mission group sent Emma Jane Wilson to Mayesville to open a school for former slaves. Mary eagerly walked five miles to the one-room schoolhouse. There, she realized her dream and learned to read.

Now when she went with her father to sell the cotton they'd picked, she could tell when the buyer was cheating them. Since she could read the weight on the scale, when the buyer told her father that he had 280 pounds, she corrected him by saying, "Isn't it 480 pounds?"

In 1886, when she was 11 years old, Mary had gone as far as she could at the Mayesville missionary school. Because there were no other schools nearby, she returned to the cotton fields to work with her parents. But because she could now read, write, add, and subtract, she could help other farmers get fair prices for their crops.

When Mary was 12, her former teacher visited the McLeods. She told them that a women named Mary Chrissman wanted to offer a scholarship to one of the Mayesville mission school students to continue their education. Mary McLeod received the scholarship.

Generous neighbors helped supply Mary with the school supplies and clothing she would need to attend the Scotia Seminary in Concord, North Carolina. The day she left on the train, the whole community went to the station to send her off.

The Scotia Seminary seemed elegant to Mary. Brick buildings with glass windows, white tablecloths and water glasses—these were things unknown to her. She was also surprised to find black and white teachers sitting side by side at the tables.

Mary made friends easily and quickly became a leader among the students. She was a good student and had a beautiful singing voice. In 1890 she was promoted to the Normal and Scientific Course where she studied to become a teacher. She also had a goal to become a missionary and go to Africa.

THE MOODY BIBLE INSTITUTE: Before graduating from Scotia, Mary applied to the Moody Bible Institute in Chicago. She felt that proper Bible study would help her achieve her goal of going to Africa. Once again, Miss Chrissman paid the tuition.

Mary arrived in Chicago to find herself the only African-American among 1,000 students. But it was here, Mary later said, that she learned "a love for the whole human race." She studied hard and found her faith deepening.

At the end of her study at Moody, Mary applied to the Presbyterian Mission for an assignment in Africa. But there were no positions available for an African-American missionary. Mary returned home to Mayesville and became an assistant teacher with Emma Wilson, her former teacher. One year later she took a teaching position at the Haines Normal and Industrial Institute in Augusta, Georgia.

A YOUNG TEACHER: Lucy Craft Laney, a black educator and the first woman to graduate from Atlanta University, founded the Haines Institute. Bethune taught eighth grade there. In her spare time, she helped families in the poor community surrounding the school.

Bethune also became a Sunday School teacher with an unusual program. On Sunday mornings she and her students went to the homes of the poor. They bathed children and gave out clothing, soap, toothbrushes, combs, and towels.

Inspired by Lucy Laney, Mary discovered her new mission. She became determined to work toward providing education for young black girls—in her own country.

MARRIAGE AND MOTHERHOOD: In 1897, at the age of 22, Mary took another teaching position at the Kindell Institute in Sumter, South Carolina. While singing in the choir, she met a fellow teacher named Albertus Bethune. Within a year they were married and soon moved to Savannah, Georgia. In 1899 their son, Albertus McLeod Bethune, was born. Mary took time off from teaching to take care of her baby.

MOVING TO FLORIDA: Six months after Albertus's birth, a pastor from Palatka, Florida, asked Mary to teach at his school. Her husband encouraged her to take the offer. With infant son in tow, Bethune moved to Florida. Once again she organized a Sunday School program and sang in the choir.

Bethune began reading about Booker T. Washington. He was a former slave who had founded the Tuskegee Normal and Industrial Institute in Alabama. Washington believed that blacks could better themselves and their lives by learning practical skills like farming and carpentry. At his Institute and through workshops and fairs, Washington educated thousands of black farmers. His writings inspired Bethune. They fueled her passion to start her own school for black girls.

DAYTONA BEACH: Construction on the Florida East Coast Railway provided work for black laborers who came from all over the South. The children of these workers needed a school. In 1904, Bethune and her young son took a train from Palatka to Daytona Beach. She had only $1.50 in cash. But she had a burning desire to create a school.

Bethune noticed that all the towns she saw had something in common. They all had a black section and a white section. And the black section was always the poorer of the two. When she reached Daytona Beach and walked through the black section she knew this would be the perfect place to start her school.

THE DAYTONA NORMAL AND INDUSTRIAL INSTITUTE FOR NEGRO GIRLS: On October 4, 1904, Mary McLeod Bethune rang a bell to signal the opening of her school. She'd rented a two-story cottage by the railroad tracks with her $1.50. Five little girls, ages eight to 12, were the first students. Tuition was 50 cents a month.

But even as the school accepted more and more students, the tuition was not enough to pay all the bills. Bethune asked for help from community members. She raised money and found supplies wherever she could. She looked through the dump and trash piles. She wrote letters to wealthy vacationers in Daytona Beach. One man, James Gamble, was impressed with Bethune. He became a strong supporter, donating money and legal services. He was the son of one of the founders of Proctor & Gamble.

Within two years the school had 250 students. Bethune needed more space. She found a piece of land in the black section of town for sale for $200.00. The owner agreed to sell it to her with only $5.00 down. Volunteers cleaned up the land while Bethune found donations of bricks and lumber.

In October 1907 the school moved to its new site. The motto of the school was displayed over the doorways: "Enter to Learn. Depart to Serve."

Bethune began speaking at hotels, asking rich vacationers to help her school. One gentleman gave her a $20 bill, a lot of money in those days. The next day he came to Mary's school and asked for a tour. He came back the next morning with a brand new sewing machine and workmen to finish the main building. The man was Thomas H. White of Dayton, Ohio, owner of the White Sewing Machine Company.

Throughout the years White was a regular visitor to the school and helped with gifts of money. He and James Gamble even got together and bought a two-story house for Bethune. She called it "The Retreat" and lived there until she died.

Mary Bethune in front of White Hall at Bethune-Cookman College, Daytona Beach, Florida

But Bethune's husband was unhappy. He felt she was spending too much time trying to help others instead of concentrating on her family. In 1908 Albertus Bethune left Mary and their son and moved to South Carolina. He died in 1919 without ever seeing them again.

SEPARATE BUT NOT EQUAL: Even as a young girl Bethune realized that black people did not have the same opportunities that white people did. Her school was the first of her efforts to help improve the quality of life for the children of former slaves.

She worked tirelessly to help those in need. One project saw the students from The Daytona Institute teaching black laborers in

*Mary Bethune turns the presidency of Bethune-
Cookman College over to James Colston, 1943.*

the turpentine camps how to read and write.

When a student at the Daytona School became ill with appendicitis, she was not allowed to go to the nearest hospital because she was black. Bethune pleaded with the white doctor to treat the girl and he finally agreed. After the operation Bethune went to visit the young girl and found she was not being cared for.

Bethune took action. She bought a small house and converted it into a hospital. She caught the attention of Andrew Carnegie, one of the wealthiest men in America. He gave Bethune the money she needed to complete the hospital. She named it after her mother,

Patsy McLeod. It had only two beds when it opened. Before long it grew into a 26-bed hospital.

In 1908, Booker T. Washington visited Bethune's school. They talked about their goals as teachers. Both dreamed of a world where blacks would have the same rights as whites and become leaders in America. They both knew that education was the key and hoped that the work they were doing would help this dream come true.

In 1923, the Daytona Normal Institute merged with the Cookman Institute in Jacksonville, Florida, a school for boys. The merger helped save both schools. When Bethune-Cookman College opened its doors, Bethune knew she had accomplished what she had set out to do. She served as college president until 1943.

A WOMAN OF FIRSTS: Bethune spent her entire life working to help African- Americans achieve the same rights as white people. She strongly believed in the words "All people are created equal." She traveled the country speaking out for equality.

A woman of incredible energy and accomplishment, Bethune helped to change society in many ways. During World War I, she helped integrate the Red Cross. In the 1930s, President Franklin D. Roosevelt named her Director of the Office of Negro Affairs. She became the first African-American and the first woman ever run a national agency.

Bethune founded the National Council of Negro Women in 1935. Its purpose is to promote community support for African-American women.

Bethune also helped integrate the armed forces. As a result of her efforts, 10 percent of the officers in the Women's Army

Mary Bethune with singer Marian Anderson and a group of soldiers, at the launch of the SS Booker T. Washington, the first Liberty Ship to be named for an African-American, 1943.

Auxiliary Corps (WAAC) were African-American women. She established a pilot training program at Tuskegee University that graduated black pilots who fought in World War II.

LATER YEARS: In 1952 Bethune was finally able to travel to Africa. She visited the nation of Liberia and attended the inauguration of its president. She spoke at the American Embassy and was awarded the country's Star of Africa medal.

But her health was failing. She spent her last days at her home, the Retreat. She died on May 18, 1955, at the age of 79. She was buried on the campus of Bethune-Cookman College.

HER LEGACY: Bethune is remembered as a tireless advocate for equality for African-Americans. She was determined to provide equal education to blacks, and spoke out about the rights of minorities and women. In 1974, A bronze statue of Mary McLeod Bethune was dedicated in Washington, D.C., the first monument to an African-American, and the first to a woman, in the nation's capitol.

WORLD WIDE WEB SITES

http://www.lkwdpl.org/wihohio/beth-mar.htm

http://www.nahc.org/NAHC/

http://www.nps.org http://www.usca.edu/aasc/bethune.htm

Elizabeth Blackwell

1821-1910
American Medical Doctor
First Woman to Receive a Degree from
an American Medical School
Founded the First Medical School for Women in the U. S.

ELIZABETH BLACKWELL WAS BORN on February 3, 1821, in Bristol, England. Her parents were Samuel and Hannah Blackwell. Samuel ran a sugar refinery and Hannah was a homemaker. Elizabeth was the third of nine children.

ELIZABETH BLACKWELL GREW UP in a family that believed in social reform. Her parents believed in women's equality, and were members of the **TEMPERANCE** and **ABOLITIONIST** movements.

ELIZABETH BLACKWELL WENT TO SCHOOL at home, and was educated by tutors. Because her parents believed in the equality of men and women, Elizabeth and her siblings studied all the same subjects.

MOVING TO THE U.S.: In 1832, when Elizabeth was 11, her father's sugar business failed. The family decided to move to the U.S. to start a new life. They first moved to New York, where they lived for several years. They moved to Ohio in 1838, where they settled in Cincinnati. Sadly, Elizabeth's father died the same year.

FIRST JOBS: Blackwell first made her living as a teacher. She and her mother and sisters founded a school in Cincinnati, where they taught for several years. While she worked as a teacher, Blackwell began to think about becoming a doctor.

STUDYING MEDICINE: In the 19th century, women were barred from attending college and medical school. But Blackwell decided to challenge that tradition.

She had a good friend named Mary Donaldson who was dying of cancer. Donaldson told Blackwell she believed that if she'd had a female doctor, she would have received better medical treatment. Blackwell decided she would become a doctor, to prevent the suffering of patients like Mary.

Blackwell first began to study medicine privately. Then, in 1847, she applied to 29 medical schools. All but one rejected her. That school, Geneva Medical College in New York, accepted her, but only because the students thought her application was a joke.

When she first started classes at Geneva, she faced discrimination from the students and faculty. But she refused to let it affect her studies. In 1849, Elizabeth Blackwell became the first woman to receive a medical degree in the U.S. And she graduated at the top of her class.

WORKING AS A DOCTOR: After graduating from medical school, Blackwell worked at a charity hospital in Philadelphia. But she wanted to become a surgeon. In the U.S., she couldn't find the additional medical training she needed. So she moved to France.

In Paris, Blackwell once again faced discrimination from male doctors who refused to train her in surgery. So she studied "midwifery"—the practice of delivering babies. Then, she came down with an infection that left her blind in one eye. Forced to give up her goal of becoming a surgeon, she moved to London.

Blackwell spent two years working in a clinic in London. She continued to learn as much as she could about medicine. She attended lectures, observed operations, and treated patients.

In 1851, Blackwell returned to the U.S. She tried to open her own medical practice, but once again faced discrimination. She had a hard time finding an office to rent, and getting patients to accept a woman doctor.

THE NEW YORK INFIRMARY FOR WOMEN AND CHILDREN: Finally, in 1853, Blackwell realized her dream. She opened a clinic, called the Dispensary for Poor Women and Children, in one of the poorest areas of New York City.

One year later, Blackwell bought a house in New York and moved the clinic there. On staff with her was her sister, Emily, who had just graduated from medical school. They were joined by another woman physician, Dr. Marie Zarkrzewska. In 1857, the facility was renamed the New York Infirmary for Women and Children. It was the first hospital in the country run for women patients, by women doctors.

The hospital was a great success, and provided medical care to the community. Many of the patients received medical treatment for the first time in their lives.

This stamp cover was created to commemorate the Elizabeth Blackwell postage stamp, released Jan. 23, 1974.

Meanwhile, Blackwell's medical colleagues in Britain asked for her help in training women doctors. So she spent 1858 in England setting up medical classes and training female students.

CREATING THE FIRST MEDICAL SCHOOL FOR WOMEN: Returning to the U.S., Blackwell worked to realize another goal. She wanted to create a medical school for women. That goal had to wait until the end of the Civil War (1861-1865). During the war years, Blackwell helped train field nurses for the Union army.

When the war ended, Blackwell restarted her efforts. Finally, in 1868, she opened the Women's Medical College of the New York

Infirmary. She headed the school and taught classes for several years.

RETURNING TO ENGLAND: Once again, Blackwell's English colleagues asked for her help. This time, they wanted her to open a medical school for women in Britain. So Blackwell returned to her native country in 1869.

She lectured, wrote, and started her own practice. She focused in particular on "hygiene." That's the practice of absolute cleanliness in medicine. Blackwell knew that it was crucial to patient health, and the prevention of illness. She encouraged all her doctors and students to promote it, too.

In 1874, she helped found the London School of Medicine for Women. She taught there for several years, while continuing to write and lecture.

Bronze statue of Elizabeth Blackwell at Hobart and William Smith Colleges in Geneva, New York, where Blackwell attended medial school.

Blackwell also promoted several major social reforms. She supported the movement for women's rights and the work of **Susan B. Anthony**. She spoke out against poverty and lack of education, because she believed that both led to disease, especially among poor people in large cities.

LATER YEARS: Blackwell visited the U.S. for the last time in 1906. In 1907, at the age of 86, she had a bad fall and never fully recovered. She died at her home in Hastings, England, on May 31, 1910, at the age of 89.

ELIZABETH BLACKWELL'S HOME AND FAMILY: Blackwell never married, but she did adopt a child, named Katherine, whom she raised. Katherine, called Kitty, lived with Blackwell until her death.

HER LEGACY: As the first woman to earn a medical degree in the U.S., Elizabeth Blackwell is a hero to women everywhere. She fought against prejudice her entire life, breaking barriers and establishing a path for women to achieve in science, medicine, and all fields. She wrote:

"I do not wish to give women first place, still less a second one—but the most complete freedom to take their *true* place, whatever it may be."

WORLD WIDE WEB SITES

http://campus.hws.edu/his/blackwell/biography.html

http://www.nlm.nih.gov/changingthefaceofmedicine/physicians/
  biography

Nellie Bly

1864-1922
American Journalist, Author, and Activist
One of the First Women Journalists in the United States

NELLIE BLY WAS BORN on May 5, 1864, in Cochran's Mills, Pennsylvania. "Nellie Bly" was a pseudonym (SOO-doe-nim). She took the name when she became a writer. Her real name was Elizabeth Jane Cochran. Her father was Michael Cochran and her mother was Mary Jane Cochran.

Michael Cochran was a wealthy businessman and judge. He was so successful that the town of Cochran's Mills was named for him. Mary Jane was Michael's second wife. He married Mary Jane after his first wife died.

GROWING UP: Elizabeth, called "Pink," grew up in a large extended family. Her father had 10 children from his first marriage. Pink was the third of five children from the second marriage. She was feisty and lively, and the most rebellious of all the children.

When Pink was only six, her father died. It was the beginning of years of difficulties for her family. Her father had died without a will to provide for the family of his second marriage. They faced desperate times. They had to sell their home. Her mother married a man whom she hoped would bring financial and emotional stability to the family. Instead, he abused her.

After years of abuse, her mother decided to divorce her husband. Pink testified at the divorce trial. She told the court how her stepfather, an alcoholic, abused her mother.

GOING TO SCHOOL: Pink was educated mostly at home, then went to boarding school for one year. When she was 15, she went to the Indiana Normal School, a teacher's college. She chose that because teaching was one of the few jobs open to women at that time. But after one semester, her money ran out. She moved back home and lived with her mother.

FIRST JOBS: In the mid-1880s, Bly and her mother moved to Pittsburgh. They ran a boarding house, and Pink tried to find full-time work. But she had little luck finding a job, until a column in the local newspaper caught her eye.

The local newspaper, the *Pittsburgh Dispatch*, had a regular column by a writer who called himself "The Quiet Observer," or "Q.O." One day, he wrote a column titled "What Girls Are Good For." He called working women "a monstrosity." Instead of working, he claimed, women should be content with washing, sewing, and raising children.

A LETTER TO THE EDITOR: Furious, Bly fired off a letter to the editor. The editor, George Madden replied: "This writer, who has signed herself, Lonely Orphan Girl (so he probably has an idea that it's a woman), has no style, no punctuation, no grammar, but I see a spirit here. I see a spirit here." He placed an ad in the paper, asking the author to come forward. Bly showed up at Madden's office in person, and he offered her a job, as the paper's first female reporter.

BECOMING NELLIE BLY: She accepted, and began to write the newspaper stories that would make her famous. She took the pseudonym "Nellie Bly," probably taken from a popular song of the time by Stephen Foster.

AN INVESTIGATIVE REPORTER: From the beginning of Bly's career, her stories focused on the lives of the poor and downtrodden. She wrote in the first person, with passion and style, unlike most reporters of the time. She also interviewed her subjects, and transcribed their conversations. In doing that, she allowed people to speak in their own voices.

Bly's early stories chronicled the lives of poor people from the slums of Pittsburgh. The first described the lives of women who worked in factories. It was a great success. Newspaper readers of the day, most of them from the middle- and upper-classes, had no idea about the poverty and suffering going on around them. Bly's reporting caused a public outcry. People demanded better living conditions for the poor.

Nellie Bly had established a name for herself. She had also made enemies. Factory owners and city leaders didn't like her stories, because they were blamed for the suffering of the poor. They complained to the newspaper, which backed down under the pressure. Bly was soon writing typical "women's" stories, about fashion and the arts.

Bly fought back. She wanted to write important stories. She asked to go to Mexico to cover conditions there, and Madden approved. She spent the next several months writing stories about the corrupt government of Mexico and the poverty of the people. The Mexican government was angry, and Bly's life was threatened. She returned to the U.S. full of new energy. She was ready for even more challenges.

Photograph of Nellie Bly, c. 1890.

THE NEW YORK WORLD: In 1887, Bly decided to head for New York, where she tried to find work as a reporter. After six months, she landed a job at the *New York World*. It was owned by the famous newspaperman Joseph Pulitzer. Her first assignment was to investigate the

PRESENTING THE GLOBE-GIRDLER A GOLDEN GLOBE.   THE ARRIVAL IN PHILADELPHIA.

AROUND THE WORLD IN SEVENTY-TWO DAYS AND SIX HOURS—RECEPTION OF NELLIE BLY AT JERSEY CITY ON THE COMPLETION OF HER JOURNEY—From Sketches by C. Bunnell.—[See Page 7.]

Engraving commemorating the completion of Nellie Bly's trip around the world, 1890.

conditions at Blackwell's Island, a notorious asylum for the mentally ill in New York.

LIVING IN AN ASYLUM: Bly pretended she was mentally ill, and was successful in getting herself placed in Blackwell's Island Madhouse. There, she was subjected to horrible treatment. The facility was filthy, the patients were given rotten food and treated inhumanely by the staff. Bly also saw patients who were poor, and physically sick, but clearly not mentally ill.

Bly feared for her own sanity, but nevertheless lasted for 10 days. The newspaper got her released, and she wrote a blistering expose of conditions at the asylum. She called Blackwell's "a human rat-trap, easy to get into, impossible to get out of." The story was a sensation, and led to immediate reforms at the hospital. Once again Nellie Bly was a famous name.

Over the next several years, Bly added to her fame. She wrote stories that exposed political corruption. She wrote about how the police abused female prisoners. She traveled to Chicago to report on a railroad strike. In all these stores, she reported from the point of view of the workers, not the owners.

AROUND THE WORLD IN 72 DAYS: In 1889, Nellie Bly reported a story that made her a legend worldwide. At that time, *Around the World in 80 Days*, a novel by Jules Verne, was an international best-seller. It told the story of Phileas Fogg, who traveled around the entire globe in 80 days.

Bly decided she was going to try to beat Fogg's record. She began her round the world journey from New York. She left at 9:40 a.m. on November 14, 1889, and traveled by boat, train, and even on the back of a donkey in pursuit of the record. American readers eagerly followed the news of her journey, and she met encouraging crowds wherever she went. When she returned to New Jersey, on January 25, 1890, she had beat Fogg's record. She had gone around the world in a just 72 days, 6 hours, and 10 minutes.

HOME AND FAMILY: In 1894, Bly met millionaire businessman Robert Seaman, who was 40 years older than she. They married in 1895, and Bly stopped writing for ten years. When Seaman died in 1904, Bly tried to run his iron manufacturing company. But the company went bankrupt, and she lost all her money.

LATER YEARS: Bly moved to Austria, and was there for the outbreak of World War I (1914-1918). She reported from Europe

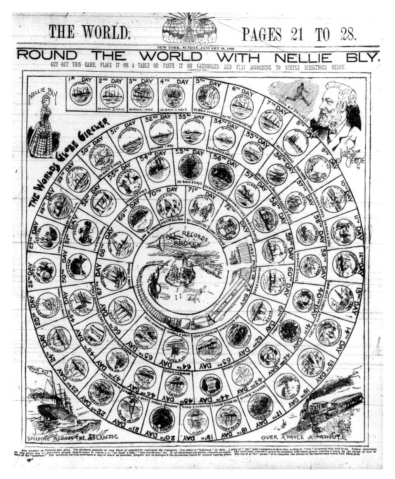

Board game about Nellie Bly's trip around the world.

throughout the war, and returned to New York in 1919.

Bly got another newspaper job, this time at the *New York Evening Journal*. She continued to write newspaper pieces, and became an advocate for abandoned children. She died of pneumonia on January 22, 1922, in New York City, at age 57.

HER LEGACY: Nellie Bly was one of the most famous journalists of her era, and one of the first women reporters in the country. Unlike most reporters, she wrote about the poor underclass of America. She became their voice and their champion, in first-person stories full of passion and detail. Her work brought to light the horrors of slums, mental asylums, and political corruption. They brought about much-needed change to the country, and fame to one of the first investigative journalists in the world.

WORLD WIDE WEB SITES

http://www.julesverne.ca/nelliebly_pbs.html

http://www.pbs.org/wgbh/amex/world

Anne Bradstreet

1612-1672
American Poet
First Woman To Be a Published Author in America

ANNE BRADSTREET WAS BORN in 1612 in Northampton, England. Her name when she was born was Anne Dudley. Her parents were Thomas and Dorothy Yorke Dudley. Thomas was a former soldier of Queen Elizabeth I, and he ran the estate of the Earl of Lincoln.

ANNE BRADSTREET GREW UP in England on the estate of the Earl of Lincoln, where her father worked. She did not go to school, but she was educated at home. The Earl of Lincoln had a large library, and Anne read classic works of history and literature. She also studied several languages, and could read Greek, Latin, French, and Hebrew.

When Anne was 16, she married a man named Simon

Bradstreet. Simon worked with her father. They lived with her family on the Lincoln estate for two years.

COMING TO THE NEW WORLD: In 1630, at the age of 18, Bradstreet emigrated to the New World with her husband and parents. They left on the ship *Arbella*, and sailed for three months. It was a perilous journey, and many died during the passage. They arrived at last at what is now Salem, Massachusetts. It was then known as the Massachusetts Bay Colony.

When Bradstreet and her family arrived in what would become New England, the colony was in its earliest years. There was only a basic settlement, and none of the comforts of the estate she was used to.

PURITAN LIFE IN NEW ENGLAND: Bradstreet was from a Puritan family. They were part of a great migration of people from England who had come to the New World seeking relief from a difficult political situation.

As Puritans, they wanted to "purify" the Church of England, the official religion of their country. They thought that their Christian religion had become corrupt, and needed to be changed. They had come to the New World to create a new life, based on their Puritan faith.

Bradstreet's father and husband were officials in the Massachusetts Bay Colony. When they arrived, the colony was in dire straits. The people had very little food; some were starving, and many were ill. The housing that was available was very limited. Bradstreet, her husband, and parents shared a house for many months, with only one room warmed by a fireplace. It was a difficult life, and at first Bradstreet was overwhelmed. She wrote later to her children, "I found a new world and new manners at which my heart rose" in protest.

Things gradually improved for Bradstreet and her family. She and her husband moved from Salem to their own home in Charlestown. She loved her husband very much, and they had eight children together. They had four sons, Samuel, Simon, Dudley, and John, and four daughters, Dorothy, Sarah, Hannah, and Mercy. Family was the center of their lives, and it became the source of her poetry, too.

STARTING TO WRITE POETRY: Bradstreet began to write poetry while raising her large family. Most of her poems are about her family, including poems to her husband and children. When her mother died, in 1643, and her father, in 1653, she wrote loving remembrances of them.

Bradstreet's poetry was well-written and thoughtful. It reflected the style of the major poets of her time, and also her wide reading in history and classic literature.

Bradstreet also wrote many poems about her love of nature, and of her faith. Yet some of what she wrote indicates that she questioned some Puritan beliefs. The Puritan faith placed all power and authority with men. Women were supposed to be quiet, modest, and only take part in the private world of the home.

Bradstreet had a friend, Anne Hutchinson, who dared to challenge the Puritan religious authority. She held prayer meetings in which she outlined her own religious views, which were different from those of the Puritans. When she refused to take back her beliefs, she was banished from the colony.

Bradstreet was very careful to share her poems only with family and close friends. In one poem, she remembers the greatness of Queen Elizabeth I. She challenges men to realize women's worth, and their ability to reason.

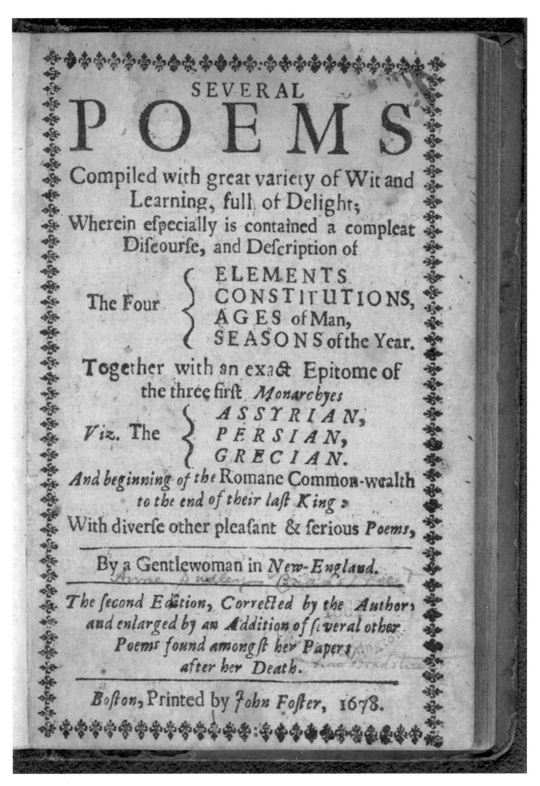

The first American edition of Bradstreet's poetry collection,
published in Boston in 1678.

A PUBLISHED POET: In 1650, Bradstreet's brother-in-law took her poems to England and had them published. (Most people believe that he did so without Bradstreet's knowledge.) The collection was called *The Tenth Muse Lately Sprung Up in America*. It was the first book by an American woman poet ever published. The book sold well in England, and was the only book by Bradstreet published in her lifetime.

The Bradstreet family moved several times in Anne's lifetime. They lived in Charlestown, Cambridge, Ipswich, and Andover, Massachusetts. As the children grew up and started lives of their own, Bradstreet wrote poetry about what it was like to witness those changes.

LATER YEARS: In her later years, Bradstreet faced tragedy and loss. In 1666, the Bradstreet home was destroyed by fire. In the following three years, three of her grandchildren died. Bradstreet's health began to fail, and she died on September 16, 1672, at the age of 60. Six years after her death, in 1678, an edition of her poetry collection was finally published in the American colonies.

HER LEGACY: Anne Bradstreet's poetry was not widely read until years after her death. Yet the depth and richness of her work make her one of the most important poets of colonial America. She is remembered for her poetry, and also as the first woman to have a book published in what would become the United States.

WORLD WIDE WEB SITES

http://www.loc.gov/exhibits/treasures/tri110.html
http://vcu.edu/engweb/eng384/bradbio.htm

Rachel Fuller Brown

1898 – 1980
American Scientist
Co-Creator of the First Anti-Fungal Antibiotic

RACHEL FULLER BROWN WAS BORN on November 23, 1898, in Springfield, Massachusetts. Her parents were Annie Fuller and George Brown. Annie was a homemaker during Rachel's early years. Later, she worked as a secretary. George sold insurance and real estate. Rachel had a younger brother named Sumner.

RACHEL FULLER BROWN GREW UP first in Springfield, then in Webster Groves, Missouri. Her family had moved there when she was young. When she was 12, her father left the family. Rachel, her mother, and brother moved back to Springfield, Massachusetts.

RACHEL FULLER BROWN WENT TO SCHOOL at the public schools in Missouri and Massachusetts. She was a fine student. When it was time for college, a family friend paid for her to attend Mount Holyoke.

Brown originally planned to major in history. But after taking a chemistry class in college, she decided she really wanted to study that, too. So she took a double major, in history and chemistry. She graduated from Mount Holyoke in 1920.

Brown went on to graduate school at the University of Chicago. She earned her master's degree in chemistry, then began to teach at a girls' school. After finishing her master's she began her PhD. She finished her research for her doctoral degree in 1926. That same year, she began a 42-year career in medical research.

STARTING TO WORK IN MEDICAL RESEARCH: Brown's first job was as a chemist for the New York State Division of Laboratories and Research. For the first 20 years of her career, she focused on finding drugs to fight infections, like pneumonia. In 1928, Alexander Fleming discovered penicillin. It was the first effective and safe antibiotic. (An "antibiotic" is a drug that fights bacterial infections.) Medical researchers everywhere worked to create other antibiotics to fight life-threatening diseases.

WORKING WITH ELIZABETH LEE HAZEN: In 1948, Brown began a very important working relationship. While working as a chemist in Albany, she was chosen to work with microbiologist **Elizabeth Lee**

Dr. Brown (left) and Dr. Hazen (right) in the lab.

Hazen to develop a drug that would fight fungal infections. Fungi are found everywhere, especially in soil and plants. Like bacteria and viruses, fungi can cause serious, life-threatening infections. Fungi cause infections of the skin, mouth, throat, digestive system, and other areas of the body. Hazen was working in New York City identifying antifungal chemicals. The two worked together to develop the first antifungal antibiotic for human use.

Over the span of two years, the two scientists conducted long-

87

distance research. Hazen collected samples of fungi found in soil. She grew cultures in her New York City lab. Then, she sent them to Brown in Albany in mason jars. In her Albany lab, Brown conducted experiments to determine the active agents in the samples. She'd identify the agents, then send them back to Hazen. Hazen would retest the sample, to see if the agent killed the fungi. If it did, she'd test the sample on animals to see if it was toxic.

The scientists faced a difficult problem. If an agent was effective against fungi, it could also be toxic to animals. To be safely used in humans, it first had to pass this important test. After two years of research, the scientists found a chemical that killed fungi, but was safe to use on animals. They named the drug Nystatin. (Named after "New York State.") Soon, it was tested on humans. It was a success. Hazen and Brown had done it. They'd invented a drug that successfully treated fungal infections.

Hazen and Brown received the patent for Nystatin in 1957. The drug made more than $13 million dollars in its first years. It is important to note that neither scientist ever earned money from their discovery. Instead, Hazen and Brown invested the money in a non-profit research foundation. That foundation still provides funding for medical research.

Nystatin proved to be effective in areas beyond human illness. It was used to fight infections in plants, like Dutch Elm Disease. Nystatin was also used to kill mold in old paintings and other art work.

Brown and Hazen continued to work together on antifungal research. In fact, they discovered two more antibiotics. The two scientists received many honors and awards, including the

Chemical Pioneer Award. It was especially important to Brown to provide scholarship and research money to deserving students. Brown continued to work at the New York State labs until she retired in 1968. A vaccine she developed to treat pneumonia is still used today.

RACHEL FULLER BROWN'S HOME AND FAMILY: Brown never married or had children. She died in Albany, New York, on January 14, 1980. She was 81 years old

In a letter written the month she died, Brown stated her hopes for the future. She wrote that she wished for "equal opportunities and accomplishments for all scientists regardless of sex."

THEIR LEGACY: Hazen and Brown's invention of Nystatin is considered one of the major breakthroughs in 20th century medicine. Nystatin has been used millions of times to treat fungal infections worldwide. Hazen and Brown also inspired young women to become scientists.

In 1994, Hazen and Brown became the second and third women to enter the National Inventors Hall of Fame. They followed **Gertrude Elion**, who created many important and life-saving medicines.

WORLD WIDE WEB SITES
http://web.mit.edu/invent/iow/HazenBrown.html
http://www.chemheritage.org/EducationalServices/pharm/
http://www.invent.org/hall_of_fame/75.html

Pearl S. Buck

1892-1973
American Author Famous for her Books on China
First American Woman to Win the
Nobel Prize in Literature

PEARL S. BUCK WAS BORN on June 26, 1892, in Hillsboro, West Virginia. "Buck" became her last name when she married. Her name when she was born was Pearl Comfort Sydenstricker. Her parents were Absalom and Caroline Sydenstricker. They were Presbyterian missionaries, who spent most of their lives in China. Pearl was the fourth of seven children. Only three lived to be adults.

PEARL S. BUCK GREW UP in China. She moved there with her family when she was only three months old. She would live there for most of the next 40 years.

GROWING UP IN CHINA: Pearl grew up in several places in China: in Chickiang, Kiangsu, and a small city on the Yangtze River. While she was growing up, her father was often gone, preaching the Christian faith to Chinese people in the countryside. Her mother raised her and her siblings, and also preached to local people.

Like her siblings, Pearl was raised to speak Chinese and English. She played with Chinese children and got to know their way of life and culture. Pearl loved to read. The family didn't have many books, but she was able to read a long, adult novel, *Oliver Twist* by Charles Dickens, when she was only seven. Soon, she'd read every one of Dickens's books.

PEARL S. BUCK WENT TO SCHOOL at home. She was taught by her mother and a tutor. Her mother gave her a weekly writing assignment when she was very young. At six, Pearl had a piece published in a local English-language newspaper.

In 1910, Pearl returned to the U.S. for college. She studied at Randolph-Macon Women's College in Lynchburg, Virginia. After graduating in 1914, she returned to China, because her mother was very sick.

BACK TO CHINA: While her mother recovered, Pearl met a young missionary from America named John Lossing Buck. He was working in China as an agricultural missionary. They fell in love and married in 1917.

The Bucks moved to northern China, where they worked in a peasant village. Those experiences would influence Buck's later novels.

In 1920, Buck had a daughter, Carol. Carol was born with a condition called "PKU." It causes profound mental delays. There wasn't adequate diagnosis or treatment available when Carol was born. Over the next several years, Buck divided her time between Carol's care and her work.

TEACHING AND WRITING: Buck began teaching at Nanking University in 1920. In 1924, the family moved back to the U.S. for one year. She studied at Cornell University, and earned a master's degree. She and her husband also adopted a daughter, Janice. They moved back to China in 1925.

These were very difficult times for Buck. Her daughter Carol had severe disabilities and needed special care. Her mother died, and her father moved in with her family. All around them, there was political and social turmoil. In 1927, they had to leave China for a year, to avoid the violent political demonstrations that were taking place.

Throughout all of these challenges in her life, Buck wrote and published. She contributed short stories and

essays to American magazines. She wrote a novel about her experiences in China, *East Wind, West Wind*, in part to help pay for Carol's medical care. With the money from her writings, Buck took Carol back to the U.S., and placed her in a treatment facility where she lived for the rest of her life.

THE GOOD EARTH: In 1931, Buck published the novel for which she is best known, *The Good Earth*. It was the first of three novels about a Chinese family, the Wangs. The novel was a worldwide success, and was the best-selling book in the U.S. for two years. In her clear, warm style, Buck introduced China, its people, and its culture to readers all over the world.

Buck continued the story of the Wang family in *Sons*, published in 1932, and *A House Divided*, in 1935. These and her later novels made her one of the most popular novelists in the world. Her work was translated into many languages.

In 1934, Buck moved back to the U.S. with her daughter Janice. John Buck remained in China. In 1935, she divorced John and married Richard Walsh. She purchased an 1825 farmhouse, Green Hills Farm, in Bucks County, Pennsylvania. She and Walsh also began adopting children, and their family grew to include seven children.

A PIONEER IN EDUCATION AND ADOPTION: Buck's experiences in China made her keenly aware of racial discrimination. She was an early advocate for civil rights, and wrote and spoke about the topic. Buck and her husband also wanted to foster peace and understanding between the U.S. and the countries of Asia. So in 1942, they founded the East West Association, to create peaceful cultural exchanges and education programs.

Group of children at Welcome House, Pearl Buck's inter-racial adoption agency.

Buck and her husband also became advocates for adoption, especially for children of Asian and mixed-race descent. At that time, there was open prejudice against the adoption of non-white children in America. In 1949, she founded Welcome House, the first organization to promote the adoption of inter-racial children. It is still an active adoption agency today.

WINNING THE NOBEL PRIZE IN LITERATURE: In 1938, Pearl Buck received the Nobel Prize in Literature. She was the first American woman to receive the award. It is considered one of the greatest honors an author can receive.

Pearl Buck with her daughter and grandchildren.

95

LATER YEARS: Buck continued to write well into her later years. She authored more than 120 books and over 1,000 publications, including novels, short stories, biographies, poetry, and children's literature. As part of her concern for the lives of mixed-race children, she started another organization. The Pearl S. Buck Foundation, which she established in 1964, helps fund education, health, and job training programs for children in Asian countries.

PEARL S. BUCK'S HOME AND FAMILY: Buck was married twice. Her first husband was named John Lossing Buck. They had two children, Carol and Janice. They divorced in 1935. Buck then married Richard Walsh. They adopted six children and became the foster parents of 10 more. The family lived at her home, Green Hills Farm. Pearl S. Buck died on March 6, 1973. She was 80 years old.

HER LEGACY: Pearl S. Buck is known around the world for her novel *The Good Earth.* It introduced millions of readers to China, many for the first time. She is remembered today for her novels, her devotion to the adoption of children, and for fostering cultural understanding between the U.S. and the nations of Asia.

WORLD WIDE WEB SITES

http://www.english.upenn.edu/Projects/Buck/biography.html
http://www.psbi.org/

Rachel Carson

1907-1964
American Biologist and Nature Writer
Author of *Silent Spring*

RACHEL LOUISE CARSON WAS BORN on May 27, 1907, in Springdale, Pennsylvania. Her parents were Robert Warden Carson and Maria McLean Carson. She was the youngest of three children in her family.

RACHEL CARSON GREW UP in Springdale, a small town about 20 miles north of Pittsburgh. Her family owned 65 acres of land outside of town. They kept horses, cows, and chickens. Rachel loved exploring the natural areas near her home. "As a child I spent long days out-of-doors in fields and woods, happiest with wild birds and creatures as companions," she remembered.

Rachel's other love was writing stories and poems. She showed talent as a writer from an early age. One of her stories was published in a national magazine when she was just ten years old.

RACHEL CARSON WENT TO SCHOOL at the Pennsylvania College for Women (now Chatham College) in Pittsburgh. She planned to study English and become a writer. But then she took a class in biology (the study of living things) taught by Mary Scott Skinker. Carson found the class so interesting that she decided to study biology instead. "Eventually it dawned on me, that by becoming a biologist I had given myself something to write about," she explained. Carson earned her college degree with honors in 1928.

Carson continued her education at Johns Hopkins University in Baltimore, Maryland. She earned a master's degree in zoology (the study of animals) in 1932. During the summers, she studied ocean life at the Woods Hole Marine Biological Laboratory in Massachusetts. She developed a love for the sea and its creatures that lasted the rest of her life.

FIRST JOBS: After she finished college, Carson taught classes at Johns Hopkins and the University of Maryland. In 1936 she got a job with the U.S. Bureau of Fisheries (which later became the U.S. Fish and Wildlife Service, or FWS). The FWS is a government agency that manages the country's fish and wildlife. It uses laws like the Endangered Species Act and the Marine Mammal Protection Act to help conserve these natural resources.

Carson worked as a science writer for the agency. She wrote scripts for radio programs, articles for scientific journals, and pamphlets telling people how to cook fish. Carson was a great writ-

Carson in the lab, looking through a microscope, 1951.

er. She used beautiful, flowing language that made dry, scientific topics seem more interesting.

WRITING HER FIRST BOOK: One of Carson's scripts was too fancy for the FWS radio program. Her boss suggested that she turn it into a magazine article. Carson sent the article to the *Atlantic Monthly,* one of the nation's top magazines. To Carson's surprise, it was published as "Undersea" in 1937. A publisher saw the article and asked Carson to expand it into a book. She worked on the project in the evenings for three years.

Carson's first book, *Under the Sea-Wind,* was finally published in 1941. It told readers all about life along the sea shore and on the ocean bottom. The book got good reviews. Unfortunately, it did not sell many copies. The United States entered World War II a few weeks after it was published. Most Americans lost interest in buying books at that time.

BECOMING A BEST-SELLING AUTHOR: After the war ended in 1945, Carson started working on a new book. *The Sea around Us* explored the history of the world's oceans. It was published in 1951 and became a best-seller. Critics said Carson explained complex scientific topics in a clear, understandable way. Many of them praised her lovely, poetic language. *The Sea around Us* won the National Book Award. Carson became a famous writer. She retired from her job at FWS in 1952.

Carson did lots of traveling for her next book, *The Edge of the Sea.* It gave readers a close-up look at the coast of the Atlantic Ocean from Maine to Florida. *The Edge of the Sea* became a best-seller when it was published in 1955. The book was also turned into an award-winning film.

ASKING QUESTIONS ABOUT PESTICIDE USE: Around this time, Carson started to worry about the growing use of dangerous chemi-

Carson at Hawk Mountain, Pennsylvania, c. 1947.

cals known as pesticides. During the late 1940s and 1950s, pesticides were commonly sprayed on food crops and in homes. People used pesticides to get rid of unwanted "pests" like insects, rodents, and weeds. But these chemicals were often toxic or poisonous to other creatures, including birds, fish, and humans.

The most popular pesticide was Dichloro-Diphenyl-Trichloroethane (DDT). DDT was very effective in killing mosquitoes and other insects. The U.S. government claimed that DDT helped reduce disease and increase food production. Big chemical companies made lots of money selling DDT. Few people questioned whether using DDT was a good idea.

Carson saw news stories that made her wonder about the safety of pesticides. Sometimes wildlife died in places where the chemicals were sprayed. Carson's old friends Stuart and Olga Huckins ran a bird sanctuary in Massachusetts. They told her how their birds had disappeared after DDT was sprayed in the area.

Carson decided to take action. "The more I learned about the use of pesticides, the more appalled [upset] I became," she said. "I realized that here was material for a book. What I discovered was that everything which meant most to me as a naturalist was being threatened, and that nothing I could do would be more important."

SILENT SPRING: For four years, Carson gathered data and talked with scientific experts. She learned that pesticides built up in soil, water, and the bodies of animals over time. "Chemicals sprayed on croplands or forests or gardens lie long in soil, entering into living organisms [creatures], passing from one to another in a chain of poisoning and death," she explained.

The buildup of DDT was especially harmful to predators (animals that eat other animals), like bald eagles. Eagles ate fish that were full of DDT. The toxic chemicals made the eagles'

Carson doing research on Cobb Island, Virginia, 1947.

eggshells thin and weak. The eggs often broke before the baby birds were ready to hatch. This problem led to a dangerous drop in the number of bald eagles.

In 1962 Carson published her findings in a book called *Silent Spring*. She painted a scary picture of what might happen if the reckless use of pesticides continued. Carson warned that the chemicals would poison the soil and water and kill many plants and animals. She imagined a day when no birds would sing in the springtime. "On the mornings that had once throbbed with the dawn chorus of scores of bird voices there was now no sound," she wrote. "Only silence lay over the fields and woods and marsh."

Carson pointed out that humans were part of the natural world. She argued that people would suffer the harmful effects of chemical pollution as well. Still, Carson did not call for an end to all pesticide use. She thought the chemicals could be helpful if they were used carefully. But she wanted the American people to know about the dangers involved.

LAUNCHING THE ENVIRONMENTAL MOVEMENT: *Silent Spring* became a best-seller. It brought national attention to the dangers of pesticides. Carson's clear writing style helped ordinary readers understand the scientific facts. Millions of people who read the book felt concerned about the environment for the first time. *Silent Spring* inspired them to take action to protect the Earth and its creatures. Many people believe that the book helped launch the environmental movement in the United States.

Not everyone liked Carson's book. It became the center of a big argument. The big chemical companies that sold DDT attacked Carson. They questioned her data and her ability as a scientist. Carson bravely defended herself and her book. In 1963 she appeared on a CBS television special called "The Silent Spring of

Carson testifying before the U.S. Congress, June 4, 1963.

Rachel Carson." She debated a chemical industry spokesman about pesticides. She impressed many viewers with her calm, common-sense answers. In the end, the attacks only drew more attention to *Silent Spring.*

The U.S. Congress formed a special committee to investigate the use of pesticides. The committee agreed with all of Carson's findings. It said that DDT and other pesticides had harmful effects on the environment. It recommended passing new laws to control pesticide use. By the end of 1963, 40 states were considering such laws. In 1972 DDT was banned from use in the United States. Many other countries placed strict limits on the chemical as well.

Today, some people want DDT to be legal again. They say it is needed to control mosquitoes in Africa. These mosquitoes carry a deadly disease called malaria. Millions of people in Africa get malaria each year. But many people think DDT is not the answer. They worry that the pesticide might harm as many Africans as malaria does. They say that safer chemicals should be used instead.

RACHEL CARSON'S HOME AND FAMILY: Carson never married or had children of her own. But she still ended up raising three children. She took care of her sister Marian's two daughters, Marjorie and Virginia Williams, after their mother died in 1937. Years later, when her niece Marjorie died, Carson adopted her young son, Roger Christie.

Carson lived in Silver Spring, Maryland. She also built a summer home on a large piece of land along the coast of Maine. In her spare time, she enjoyed flower gardening and bird watching. While Carson was leading the fight against pesticides, she was also battling breast cancer and heart disease. She died on April 14, 1964, at the age of 56.

HER LEGACY: Carson is remembered as one of the greatest nature writers in American history. She lived long enough to know that *Silent Spring* had a major impact. "Now I can believe that I have at least helped a little," she said. "It would be unrealistic to believe that one book could bring a complete change."

Carson received many important awards and honors, even after death. She won the Audubon Medal, and she was elected to the American Academy of Arts and Sciences. In 1980, she received the Presidential Medal of Freedom. The next year, her picture appeared on a U.S. postage stamp.

Carson's courageous fight against pesticides inspired many future environmental leaders. "Rachel Carson was one of the reasons why I became so conscious of the environment and so involved with environmental issues," said Al Gore, who earned the Nobel Peace Prize for his fight against global warming. "Her picture hangs on my office wall among those of the political leaders, the presidents, and the prime ministers. Carson has had as much or more effect on me than any of them, and perhaps all of them together."

WORLD WIDE WEB SITES

http://www.rachelcarson.org/biography.aspx

http://www.rachelcarsonhomestead.org/

http://www.fws.gov/northeast/rachelcarson/carsonbio.html

http://www.ecotopia.org/ehof/carson/

Mary Cassatt

1844-1926
American Painter

MARY CASSATT WAS BORN on May 22, 1844, in Allegheny City, Pennsylvania. Her full name was Mary Stevenson Cassatt, and her last name is pronounced cah-SAT. Her parents were Robert and Katherine Cassatt. Robert was a successful banker and Katherine was a homemaker, who raised Mary and her four siblings.

MARY CASSATT GREW UP in Philadelphia, where her family moved when she was very young. Her parents valued education and travel. When she was seven years old, her family moved to

France, where they lived for three years. By the time she was 10 years old, Mary had visited most of the major cities of Europe.

MARY CASSATT WENT TO SCHOOL in Philadelphia and Paris. By the time she was a teenager, she knew she wanted to be an artist. Her parents, especially her father, didn't like the idea. At that time, young women from wealthy families were not supposed to have careers. They were expected to become wives and mothers. But Mary knew what she wanted, and when she was 15, she began studying at the Pennsylvania Academy of the Fine Arts in Philadelphia.

Art school was a disappointment to Cassatt. She complained that the teachers taught her nothing. She began to study the art of the "Old Masters" on her own. These works, by great artists of the 1400s and later, were the first major influences on her own painting.

MOVING TO PARIS: In 1866, Cassatt left the U.S. and moved to Paris to study art. She couldn't study at the art schools in Paris, because they didn't allow women. So she studied privately with artists. She also went to the Louvre, the great museum in Paris, where she copied the works of the Old Masters.

After a few years in France, Cassatt returned to the U.S. France was at war, and she moved home with her parents. Her father, still unsupportive of her work, refused to pay for her art supplies. It was a difficult time for Cassatt. But in 1872, a local bishop commissioned her to make copies of two famous Italian paintings for him. She moved to Italy and made the copies, which were of paintings by the Renaissance master Correggio, who was one of her favorites. With the money she earned from the work, she was able to move back to Paris.

A drawing of Mary Cassatt looking at paintings at the Louvre in Paris, by French artist Edgar Degas, 1879.

IMPRESSIONISM AND EDGAR DEGAS: In 1874, Cassatt saw the work of Edgar Degas for the first time. It was a life-changing event. The paintings were of ballet dancers. But it was his treatment of his subject, especially the technique, that impressed her. "I saw art as I wanted to scc it," she wrote. "I began to live."

She became a close friend and student of Degas. He introduced her to the art movement called "Impressionism." The Impressionists took a different approach to the classical style of art popular at the time. They used bold colors, and emphasized the way that light struck objects in a painting. They didn't aim for a "realistic" effect. They wanted to capture the "impression" suggested by a work of art.

Cassatt began to exhibit her art with the Impressionists in the late 1870s. She was the only American, and one of only three women, to do so. She met the famous Impressionists Claude Monet and Camille Pissarro. Learning from Degas, she became expert in her use of pastels, and also learned the technique of copper engraving.

Cassatt was developing as an artist, and also as a spokesperson for Impressionism. She convinced several collectors of the importance of their art. Museums in America also began to purchase Impressionist works. In this way, she helped spread the influence of the Impressionist movement.

Cassatt's art work was interrupted over the years because of family illness. Her family came to live with her in 1877, but soon both her mother and sister became ill. She cared for both of them until their deaths.

A FAMOUS ARTIST: By the late 1880s, Cassatt had established herself as one of the finest artists in France. Though little known in her own country, she was famous in Paris, especially for her pastel and oil paintings of simple domestic scenes.

Cassatt was best known for her paintings of mothers and children. She presented them in everyday settings, and in everyday clothes. What she captured was the closeness and the love between them. Her portraits weren't sentimental or simple. Instead, they showed the natural, tender feelings between mothers and their children.

Sometimes she painted people she knew, including friends and family. Sometimes, she hired models. Cassatt always was very careful in the design of her paintings. She planned everything with great care, to achieve art that was honest, moving, and true to life.

In the 1890s, Cassatt saw an exhibition of Japanese art. It had a

"Mother's Kiss" by Mary Cassatt, 1890–1891.

great influence on her later work, especially in her use of bold color. It also influenced her print-making technique, which became a focus for her later work.

Mary Cassatt self-portrait, 1880.

LATER YEARS: Cassatt became ill in her later years. She developed diabetes, and then became nearly blind. She stopped painting in 1914. She came to the U.S. and became involved in the movement for **WOMEN'S SUFFRAGE**. She even hosted an exhibition in New York, and gave the money she made from the sale of her paintings to the movement.

Cassatt's final years were very difficult for her. She had lost her sight, so could no longer paint. She died at her home near Paris on June 14, 1926.

MARY CASSATT'S HOME AND FAMILY: Cassatt never married or had children. She lived most of her life in France, where she was a treasured member of the artist community.

HER LEGACY: Cassatt is widely considered to be one of the most accomplished painters of her generation. She broke barriers for women, choosing to have a career as an artist, and accomplishing that goal in a male-dominated profession. She is remembered for her paintings of mothers and children that indicate the deep love between them, with artistic grace and without sentimentality.

WORLD WIDE WEB SITES

http://www.artic.edu/aic/resources/resource/467

http://www.butlerart.com/pc_book/pages/mary_stevenson_
  cassatt_1845.htm

Catherine the Great

1729-1796
Empress of Russia

CATHERINE THE GREAT WAS BORN on April 21, 1729, in the German city of Stettin. Her name when she was born was Sophia Augusta Fredericka, and she was known as Princess Sophia. She was the daughter of two members of European royal families. Her father was Prince Christian August of Anhalt-Zerbst. Her mother was Princess Johanna Elizabeth of Holstein-Gottorp.

CATHERINE THE GREAT GREW UP in a wealthy, privileged family. She had private tutors and learned several languages. She also studied history, literature, art, music, and religion. At that time, she was a Protestant.

MARRIAGE: In 1744, Princess Sophia and her mother were invited to the court of Empress Elizabeth of Russia. Elizabeth hoped that a marriage could be arranged between her son, Peter, and Sophia. Throughout history, marriages have been arranged between members of royal families as a way of creating political alliances. Both Empress Elizabeth and Sophia's parents hoped that her marriage to Peter would strengthen Russia's influence in Europe.

Sophia and Peter were married in 1745. In marrying a member of the Russian royal family, Sophia had to convert to the Russian Orthodox faith. She took the name Catherine, as another part of becoming a member of the Russian royal family.

Catherine's marriage to Peter was very unhappy. They didn't love each other, and Peter was widely disliked by the Russian people. Even though he was the grandson of the former czar Peter the Great, he didn't think of himself as Russian. He refused to join the Russion Orthodox faith, and was very open about his dislike of the Russians. Peter was also closely allied with Prussia (a country that is now Germany and Poland), which was an enemy of Russia. He even praised its ruler, Frederick the Great.

Catherine took a different path. She learned Russian and became a devout member of the Orthodox faith. She learned the ways of power in the Russian court. And she developed powerful political allies in the army and government.

BECOMING EMPRESS OF RUSSIA: When Empress Elizabeth died in

Portrait of Catherine the Great, c. 1796.

1761, Peter became Emperor Peter III, and Catherine became Empress. Peter was very unpopular with the military, the nobility, and the people. Within a few months, there were plots to overthrow him.

Catherine learned of these plots, and decided she wanted to rule Russia herself. In 1762, with the military supporting her, she declared herself Catherine II, ruler of Russia. She had Peter removed from power and arrested. He died eight days later. She became the sole ruler of Russia.

RULING RUSSIA: When Catherine took over in Russia, she had plans to make changes in education, the legal system, and the arts. But first, she had to make sure her of her control of the country. She formed alliances with powerful nobles and military leaders. She won their loyalty, then was able to pursue her goals.

Catherine was a believer in the theories of the "Enlightenment." That is a philosophy that became important in the 1700s throughout Europe. Enlightenment thinkers believed in the importance of reason and science. Under its influence, Catherine began a series of reforms in Russia. She created many schools, from the elementary to the college level. She reformed the legal system, establishing courts and revising laws. She also established policies for medical care.

Catherine was also a great patron of the arts. She encouraged writers, painters, and musicians. She collected art from all over Europe and built museums to display it. She made St. Petersburg an important center for the arts.

During Catherine's reign, Russia battled neighboring countries. Russia went to war several times against Turkey to gain land. Catherine and her advisors wanted to establish routes to the Black Sea. That way they could trade goods with other countries, using

One of Catherine the Great's coaches.

land and water routes. Russia succeeded in their goal, defeating Turkey and establishing the Russian port of Odessa on the Black Sea.

Catherine could be ruthless in her determination to expand Russian lands. With Prussia and Austria, Russian forces took land from Poland by force. Russia also added the Crimean provinces to its holdings, expanding its boundaries even further.

Catherine also had to deal with threats from within her own country. In 1774, a rebellion began, under a man named Yemelyan Pugachev. He claimed to be Peter III, and rallied soldiers and serfs to his cause. Catherine's troops defeated Pugachev after several battles, but the threat concerned her. Many of Pugachev's supporters were peasants, called serfs. She decided to severely limit any rights the serfs had. She wanted to punish them and protect herself against any future rebellion.

Catherine was an ambitious ruler. Still bent on extending Russian lands and influence, she went to war with Turkey again in 1787. She wanted to capture its main city, Constantinople, and other territories. She won land for Russia in the treaty that ended the war.

To extend Russia's strength, Catherine encouraged farmers to move to the new lands she had conquered. The population and the economy of Russia grew greatly during her reign. At the same time, she was worried about the revolutions in France and the United States that took place during her reign. She thought she had the right to rule with absolute authority. Catherine the Great ruled Russia with a firm hand until she suffered a stroke and died, in November 1796.

HER LEGACY: Catherine the Great is remembered as a powerful ruler, who wanted to expand Russia's strength and influence. She could be harsh and punishing to her enemies, inside and outside of Russia. But she also began major reforms that helped modernize the country in law, education, and the arts.

WORLD WIDE WEB SITE

http://countrystudies.us/russia/4.htm

Cleopatra

69 B.C.E.–30 B.C.E.
Queen of Egypt
Last of the Pharaohs

CLEOPATRA WAS BORN in January 69 B.C.E. in Alexandria, Egypt. Although she was a member of the Egyptian royal family, she was Greek. She was descended from Ptolemy (TOL-uh-me), a Greek general who had served Alexander the Great, who conquered Egypt in 332 B.C.E. The Ptolemies had ruled Egypt since 305 B.C.E.

Cleopatra, whose full title was Cleopatra VII, was the daughter of Ptolemy Auletes. At that time, Egyptian rulers often gave several of their children the same name, to indicate their royal background. So she had two older sisters, Cleopatra VI and Berenice IV, and a younger sister, Arsinoe IV, and three younger brothers, Ptolemy XII, Ptolemy XIII, and Ptolemy XIV.

CLEOPATRA GREW UP in Alexandria, which the Ptolemy royal family had made a center of culture and power. It was the home of the first great library in the ancient world. It was also Egypt's seaport on the Mediterranean Sea.

Much of what we know about Cleopatra is part legend and part history, but it appears that she was very intelligent. She knew seven languages, and was the first and only Ptolemy to learn Egyptian. She also wrote books, and learned all she could about Egyptian history. Cleopatra followed the Egyptian religion. She saw herself as a reincarnation of Isis, who is the Egyptian goddess of wisdom.

BECOMING QUEEN OF EGYPT: When Cleopatra was 18, her father, Ptolemy Auletes, died. He left the kingdom to Cleopatra and her brother Ptolemy XIII, who was 12 years old at the time, with his counselor Pompey overseeing them. They were to be co-rulers of Egypt, and by custom, they were married to one another. But Cleopatra wanted to rule alone. She declared that she was ruler, or Pharaoh, of Egypt. She was only the third woman to rule as Pharaoh, a title usually limited to male kings. (You can read about the first female Pharoah, **Hatshepsut**, in this volume.)

THE WORLD OF CLEOPATRA: During Cleopatra's time, Rome was the leading power of the world. Egypt was weak, and Cleopatra wanted to strengthen her country. She wanted to build a strong alliance with Rome, for economic and political reasons.

Cleopatra knew that Egypt needed to develop trade with Rome, and she needed Rome's protection, too. She had two famous lovers, Julius Caesar and Mark Antony, who were two of the most powerful leaders of the era. Whether she loved them, or whether she had the relationships for the power and protection of Egypt is not known. But in those relationships and their outcome, she became one of the most famous women rulers of all time.

Portrait sculpture of Queen Cleopatra.

From the beginning of her reign, Cleopatra could not rule Egypt without a struggle. Her brother's advisors didn't trust Cleopatra. In 48 B.C.E., they drove her from Egypt, and she lived in exile.

JULIUS CAESAR: Cleopatra saw her chance to return to power in Julius Caesar, the powerful general who ruled Rome. He came to Alexandria in 48 B.C.E. to challenge her former guardian, Pompey. Cleopatra had herself delivered to Caesar at his palace, wrapped in a carpet. Caesar fell in love with her, and he took her side in the struggle against her brother.

With Caesar's help, Cleopatra regained power. Her brother, Ptolemy XIII, drowned, and Caesar made her next youngest brother, Ptolemy XIV, her co-ruler. Caesar and Cleopatra had a son together, Caesarion.

Cleopatra left Egypt and lived in Rome with Caesar for two years, from 46 B.C.E. to 44 B.C.E. But Caesar had strong political enemies. He was assassinated in 44 B.C.E. and Cleopatra and Caesarion returned to Egypt. To further strengthen her power, she had Caesarion named her co-ruler.

MARK ANTONY: After Caesar's murder, Rome was torn by civil war. One of the factions was led by the military leader Mark Antony. Antony demanded that Cleopatra meet him in the city of Tarsus. He wanted taxes from Egypt, and her loyalty.

Cleopatra arrived in a barge, dressed as Venus, the goddess of love. Like Caesar before him, Antony fell in love with Cleopatra. He returned to Alexandria with her and they lived together. Cleopatra and Antony had twins, Cleopatra Selene II and Alexander Helios, and a son, Ptolemy Philadelphius.

Mark Antony had enemies of his own. Julius Caesar's son, Octavian, was head of the other major faction in Rome's civil war. He planned to attack Egypt, and rule the entire Mediterranean.

ACTIUM: Cleopatra and Antony had ambitions to rule of their own. They joined forces to fight Octavian. Cleopatra was wealthy, and had a large naval fleet. In 31 B.C.E., Octavian

A hieroglyph of Cleopatra and her son Caesarion at the Temple of Dendera, Egypt.

Coin showing a likeness of Cleopatra.

fought the combined forces of Cleopatra and Antony at the battle of Actium. He won in an overwhelming show of force. Shortly afterward, Antony committed suicide.

DEATH: Crushed by the death of the man she loved, Cleopatra took her own life. No one is exactly sure how she died, but on August 10, 30 B. C. E., Cleopatra was found dead, possibly from a snake bite.

THE END OF THE EGYPTIAN MONARCHS: With Cleopatra, the age of the Egyptian Pharaohs came to an end, and was followed by Roman rule. But her memory, especially the legend of her life, lives on.

HER LEGACY: Cleopatra is one of the most famous women who ever lived. She has passed into legend as beautiful, powerful, ambitious, and intelligent. Famous writers, including William Shakespeare, have left stories of her life that have contributed to her legend. In modern times, she continues to fascinate, and movies and books based on her life are always popular. While certain facts of her life—and death—remain unknown, Cleopatra has left a legacy that continues to captivate people, 2,000 years after her reign.

WORLD WIDE WEB SITES

http:// www.fi.edu/cleopatra

http://www.fieldmuseum.org/cleopatra/whocleo10a.html

http://www.touregypt.net/cleopatr.htm

Hillary Rodham Clinton

1947-
American Secretary of State, Former U.S. Senator and Former First Lady

HILLARY RODHAM CLINTON WAS BORN October 26, 1947, in Chicago, Illinois. Clinton became her last name when she married. Her name when she was born was Hillary Rodham. Her parents were Hugh and Dorothy Rodham. Her father was a salesman and business owner and her mother was a homemaker. Hillary has two younger bothers, Hugh and Tony.

HILLARY RODHAM CLINTON GREW UP in Park Ridge, Illinois, a suburb of Chicago. She enjoyed a lot of activities growing up, including sports, Girl Scouts, ballet, and piano. She remembers that she was encouraged by her family to do well. Her mom and dad told her, "You can do or be whatever you choose, as long as you're willing to work for it."

Her mother also helped all the children to have faith in themselves. "She encouraged us to speak out and not worry about what anybody else thought, just be ourselves," Clinton remembers.

HILLARY RODHAM CLINTON WENT TO SCHOOL at the public schools in Park Ridge. She always did very well in school. In high school, she was involved in many things, including student government and the debate team.

Hillary was also very active in her church group. Even as a teenager, she cared about poor people, especially poor children. She became involved with organizations that worked to help people in need.

After high school, Hillary attended Wellesley College, an excellent school near Boston. When she went to Wellesley, it was an all-girl's school, but now it has both male and female students. In college she studied political science—the study of how government works. After college, she went to law school at Yale University. While in law school, she worked for organizations that helped to improve the lives of the poor.

FIRST JOBS: When she finished law school, Clinton began to work in Boston with Marian Wright Edelman. Edelman was head of the Children's Defense Fund, a group that works to help children. After working on the problems of poor families with that organization, she moved to Washington, D. C., then to Arkansas.

At Yale, she had met Bill Clinton, and they had fallen in love. After working far away from each other, they decided to live closer together. So Hillary took a job teaching law in Arkansas. Soon after, Bill and Hillary got married.

LIFE IN ARKANSAS: Bill had been interested in politics all his life. A lifelong Democrat, he was elected governor of Arkansas in 1978. Hillary took a job as an attorney in Arkansas. Even though she had a full-time job in law, she continued her work with children. As First Lady of Arkansas, she was head of the state's Education Standards Committee. She also co-founded the Arkansas Advocates for Children and Families.

Secretary of State Hillary Clinton addresses the UN Security Council on the 10th anniversay of Council Resolution 1325 on Women, Peace, and Security.

In 1991, Bill Clinton decided to run for President of the United States. Hillary took part in the campaign, and gave speeches all over the country. Bill Clinton won the election in 1992 and was president for eight years.

FIRST LADY OF THE UNITED STATES: During Bill Clinton's years as president, Hillary Clinton was active in many roles. She was an advocate for health care reform, and helped develop the Children's Health Insurance Program. That program provides health care to millions of poor children. She was also involved in improving the adoption and foster care system in the country.

Clinton traveled to more than 80 different countries as First Lady. She gave speeches as an advocate for democracy, human rights, and especially women's rights. In 1995, she gave a rousing speech in Beijing. She said, "human rights are women's rights, and women's rights are human rights."

President Clinton chose **Madeleine Albright** to be his Secretary of State. She was the first woman to hold the position. Albright and Hillary Clinton formed an organization called Vital Voices Democracy Initiative. It trains women for leadership roles all over the world.

SENATOR FROM NEW YORK: After Bill Clinton's second term was over, the family moved to Chappaqua, New York. Hillary Clinton began a "listening tour" of the state. She listened to the problems and political concerns of New Yorkers. She decided she could help them, and ran for the U.S. Senate as the candidate of the Democratic Party.

In 2000, Hillary Clinton was elected Senator for New York. She was the only First Lady in history to be elected to the Senate,

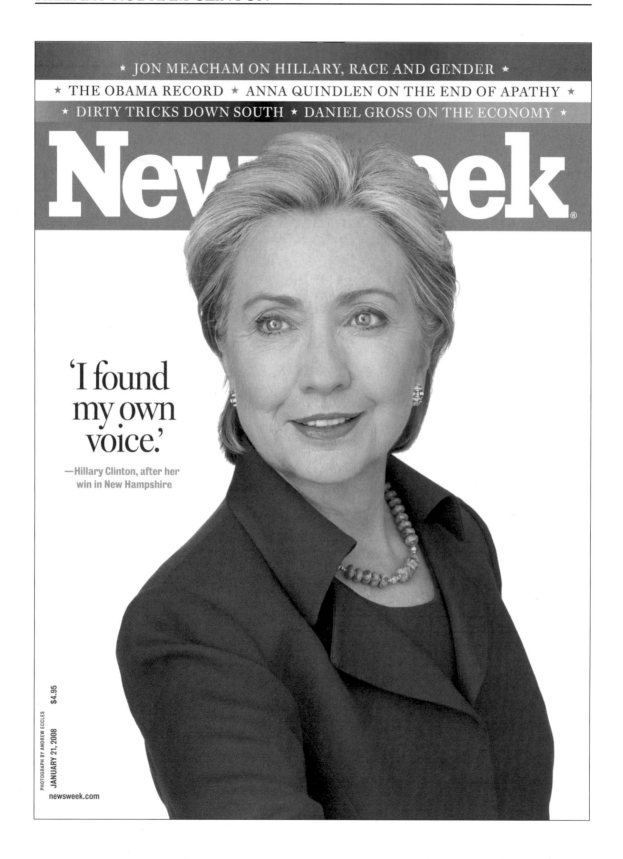

and also the first woman to be elected statewide from the state of New York. Clinton held a series of important committee jobs in the Senate, including the Armed Services Committee, the Health, Education, Labor, and Pensions Committee, the Environment and Public Works Committee, the Budget Committee, and the Select Committee on Aging. She developed a reputation for hard work, and for being able to work well with both Democrats and Republicans.

On domestic issues, she also continued to be a staunch advocate for health care and economic opportunity for all Americans. On international issues, Clinton worked with the Department of Defense Joint Forces Command, and served on the Commission on Security and Cooperation in Europe. She ran for re-election in 2006, and won.

HILLARY CLINTON'S HISTORIC RUN FOR THE PRESIDENCY:
In 2007, Hillary Clinton decided to run for President. She ran for the Democratic nomination, and her main opponent was Barack Obama. Soon it was clear that they were the frontrunners. It was an historic race. It was the first time that a woman and an African-American were competing for the nomination of a major party. Clinton won several early primaries and many dedicated delegates. By June 2008, Obama had enough delegates to win the nomination, and Clinton campaigned for him vigorously.

After Obama won the election in November 2008, he chose Clinton to be his Secretary of State.

SECRETARY OF STATE: As Secretary of State, Clinton is in charge of the U.S. State Department. She is a member of the President's cabinet, and helps to determine U.S. foreign policy around the world.

She travels constantly, meeting with the country's allies. She helps to forge agreements between countries, to advance America's interests, and to foster peace around the world.

HOME AND FAMILY: Hillary married Bill Clinton in 1975. In 1980, they had a daughter, Chelsea. Chelsea lived in the White House when she was a teenager. In the summer of 2010, the Clinton's hosted Chelsea's marriage to Mark Mezvinsky. When they're not in Washington, D.C., the Clintons live in Chappaqua, New York, where they have a home.

HER LEGACY: Hillary Rodham Clinton is continuing to add to a legacy that includes a number of ground-breaking achievements. She is the only former First Lady elected to the U.S. Senate. She is the second woman to run for the presidential nomination for a major U.S. political party. (The first was **Margaret Chase Smith).** And she is only the third woman to serve as U.S. Secretary of State.

WORLD WIDE WEB SITES

http://www.state.gov/secretary/

http://www.whitehouse.gov/about/first-ladies/hillaryclinton

Marie Curie

1867-1934
**Polish Scientist Who Co-Discovered
Radium and Polonium
First Person to Win Two Nobel Prizes**

MARIE CURIE WAS BORN on November 7, 1867, in Warsaw, Poland. Her name when she was born was Maria Sklodowska. Her parents were both teachers. She had four siblings: sisters Zosia, Hela, and Bronya, and a brother, Jozef.

MARIE CURIE GREW UP in a family that valued education and their Polish heritage. When Maria was growing up, Poland had been partitioned into three provinces, and was no long a country. The city in Poland that she grew up in, Warsaw, was then in a Russian province. Like her father, she became active in Polish patriotic organizations.

MARIE CURIE WENT TO SCHOOL at local schools and at home. Her father taught her physics and chemistry, and she was an excellent student. She graduated from high school with highest honors at 15, but, at that time in Poland, women could not attend college. So she and her sister Bronya attended what were called "floating universities." The classes were held in secret, often at night, so that women could study for degrees.

Maria and Bronya wanted to study at the Sorbonne in Paris. That is one of the finest universities in the world. They knew it was very expensive. So they developed a plan: Maria would work as a governess to raise the money for Bronya to go to the Sorbonne. Then, when Bronya got her degree, she would help pay for Maria's college.

Maria worked as a governess for three years, while Bronya finished her medical degree. She taught the children of a beet farmer. She also taught the children of the Polish peasants who worked the farmer's land. That was against the law at that time, because the Russians forbade Polish peasants to be educated.

Finally, at the age of 24, Maria went to Paris, where she studied mathematics and physics. Now known by the French form of her name, "Marie," she rented a tiny attic room that was so cold that she wore all her clothes to bed at night, to stay warm. Although she had been away from school for years and the classes were given in French, she was an outstanding student.

Marie loved her studies. "It was like a new world opened to me, the world of science, which I was at last permitted to know in all liberty," she recalled. Marie received a degree in physics in 1893, and in mathematics in 1894.

MEETING PIERRE CURIE: In 1894, Marie met Pierre Curie. He was a professor of physics and an internationally known scientist. They shared a great passion for science, and fell in love, marrying in 1895. Unlike many men of his era, Pierre Curie considered Marie his equal in every way. He considered her intellect and ability equal to his own. When their daughter Irene was born, Pierre's grandfather

Marie and Pierre Curie in their garden, 1895.

became her primary caregiver. That way, Marie and Pierre could both continue their scientific work.

INVESTIGATING "RAYS": Marie and Pierre Curie were fascinated by the recent discovery of "rays," the energy and light that some materials gave off. "X-rays" had been discovered by Wilhelm Roentgen in 1895. While doing experiments on cathode rays, Roentgen discovered that these mysterious rays could go through paper, wood, skin, and other materials. But they didn't penetrate bone. The rays also made an image on a photographic plate. This meant that scientists could take pictures of things not visible to the eye. It led to the invention of the "x-ray" machine, which became an invaluable diagnostic tool for medicine. It allowed doctors to see inside a patient, and diagnose diseases, for the very first time.

The Curies were also inspired by the discovery of radioactivity by Henril Becquerel in 1896. Becquerel had discovered that minerals that contained the element uranium gave off rays, too. Marie decided to focus her research on the rays given off by uranium.

Working out of a simple lab created out of a school storeroom, Marie set to work. She investigated the properties of the rays produced by different compounds containing uranium. She discovered that the strength of the rays didn't vary, no matter what the source of the uranium was.

This discovery led her to a revolutionary new theory. She proposed that the key to the strength of the rays was in the *atomic structure* of the uranium. At that point, scientists thought that the atom was the basic unit of matter. Curie suggested that the atom itself was made up of unique particles, and that the atomic structure of each element was distinct.

Marie Curie in her laboratory.

Next, she went through the entire table of elements to test the radioactive qualities of each one. She found that only two of the known elements, uranium and thorium, were radioactive.

DISCOVERING POLONIUM: Pierre now joined Marie in her experiments. They decided to evaluate natural ores that contained both uranium and thorium. They discovered that two ores, called pitchblende and chalcolite, were much more radioactive than uranium alone. Marie proposed that the high level of radioactivity might be caused by an additional radioactive element, one that had not yet been discovered.

The Curies conducted experiments on the radioactive ores that proved that they had indeed discovered a new element. They published a paper to announce their discovery in July 1898. They named the new element "polonium," to honor Marie's home country of Poland.

DISCOVERING RADIUM: Within months, the Curies announced a new discovery. They found another radioactive element, which they named "radium," from the Latin world for "ray." They spent much of the next few years refining their experiments, and proving their findings.

They worked long days in a new lab, separating chemicals, measuring the results, and checking their work for accuracy. It was backbreaking work. "Sometimes I had to spend the whole day stirring a boiling mass with a heavy iron rod nearly as big as myself," Marie recalled.

When the Curies were doing their ground-breaking work, no one knew of the deadly nature of radiation. But they were exposing themselves to lethal levels every day. It would eventually lead to illness and extreme fatigue for them both.

While they conducted their experiments on radium and polonium, both the Curies continued to teach. Marie also completed her doctoral degree in 1903. She was the first woman to receive a Ph.D. in science in France. The professors who granted her degree said that her thesis represented the greatest scientific contribution ever made by a doctoral candidate.

FIRST NOBEL PRIZE: In 1903, Marie and Pierre Curie won the Nobel Prize in Physics. That is one of the most important awards in the world of science. They received the award for their research into radioactivity. They became famous around the world.

THE DEATH OF PIERRE CURIE:
In 1906, tragedy struck. On April 19, Pierre Curie was run over by a horse-drawn cart and killed. Marie was overwhelmed with grief at the loss of her husband, friend, and scientific partner. "It is impossible for me to express the profoundness and importance of the crisis brought into my life by the loss of the one who had been my closest companion and best friend," she wrote. "Crushed by the blow, I did not feel able to face the future. I could not forget, however, what my husband used sometimes to say that,

Marie and Pierre Curie in their laboratory, 1896.

Marie and her daughter Irene at work in the laboratory, 1921.

even deprived of him, I ought to continue my work."

FIRST WOMAN TO TEACH AT THE SORBONNE: Marie Curie did continue her work. She took over Pierre's laboratory, and his teaching position. In doing that, she became the first woman ever to teach at the Sorbonne.

She devoted herself to the education of her own children, too. She and Pierre had two girls, Irene and Eve. Marie established a private school for them and the children of several colleagues. The students learned many subjects, with an emphasis on science. But they were encouraged to learn at their own pace, and the school also encouraged games and play.

SECOND NOBEL PRIZE: In 1911, Marie Curie became the first person to win two Nobel Prizes. That year, she was awarded the prize in chemistry, based on her discovery of radium and polonium. She traveled to Sweden to accept the award, but she was very ill. She spent much of the next year recuperating.

LATER YEARS: Curie wanted to build an institute to honor her husband, and in 1914, the Radium Institute was completed. She hired scientists and created a center for research that became one of the finest in the world.

Curie wanted the institute to focus on the medical use of radium. She helped promote the use of x-ray machines in the detection of illnesses. During World War I (1914-1918), Curie equipped 20 vans with x-ray machines to diagnose wounded soldiers.

Curie also led research into radiation as a treatment for cancer and other diseases. It became a widespread treatment that has been used around the world to treat cancer for nearly 100 years, and has saved millions of lives.

Curie was gratified by the results of her work. "It may be easily understood how deeply I appreciated the privilege of realizing that our discovery had become a benefit to mankind, not only through its great scientific importance, but also by its power of efficient action against human suffering and terrible disease. This was indeed a splendid reward for our years of hard toil."

Curie was very popular in America. She traveled to the U.S. in the 1920s and received a hero's welcome. She received honorary degrees and awards. President Warren Harding presented her with a gram of pure radium in support of her research. In 1929, President Herbert Hoover presented her with a check for $50,000, to continue her research.

But the years of working with radioactive materials had taken their toll on Curie. She developed serious health conditions, including aplastic anemia, which is linked to exposure to radiation. Marie Curie died on July 4, 1934, at the age of 67.

Just one year later, her daughter, Irene Curie Joliot, and her husband, Frederic Joliot, won another Nobel Prize for the family, for their discoveries in radioactive science.

HER LEGACY: Marie Curie is one of the most important scientists in history. As the first woman to receive a doctoral degree in France, and the first person to win two Nobel Prizes, she is honored throughout the world for her scientific achievements. She was also a great humanitarian, whose research led to the successful use of radiation therapy for cancer and other diseases.

WORLD WIDE WEB SITES

http://www.aip.org/history/curie/contents.htm

http://nobelprize.org/nobel_prizes/physics/laureates/1903/marie-curie-bio.html

Emily Dickinson
1830-1886
American Poet

EMILY DICKINSON WAS BORN on December 10, 1930, in Amherst, Massachusetts. Her parents were Edward and Emily Norcross Dickinson. Her father was a lawyer and her mother was a home-maker. Emily had a sister, Lavinia, and a brother, Austin.

EMILY DICKINSON GREW UP in Amherst. When she was young, she had an active social life, and enjoyed friends and activities. She enjoyed baking and gardening especially, as well as singing and playing the piano.

Although Dickinson became very shy as an adult, she was very outgoing as a young person. "I am growing handsome very fast indeed!" she wrote as a teenager. "I expect I shall be the belle of Amherst when I reach my 17th year."

EMILY DICKINSON WENT TO SCHOOL at the local schools in Amherst for several years. Then, she went to Amherst Academy for what we would think of as middle school and high school. She went to college at Mount Holyoke, in South Hadley, Massachusetts, for one year. When she went there, it was an all-women's school, called the Mount Holyoke Female Seminary.

A QUIET LIFE: Except for college, Dickinson lived most of her life in her parents' house. She traveled very little, and she rarely left the house. She preferred to live a quiet life, out of the public eye. When guests visited the house, she often retired to her room, because she was too shy to meet with them.

Dickinson was close to her brother, Austin, and sister-in-law, Susan Gilbert. They lived next door to Dickinson, and she enjoyed spending time with them, and with their three children.

BEGINNING TO WRITE POETRY: Sometime in her 20s, Dickinson began to write poetry. But during her lifetime, she shared only a few of her poems, and only with a few people. One of them was her sister-in-law, Susan Gilbert, who was a close friend.

In 1862, Dickinson began to write letters to an essayist named Thomas Wentworth Higginson. She sent him a few poems and asked for his advice. Her poems were unlike anything Higginson had read before. He didn't seem to understand them, or her talent. Years after her death, Dickinson scholars examined the letters searching for clues to understand the poet and her work.

Emily Dickinson's home in Amherst, Mass.

Dickinson's letters, to Higginson and others, are a way to understand her poetry, and how she saw herself. In one letter, she described herself to him. It is a remarkable description: "I am small, like the wren; and my hair is bold, like the chestnut burr; and my eyes, like the sherry in the glass that the guest leaves."

In another letter to Higginson, Dickinson described what she thought poetry was. "If I read a book, and it makes my whole body so cold that no fire ever can warm me, I know *that* is poetry. If I feel physically as if the top of my head were taken off, I know *that* is poetry. These are the only ways I know. Is there any other way?"

Dickinson did have a few poems published in her lifetime, but she didn't sign them. They appeared in newspapers, without a name. They were most likely sent to the newspapers by friends or family.

LATER YEARS: In 1864 and 1865, Dickinson had to have medical attention for an eye condition. She traveled to Boston. While she underwent treatment, she lived with her cousins. When she returned to Amherst, she rarely left her home.

Dickinson never married or had children, but she had several close male friends. She did have a romance with a family friend, Judge Otis Lord. There are letters between them that indicate she might have married him.

Dickinson also faced the loss of several beloved family members in her later years. Her father died in 1874, and her beloved nephew Gilbert died suddenly in 1883. Dickinson never recovered from his death, and soon became ill. She died on May 15, 1886, at the age of 55.

THE DISCOVERY OF HER POETRY: Emily Dickinson wrote some of the most beautiful, moving poetry ever composed. But the world knew nothing of her achievement until after her death.

Shortly after she died, her sister, Lavinia, discovered more than 1,800 of Dickinson's poems among her things. Some were written in small booklets she had made by hand. Some were written on scraps of paper. All were poems of great richness and depth. They were unlike any poetry that had come before.

After the discovery of the poems, Dickinson's relatives argued among themselves about how they should be published. Her poems are very unusual. She uses dashes at the ends of lines, capital letters to emphasize words, and strong imagery that must have seemed strange to her relatives.

The poems began to be published, but not in the form they were written. The first collections that were published were heavily edited. Words, lines, and entire poems were changed from Dickinson's original work. It wasn't until 1955 that an edition of her work appeared that was based on her original booklets. These poems amazed readers around the world.

Until the 1950s, Emily Dickinson had been best known for simple verse, like "I'm nobody, who are you?" Her full work showed an artist of great gifts. Her poems were about the deepest human emotions, from grief and pain to joy. She used vivid, remarkable language. She explored what it was like to love, and to lose someone your loved.

She wrote about nature, and her response to the natural world was striking and bold. She writes often about birds, and how their song is true music, taking its place in the "Human Heart." She writes about flowers, about the changing seasons, about how "Beauty is nature's fact." She writes about God, and the meaning of life, and of death. The ideas in her poems are drawn in images that amaze as they convey their meaning. They cause the reader to think about things in a new way.

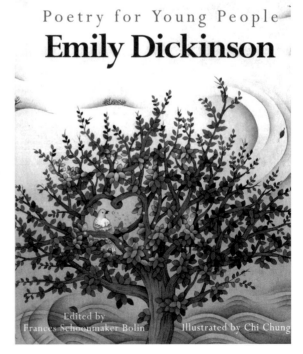

Only in the last 50 years have readers come to know Dickinson's full work, and they have taken it to their hearts. Her powerful poetry, contrasted with her simple life, continues to move readers. There are many biographies of her, and many books about her poems. Each new generation explores her work, and finds it to be powerful and meaningful.

HER LEGACY: Emily Dickinson is considered one of the finest and most original poets in the English language. Although she never shared her poems with the world at large, she wished to be remembered for what she tried to achieve. "Judge tenderly—of Me," she requested in one of them. Her poems, written in vibrant, vivid language, still have the power to startle and amaze readers. They are her achievement, and her legacy.

WORLD WIDE WEB SITES

http://www.emilydickinsonmuseum.org/

http://www.poets.org/poet.php/prmPID/155

Amelia Earhart

1897-1937
American Aviator
First Woman to Pilot a Solo Transatlantic Flight

AMELIA EARHART WAS BORN on July 24, 1897, in Atchinson, Kansas. Her full name was Amelia Mary Earhart. Her parents were Amy and Edwin Earhart. Amy was a homemaker and Edwin was a lawyer. Amelia had a younger sister named Muriel.

AMELIA EARHART GREW UP in several places. She was born at her maternal grandparent's home in Kansas and spent much of her early life there. She used to spend winters with her grandparents in

Atchinson, and summers with her parents in Kansas City, where her father practiced law.

Amelia, called Millie, was an outgoing, active girl. She was a tomboy, and she loved to climb trees and play all kinds of sports. She even knew how to shoot rats with a rifle. And she kept a scrapbook of newspaper stories about women who achieved in professions that at the time were mostly limited to men, like law and engineering.

SEEING HER FIRST AIRPLANE: When Amelia was 10, she saw an airplane for the first time. She really didn't like it. "It was a thing of rusty wire and wood and looked not at all interesting," she recalled.

AMELIA EARHART WENT TO SCHOOL at private schools for several years. When she was in the seventh grade, her family moved to Des Moines, Iowa. Those were difficult times for the family. Her father's business failed, and he began to drink heavily. Amelia's mother moved with her daughters to Chicago. Amelia graduated from Hyde Park High School in Chicago in 1916.

After high school, Amelia went to the Ogontz School, near Philadelphia, Pennsylvania. Ogontz was a "finishing school," the type of school that girls of that time attended, instead of college, to prepare for life in society. In 1917, she left school and moved to Canada, to help care for soldiers wounded in World War I (1914-1918).

When the war was over, Earhart moved to New York City. There, she started working on a degree in pre-medicine at Columbia. She left during her first year and moved to California, where her parents were living.

STARTING TO FLY: In 1920, Earhart went to a stunt-flying exhibition in California. It was an experience that changed her life. She and a friend were watching the exhibition when the pilot took a dive right for them. Earhart, ever courageous, didn't move. The plane buzzed right next to her. "I didn't understand it at the time," she recalled. "But I believe that little red airplane said something to me as it swished by."

In December 1920, she rode in a plane for the first time. It was the beginning of a lifelong passion. "By the time I had got two or three hundred feet off the ground, I knew I had to fly," she claimed.

Earhart's first flight instructor was another woman aviator, Neta Snook. In 1921, Earhart bought her first plane, a Kinner Airster, which she named the "Canary."

Soon, Earhart was breaking flying records, including setting a women's flying altitude record of 14,000 feet. She had several accidents during these early years, but was never seriously injured, or discouraged.

In 1924, Earhart sold the Canary and bought a car. She and her mother drove back East to Boston. There, Earhart got a job at a settlement house as a social worker. But she still loved flying, and longed to get back in the air.

GEORGE PUTNAM: In 1928, Earhart was contacted by publisher George Putnam. Putnam had published books by Charles Lindbergh, who had become world famous as the first person to fly across the Atlantic Ocean in 1927. Now, he wanted Earhart to become the first woman to be a passenger on a transatlantic flight. And he wanted to publish her account of what would be an historic flight, for women and America. In Earhart, he knew he had a captivating subject.

Portrait of Amelia Earhart taken around 1930.

FIRST WOMAN PASSENGER ON A TRANSATLANTIC FLIGHT:
Earhart agreed to Putnam's plan. On June 17, 1928, Earhart flew
across the Atlantic aboard the trimotor plane *Friendship,* piloted
by Wilmer Stultz, with Lou Gordon as mechanic. They left from the
Canadian province of Newfoundland and traveled 20 hours, landing
in Wales on June 18.

Amelia Earhart became famous around the world. She wrote a book about her experience, *20 Hours – 40 Minutes*, and it became a great success. She continued her flying career, buying a new airplane, an Avro Avian, and completing the first transcontinental flight by a woman in September 1928.

In 1929, Earhart got another new plane, a single-engine Lockheed Vega. She competed in the Women's Air Derby, a race from Santa Monica to Cleveland, and came in third. She also helped establish an organization called The Ninety-Nines, a group of women pilots dedicated to promoting women aviators that is still in existence today.

The year 1930 found Earhart still going strong, setting the women's world flying speed record of 181 miles per hour. The next year, she became the first president of the Ninety-Nines, and got a new kind of plane, an autogiro, in which she set a new women's altitude record of 18,415 feet.

MARRIAGE: In 1931, Earhart married George Putnam, who by that time was managing her career. He planned her appearances, published her books, and arranged her flights. He made his wife into a celebrity, beloved by people everywhere.

FIRST WOMAN TO PILOT A SOLO TRANSATLANTIC FLIGHT: In 1932, Earhart entered the history books again. On May 20, she became the first woman, and only the second person, to fly across the Atlantic Ocean alone. Once again, she was international news. Earhart thought her effort had proven that men and women were equals: "in jobs requiring intelligence, coordination, speed, coolness, and willpower."

That same year, she set the record for women for a transcon-

Earhart posing in front of an aircraft engine.

tinental flight across the U.S. The awards and honors poured in.
Earhart received the Army Air Corps Distinguished Flying Cross,
the Gold Medal of the National Geographic Society, and other
awards.

Amelia Earhart in front of her Lockheed Electra, 1937.

A FAMOUS AVIATOR: Earhart continued to fly, and to set new records. In 1933, she broke her own record for transcontinental flight. In 1935, she became the first person to fly across the Pacific Ocean alone, in a flight from Hawaii to California. That year, she also became the first woman to compete in the National Air Races.

In 1936, Earhart began preparing for her biggest challenge: she wanted to fly around the world. In March 1937, her plane, a Lockheed Electra, was damaged during a practice takeoff. She had it rebuilt and returned to her preparations. "I have a feeling that there is just about one more good flight left in my system," she said. "And I hope this trip is it."

FINAL FLIGHT—LOST AT SEA: Amelia Earhart began her final flight on June 1, 1937. She and her navigator, Fred Noonan, took off from

Miami, Florida, and headed east on a trip that was supposed to cover 29,000 miles.

Twenty eight days later, nearing the final portion of their flight, they landed in Lae, New Guinea, on June 29. With just 7,000 miles to go, Earhart and Noonan set out again on July 2, 1927, for Howland Island, which was 2,500 miles from Lae, in the middle of the Pacific. There were several ships in the area, including the U.S. Coast Guard cutter *Itasca*, that were standing by to help Earhart and Noonan.

The aviators radioed that the weather was cloudy, and asked for help in tracking their path. Although the *Itasca* sent several messages to Earhart, she could not receive them. The *Itasca* received messages from her, saying, "We must be on you, but we cannot see you. Fuel is running low. Been unable to reach you by

The last photograph of Earhart's Electra, taking off from New Guinea, June 1937.

radio. We are flying at 1,000 feet." Her last message, "We are running north and south," was received about 8:45 A.M. on July 2, 1937.

Earhart and Noonan were never heard from again. The U.S. mounted the largest rescue operation in history to find them. Ships and airplanes searched over 250,000 square miles of ocean in an attempt to find the famed aviator. Finally, after 17 days, the search was called off.

No one is sure what happened to Earhart and Noonan. Some think her plane crashed into the sea. Some think they could have been captured as spies. But whatever her fate, Earhart was mourned and celebrated all over the world.

HER LEGACY: Amelia Earhart is a symbol of courage and vision for her achievements as a pilot, and as a woman. Her legacy includes many "firsts"—first woman to fly solo across the Atlantic, across the Pacific, across the U.S., and the first to attempt to fly around the world. But it is her bravery and her spirit that are her greatest legacy. She left a letter for her husband, to be read if she died in flight, in which that spirit shines through:

"Please know I am quite aware of the hazards. I want to do it because I want to do it. Women must try to do things as men have tried. When they fail, their failure must be but a challenge to others."

WORLD WIDE WEB SITES

http://www.ameliaearhartmuseum.org

http://www.ninety-nines.org/index.cfm/amelia_earhart.htm

Sylvia Earle

1935 –
American Marine Botanist and Oceanographer
Explorer of the Oceans

SYLVIA EARLE WAS BORN on August 30, 1935, in Gibbstown, New Jersey. Her parents were Lewis and Alice Earle. Lewis was an electrician and Alice was a nurse before she had children. Sylvia has two brothers, Lewis and Evan.

SYLVIA EARLE GREW UP in New Jersey and Florida. When she was three, her family moved to a farm near Camden, New Jersey. Sylvia loved it. Her parents introduced Sylvia and her brothers to the wonders of nature.

"My parents used to bring frogs for my brothers and me to get to know. But we were very carefully told always to put them back in the pond. Or to allow a caterpillar to gently walk across you hand, and not to disturb them, because you might get stung by some of their bristles. I learned very early on that if you show respect for other creatures, they won't go out of their way to harm you."

Even as a small child, Sylvia loved to watch the creatures of the forest — squirrels, fish, and frogs — for hours. She loved to wander and think about the natural world around her. Like the scientist she would become, she "made observations and kept notebooks. Nobody had to tell me to do those things — I just did them."

When Earle was 12, her family moved to Clearwater, Florida, on the Gulf of Mexico. Their house was right on the water. "My back yard became the Gulf of Mexico," she recalls. She loved it.

"I had the pleasure of getting acquainted with salt marshes, and sea grass beds." There, she watched the "sea horses and sea urchins, and great crabs with long, spindly legs that were absolutely fascinating. You never knew what you were going to find just walking around in these squishy, but beautiful clear water areas."

SYLVIA EARLE WENT TO SCHOOL at the local public schools. She always did well in school, and she loved it, too. "I just felt this joy of discovery," she says. "I was like a big sponge, absorbing as much as I could. And I enjoyed succeeding. I liked it when I could get my mind around the math problems."

Earle also loved reading the encyclopedia. "It was like a discovery. You never knew what new things you were going to find on every page."

Earle graduated from high school at 16 and went off to college. She studied at St. Petersburg Junior College, Florida State University, and Duke University. She knew by then that she wanted to be a scientist. She wanted to study the plants of the ocean.

DECIDING TO BE A SCIENTIST: Earle studied botany, which is the study of the lives of plants. Her special area of study is marine plants, plants that grow in sea water. She remembers that one of her college professors, Harold Humm, "introduced me to the beauty and interest and common good sense of looking at plants."

THE IMPORTANCE OF MARINE PLANTS: "By knowing the plants, you get some feel for how the whole system works," says Earle. "Plants provide shelter, whether it's underwater or above. They provide food. They provide energy that supplies a whole interacting system."

Earle studied to become a marine botanist. While she was studying, she also got married and had children. Over the next several years, she earned her bachelor's, masters, and doctorate in the study of marine plants. Her specialty within the field is the study of algae (pronounced al-gee).

BECOMING AN EXPERT ON MARINE PLANTS: During the 1960s, Earle traveled all over the world to study marine plants. She became a leading expert on ocean plant life, especially the algae of the Gulf of Mexico.

In 1970, she joined a group of women scientists who lived in an underwater structure on the ocean floor for two weeks. Called

Earle examines a fish reference chart during a dive off the Florida Keys, 1997.

"Tektite II," the structure was like an underwater hotel. Tektite II was off the Virgin Islands in the Caribbean. It had air, water, and living and study areas for the scientists.

The scientists ate, slept, and worked in the area. Earle spent most of her time out in the ocean waters. There, she identified 153 plants. Twenty-six of them had never been seen before in the area.

The Tektite mission made Earle famous. She and the other scientists met the President and had parades in their honor. Earle used her fame to focus attention on the importance of ocean research.

THE "JIM DIVE": In 1979, Earle made a solo dive off the coast of Hawaii. She dove down 1,250 feet. That was the deepest dive anyone had ever made. She wore a special suit called a "Jim Suit" for its maker, Jim Jarrat. It provided oxygen and special protection from water pressure that can harm a diver.

EXPLORING THE OCEAN FLOOR: With the "Jim Suit," Earle could dive deeper and longer than anyone had before. She explored the ocean floor and discovered plants no human had ever seen. When the American astronaut Neil Armstrong landed on the moon in 1969, he had planted an American flag on the surface. Sylvia Earle did the same thing on the ocean floor off Hawaii. She planted an American flag in the ocean. She wanted to emphasize that ocean exploration was every bit as important — and exciting — as space.

HELPING TO SAVE THE OCEANS: Earle knew from her studies that the pollution that affects the air also hurts the oceans. She wrote articles for magazines like *National Geographic*. She told readers about the beauty of ocean life and the dangers of pollution.

Earle also continued to study the oceans of the world. In the

1970s, she explored the Pacific and Indian Oceans. She followed migrating whales from Hawaii to Australia and Alaska.

In the 1980s, Earle started a business called Deep Ocean Engineering. The company builds undersea vehicles. They help scientists reach ocean depths never before seen or explored.

Now in her 70s, Earle still loves her work. For her, there are endless questions about the oceans and the life they hold. "There are plants growing where people didn't expect to find plants. That leads to a whole host of questions. Why is this so? Why do they occur here? Why don't they occur somewhere else? Who eats them?"

Earle claims that "it could take ten lifetimes" to explore and learn all there is to know about the oceans. Now, she is concerned about the health of the oceans. She urges young people to study the life of the oceans and to help protect them.

SYLVIA EARLE'S HOME AND FAMILY: Sylvia Earle has been married three times. Her first husband was named Jack Taylor. They had two children, Elizabeth and John, who are grown now. Earle and Taylor divorced in 1967. Her second husband was named Giles Mead. They had one daughter, Gale. Earle married Graham Hawkes in 1986. They divorced in 1990.

She still loves to dive. In all, she has spent some 6,000 hours in the water. That's equal to an entire year of her life. "Underwater, every spoonful of water is filled with life," she says.

HER LEGACY: Eearl has brought the world's attention to the importance of improving and sustaining the health of the oceans. But, she says, there is much more to do."We're far behind the curve from where we need to be…People look at the surface, and they think that's the ocean, and because they can't see what's going on below, they think everything's just fine. But those of us with decades of exploration [experience know that] the ocean is in trouble, and therefore so are we."

WORLD WIDE WEB SITES

http://www.achievement.org/autodoc/page/ear0bio-1

http://www.nationalgeographic.com/field/explorers/sylvia-earle.
   html

Gertrude Elion

1918 – 1999
American Scientist and Inventor of Life-Saving Drugs to Treat Leukemia and Other Diseases
Winner of the Nobel Prize

GERTRUDE ELION WAS BORN on January 23, 1918, in New York City. Her parents were Robert and Bertha Elion. Her father was a dentist and her mother was a homemaker. Gertrude had a younger brother named Herbert.

GERTRUDE ELION GREW UP in the area of New York City known as the Bronx. She particularly loved the Bronx Zoo. She visited often, in the company of her beloved grandfather.

Gertrude was part of a loving family, and her parents nurtured her interests in reading and music. She remembered her father reading her "poetry, history, biography, and fiction." She especially loved the stories of famous scientists and people who "discovered things." Scientists like **Marie Curie** fascinated her.

Gertrude's mother was an important influence, too. When Gertrude was growing up, many girls were discouraged from choosing careers. But Bertha Elion encouraged her daughter to follow a career in science.

GERTRUDE ELION WENT TO SCHOOL at the local public schools. She was an outstanding student. She loved all her courses (except gym), and she got all "A's." She did so well in school that she skipped several grades. She graduated from high school at 15.

But the same year she graduated, tragedy struck. Her beloved grandfather died of cancer. Gertrude was terribly sad. But her grandfather's death made her resolve to study science and try to find a cure for a killer disease. "When I was 15, I already knew that I loved science," she recalled. "But that year I was so devastated by my grandfather's death from cancer that majoring in chemistry seemed the logical first step in committing myself to fighting the disease."

Elion studied biochemistry at Hunter College in New York City. She graduated in 1937 with highest honors. She wanted to go on to graduate school, but was rejected by all 15 colleges she applied to.

Elion knew it wasn't that she couldn't do the work. It was because those schools, and society in general, discriminated against women. "Nobody took me seriously," she said. "They wondered why in the world I wanted to be a chemist when no women were doing that."

But Gertrude Elion wouldn't give up. She tried to get a job in a laboratory. Once again, she faced discrimination. The companies she applied to wouldn't give her a chance. "I often wonder why I didn't give up then and there," she recalled. "I almost did. I actually went to secretarial school for six weeks." But then she was offered a job as a lab assistant. "I left secretarial school and never looked back," she said.

In 1939, Elion finally was admitted to New York University's graduate school. "I was the only female in my graduate chemistry class," she recalled. "But no one seemed to mind, and I didn't consider it at all strange." She studied chemistry while working two jobs to pay tuition. She received her master's degree in chemistry in 1941. Once again, she looked for a job as a scientist. But this time, she found work much more quickly.

GETTING WORK AS A SCIENTIST: Elion got her master's degree just as the U.S. was entering World War II. When the U.S. joined the war effort in 1941, millions of men left their jobs to join the armed forces.

"War changed everything," recalled Elion. "It was only when men weren't available that women were invited into the lab." For the first time, intelligent, able and educated women could find the jobs they wanted.

FIRST JOBS: Elion's first job was in a food company. She worked as a chemist, checking the quality of the foods the company produced. After a year in that job, she worked at Johnson and Johnson labs.

Next, she got a job at Burroughs Wellcome Laboratories. She remained there for the rest of her 40-year career in chemistry.

Elion and Hitchings, c. 1950

Elion was hired by George H. Hitchings. Over the next four decades, the two worked closely together. And together they developed some of the most important medicines of the 20th century.

THE CELL: Elion and Hitchings's focus was how diseases penetrated human cells. The cell is the basic unit of living things. All living things—plants, animals, and people—are made up of cells. Each cell contains the elements that allow the cell to live and reproduce.

When Elion and Hitchings began their work, drug research wasn't focused on the cell. At that time, most medical researchers started with an existing medicine that worked. Then, they would make some changes to it, and see if that improved the product.

Elion and Hitchings took a different path. They studied the differences between diseased and healthy cells. They looked at how cancer, bacteria, and viruses cause disease. Next, they developed drugs that would destroy the disease, without harming healthy cells.

DISCOVERING A DRUG TO TREAT LEUKEMIA: In the late 1940s, Elion began working on a drug to fight childhood leukemia. Leukemia is a type of cancer. At that time, it was nearly always fatal. By 1951, she had discovered a chemical that could fight leukemia.

The chemical compound that Elion created was called "6MP." That stands for "6-mercaptopurine." In its first trials, the drug helped leukemia patients live longer than they had on any previous drug. Soon, doctors were using 6MP with other drugs, to fight leukemia.

The results of using 6MP were amazing. Cases of leukemia treated with the drugs disappeared. Leukemia soon became one of the most treatable cancers. Elion was overjoyed. "What greater joy can you have than to know what an impact your work has had on people's lives? The thrill of seeing people get well who otherwise might have died cannot be described in words." Today, nearly 80% of leukemia patients are cured.

Elion praised Hitchings as her mentor. "Dr. Hitchings permitted me to learn as rapidly as I could and to take on more and more responsibility," she said. She felt she could explore all areas of medical research. In addition to chemistry, she studied biochemistry, pharmacology, immunology, and eventually virology.

OTHER IMPORTANT DISCOVERIES: Another important discovery developed from Elion's work on 6MP. A new drug, Imuran, derived from 6MP, could fight the body's rejection of transplant organs, like kidneys. The body's "immune system" helps the body fight disease. But it also attacks anything "foreign" to the body, including an organ transplanted from another person.

However, if a patient received Imuran before transplant surgery, the body accepted the new organ. So another major medical breakthrough came about through Elion's research.

Next, Elion developed a drug to treat malaria. Malaria is a disease that kills millions of people every year. Most of its victims are in Africa and Asia. And most are infants and children. Elion's new drug saved many lives.

After Hitchings retired in 1967, Elion became director of Burroughs' Department of Experimental Therapy. Heading up the lab, she oversaw the creation of even more new drugs.

And on her own, she developed the first antiviral drug, acyclovir. The drug was used to treat diseases caused by viruses. It was especially important in the treatment of herpes, a disease group that includes chicken pox. She called it "my crown jewel. That such a thing was possible wasn't even imagined up until then."

Elion retired from Burroughs in 1983. But she continued to work with researchers and medical students. One of the teams she trained developed AZT, the first drug used to treat AIDS. Over the course of her career Elion received 45 patents for her work.

THE NOBEL PRIZE: In 1988, Elion received the Nobel Prize. That is one of the most important awards in the world. Her award came in the field of "Physiology or Medicine." She shared the award with Hitchings and a British scientist, James W. Black.

Elion and Hitchings, 1988, after winning the Nobel Prize

Elion was grateful for the Prize. But she was clear about what it meant to her. "People often ask whether it wasn't what I had been aiming for all my life. Nothing could be farther from the truth. My rewards had already come in seeing children with leukemia survive, meeting patients with long-term kidney transplants, and watching acyclovir save lives and reduce suffering. What we were aiming at was getting people well. The satisfaction of that is much greater than any prize you can get."

LATER YEARS: In 1991, Elion became the first woman named to the National Inventors Hall of Fame. "I'm happy to be the first woman," she said. "But I doubt I'll be the last." In fact, she was followed three years later by **Rachel Fuller Brown** and **Elizabeth Lee Hazen**, inventors of Nystatin.

After Elion retired, she often traveled to schools to visit young students. She encouraged them to study science. "The same thing that inspired me over the years inspires me now," she told them. "I want to get sick people well. I want to get children involved in science. I want them to have the same kind of excitement and fun I've had and do something useful with their lives."

Over the years, Elion received hundreds of letters from patients who were cured by her drugs. "I treasure those letters," she said. "I keep every one of them." Gertrude Elion died suddenly of a stroke on February 21, 1999. She was 81 years old.

GERTRUDE ELION'S HOME AND FAMILY: Elion never married or had children. In 1937, she met a fellow student named Leonard Canter. She and Leonard fell in love and became engaged. But, tragically, Canter died in 1941, of a heart infection. Throughout her life, Elion remained very close to her brother and his family.

HER LEGACY: Elion is considered one of the most important medical researchers of the 20th century. In her 40-year career, she invented some of the most important life-saving drugs of the era, including drugs for leukemia, organ transplantation, and the herpes virus.

WORLD WIDE WEB SITES

http://nobelprize.org/medicine/laureates/1988/elion-autobio.html
http://web.mit.edu/invent/iow/elion2.html
http://www.invent.org/hall_of_fame/51.html

Elizabeth I

1533-1603
English Queen
One of England's Most Successful and Influential Rulers

ELIZABETH I WAS BORN on September 7, 1533, at Greenwich Palace, in England. Her parents were Henry VIII, King of England, and Anne Boleyn, Henry's second wife. Henry was part of the Tudor family, who ruled England from 1485 to 1603.

Elizabeth was one of Henry's three children, and had two half-siblings, Mary and Edward. She was part of one of the most famous royal families in history, and its final monarch.

THE REIGN OF HENRY VIII: Henry became King of England in 1509, and married Catherine of Aragon, the daughter of Ferdinand and **Isabella** of Spain, the same year. At that time, Henry was a Catholic, and it was the official religion of England. Catherine gave birth to only one child, Mary. But Henry wanted a male son, an heir, to rule after him. He asked the Pope, the head of the Catholic Church, to declare his marriage to Catherine invalid. The Pope refused.

Henry made a bold move that changed history. He divorced Catherine, and declared himself the head of a new church, the Church of England. (This later became the Anglican church). Henry married Anne Boleyn immediately after the divorce, which created great turmoil and unrest in the country. Many of his own court members remained loyal to their former Queen and their faith. The people, too, loved their former queen. Henry severely punished those he considered disloyal, and had some put to death.

Anne Boleyn became pregnant, and Henry happily looked forward to a male heir. When Elizabeth was born instead, Henry was greatly disappointed. He had Elizabeth sent away, and brought up false charges against Anne. When Elizabeth was just two-and-a-half years old, her mother was executed.

THE EDUCATION OF A PRINCESS: After her mother's death, Elizabeth was sent away from court. She was raised at a home Henry provided for her, called Hatfield House. She was well educated by tutors, and was an excellent student. She was fluent in several languages, including Greek, Latin, Italian, and French. She also studied the law, history, and religion, as well as music and art. One of her tutors said her determination was "equal to that of a man, and her memory long keeps what it quickly picks up."

Henry VIII went on to have four more wives, and one surviving male heir, Elizabeth's half-brother Edward, who was born in 1537. Most of Henry's other wives wanted little to do with Princess Elizabeth. But his last wife, Katherine Parr, took a great interest in her. She made sure that Elizabeth's education was the finest available. Princess Elizabeth was as well-educated as any prince in Europe.

THE DEATH OF HENRY VIII: When Henry VIII died in 1547, Elizabeth's half-brother Edward became king. He was sickly and died 1553. Edward was followed by Elizabeth's half-sister Mary, the daughter of Catherine of Aragon.

Mary, who became known as "Bloody Mary," was still Catholic, and made Catholicism the state religion again. She persecuted Protestants, and, suspecting Elizabeth of disloyalty, had her imprisoned for several months. Though still a young adult, Elizabeth showed much strength and grace at this time.

Mary was very unpopular with the people, and under her reign England became weak and isolated from other European countries. She died without having any children in 1558. Elizabeth, age 25, became the new Queen of England.

THE REIGN OF ELIZABETH I: The coronation of Queen Elizabeth I was a time of great joy and hope for England. She was very popular with the people, and did much to earn their love. On the way to her coronation, she stopped to talk with them. And throughout her reign, she was always concerned about their welfare.

Elizabeth began immediately to rule the country according to her own mind. First, she had to deal with the issue of marriage. She had many suitors during her lifetime, and many men who wished to

Portrait of Princess Elizabeth, 1546.

rule England tried to either marry her, or remove her from power.

Marriage was a way for a nation to form alliances. And children were a way to guarantee who would follow her to the throne. Yet Elizabeth always resisted both. She never married or had children, preferring to reign on her own. Always keeping her people first in her mind, she said, "I am already bound unto a husband which is the Kingdom of England."

Elizabeth did enjoy the company of men, and she was a charming, witty woman. She loved music and dancing, as well as horse riding and hunting. She also loved beautiful clothes and elegant jewelry. There are many portraits of her that show her taste for luxurious dresses, and her curly red hair.

Elizabeth had several close counselors. These included Sir William Cecil (called Lord Burghley). He advised her on matters of state, including alliances with other countries. Elizabeth was educated, and knew law, finance, and politics. She made laws, and she kept a careful eye on what the country spent on everything, including the military.

Elizabeth was also shrewd and intelligent in matters of politics. England's most powerful enemies were France and Spain. She encouraged powerful European princes, from countries that were also enemies of France and Spain, to form alliances with England, keeping the French and Spanish wary.

RELIGION: Elizabeth also took on the difficult issue of religion. She decreed that England was once again a Protestant nation. She kept some of the Catholic traditions in the Church of England, including the positions of bishop and archbishop. But many of her Catholic subjects still did not approve. There were also powerful Catholic rulers in Europe, particularly in Spain and France, who were her enemies. She appointed a team of spies, who kept her informed of any plots against her.

MARY QUEEN OF SCOTS: There were several plots against Elizabeth during her reign, including one surrounding a relative,

Mary Queen of Scots. Mary had been born in Scotland in 1542, the daughter of King James V. So she was, by birth, a distant heir and rival of Elizabeth. She was actually named Queen of Scotland when she was only a few days old, after her father's death.

In 1548, Mary moved to France. She married Francis, heir to the throne, and became Queen when Francis became King in 1560. But Francis died a few months later, and Mary returned to Scotland to rule the country. Elizabeth was suspicious of her, and had Mary carefully watched.

In 1568, Mary fled to England and asked for Elizabeth's protection. Wary of her cousin's true intent, Elizabeth had Mary kept a prisoner at a distant castle for 19 years. Over those years, several plots were discovered in which Mary's supporters planned to kill Elizabeth, and make Mary queen. In 1586, in a plot that was most likely made up by one of Elizabeth's counselors, Mary was accused of plotting to assassinate Elizabeth. Mary was convicted and executed in February 1587.

THE DEFEAT OF THE SPANISH ARMADA: One of Elizabeth's greatest triumphs was reestablishing England as a sea power. During her reign, Sir Walter Raleigh and Sir Francis Drake became renown for their explorations of the New World. Drake was only the second man in history to sail around the globe.

Philip of Spain had built his fleet, the Spanish Armada, into what he claimed was the greatest navy in Europe. In 1588, the Armada sailed into the English Channel to challenge England. Drake led the English forces, whose smaller, faster ships defeated the Spanish Armada in nine days. England once again ruled the waves.

The English fleet in battle against the Spanish Armada, 1588.

SHAKESPEARE AND THE ARTS IN ELIZABETHAN ENGLAND:
Elizabeth loved literature, especially poetry and plays. She encouraged the new writers of the era, including William Shakespeare, whose plays she attended, and who went on to create some of the greatest literature the world has ever known. Shakespeare was one of several writers, including Edmund Spenser, Christopher Marlowe, and others who are now called the "Elizabethan poets," for their great patroness and inspiration.

HER LEGACY: Elizabeth I is one of the most famous, and beloved, English monarchs. She came to the throne of England when the country was torn apart over religion, politics, and its future.

179

Through her intelligence, wit, and ability, she established a Golden Age of English history that now bears her name. She inspired great works of literature and the love of her people. Shortly before her death in 1603, she said to them, "This I account the glory of my crown, that I have reigned with your loves."

WORLD WIDE WEB SITES

http://www.bbc.co.uk/history/british/tudors/elizabeth_i_01.shtm

http://englishhistory.net/tudor/monarchs/eliz1.html

Jane Goodall

1934-
English Scientist
Famed Zoologist Who Has Studied
Chimpanzees in Africa for 50 Years

JANE GOODALL WAS BORN on April 3, 1934, in London, England. Her mother was Vanne Goodall and her father was Mortimer Goodall. Vanne was a homemaker and Mortimer was a business-man. They divorced when Jane was eight. Jane has one sister, Judy.

JANE GOODALL GREW UP in London. She showed an early love of chimps when her mother gave her a stuffed one. She named it "Jubilee."

When Jane was in grade school, the family moved to the seaside city of Bournemouth. Jane loved living in the country. She would spend hours playing by the sea and watching animals.

Jane was a curious and patient child. One day, she spent four hours in a chicken coop, because she wanted to know where eggs came from. "I hid in the straw at the back of the stuffy little hen house," she recalls. "And I waited and waited."

Her mother was frightened when she couldn't find Jane, and called the police. Then, she saw "this excited little girl come running across a field with shining eyes and straw all over her," Goodall recalled. "And instead of scolding me, which would have taken away all the joy, she sat down to hear my story."

JANE GOODALL WENT TO SCHOOL at a private school in Bournemouth. "Although I always did well in my studies, I never liked school," says Goodall. "I just wanted to be outdoors, watching and learning."

Young Jane Goodall with her toy chimp, Jubilee.

Even though she didn't like school, Jane loved to read. Her favorite book was *Dr. Doolittle*. It inspired her greatest dream. "I decided that someday I had to go to Africa," she recalls.

After high school, Goodall went to London to study at a

school for secretaries. When she was 23, she got an invitation to visit a friend living in Kenya. She was finally going to Africa.

GETTING INTERESTED IN CHIMPS: After her visit was over, Goodall went to Nairobi (nye-ROW-bee), the largest city in Kenya, to find a job. In Nairobi, she met Louis Leakey. Leakey was a famous anthropologist. That is a scientist who studies cultures. Leakey studied fossils to learn about ancient people and animals.

Goodall took a job with Leakey. Together they scoured the plains area of Kenya and Tanzania for fossils. She was overjoyed when she found the remains of an ancient creature. "This—this very bone—had once been part of a living, breathing animal," she recalls of her early discoveries.

Goodall makes contact with an infant chimpanzee, 1960.

But Goodall missed studying living creatures. The area was filled with lions, gazelles, zebras, rhinos, and other animals. Leakey suggested that Goodall study chimps.

Chimpanzees are the animals that are closest to humans. So, Leakey thought that Goodall could learn about early human behavior if she studied how chimps live.

Leakey told Goodall that he thought her studies would take five years. She thought it would take three. She has now been studying chimps for 50 years. "The more I learned about chimpanzees, the more I realized there was more to learn—until I couldn't stop," she says.

Goodall did return to England to study anthropology. She went to Cambridge University, and got a Ph.D. in anthropology. Then, it was back to Africa.

LIFE WITH THE CHIMPS: Jane Goodall's life work has been the first study of its kind. Hers is the first long-term study of animals in the wild. She studies chimps in their own habitat, instead of in a zoo.

When Goodall first moved to Africa full-time, her mother came with her. Goodall spent her days in the forests of Tanzania. She sat very still for hours. Sometimes she even slept outside, so that the chimps would get used to her.

Her plan paid off. Soon, the chimps would walk right up to her. They got to know her and to trust her.

SCIENTIFIC METHOD AND DISCOVERIES: Goodall carefully watched chimp behavior. She tried to get to know the chimps as individuals.

Young researcher Jane Goodall scanning the forests in Tanzania, searching for champanzees, c. 1960.

Unlike other animal scientists, she didn't refer to the chimps by number. Instead, she gave them names. For 50 years, she has watched several generations of a group of chimp families grow.

Goodall discovered many things about chimps that were never known before. She learned that they ate meat. She also discovered that they could make tools—using twigs and blades of grass. And she learned that chimps, like humans, could make war.

"People are surprised when they find out how brutal chimpanzees can be," she says. "But they shouldn't be. It's a measure of how much they're like us."

CURRENT WORK: Goodall is very concerned about the future of chimps. In Africa, the forests they live in are being cut down to make way for homes and farms. Chimps are also preyed on by poachers. The poachers will sometimes steal a baby chimp and kill its mother. They also hunt chimps for food.

Goodall is also concerned about the use of chimps in medical research. She considers it morally wrong. She speaks out about it, to scientific research organizations and government officials.

Goodall is concerned about the environment, too. She knows that the destruction of habitat, in Africa or anywhere, and the pollution of air, land, and water affect everyone, animals and humans alike. She reaches out to people to help confront and solve these problems.

Goodall started an organization, the Jane Goodall Institute, to help her reach as many people as possible with her message. She believes that the children of the world can help. As part of her institute, she started a Roots and Shoots program for children.

Goodall travels up to 300 days each year. She talks to students, telling them of her concerns for animals. She hopes the children will share her concerns. And it appears to be working.

"Everywhere I go, there are shining eyes," she says. "There are children from our Roots and Shoots program who are all so excited to meet "Dr. Jane" and tell me what they've been doing to make the world a better place.

"There's a Roots and Shoots member in the Eastern Congo, and he had an uncle who was a hunter. He persuaded the uncle to give it up and become a chicken farmer. Between them, in two years, they've changed 75 hunters. When I meet people like that, they give me energy and hope."

Goodall with the chimp she named Gregoire, in 2008.

Goodall doesn't spend as much time in Gombe as she did years ago. Now that she spends much of her time speaking and meeting with people, she gets back there a few times a year.

HOME AND FAMILY: Goodall has a home near the National Park in Tanzania where she lived and worked most of her life. She has been married twice. Her first husband was a photographer named Hugo van Lawick. They had one son, Hugo, nicknamed Grub. Grub grew up in the forests of Tanzania while his mother continued her chimp studies.

Goodall's second husband was named Derek Bryceson. He was the director of the National Park in Tanzania where she worked. He died in 1980.

HER LEGACY: Jane Goodall is one of the most famous scientists in the world. She is known around the globe for her groundbreaking studies of chimpanzees. She is also known and honored for her commitment to preserve animals and environments threatened by pollution or human intervention, and for promoting the humane treatment of animals everywhere.

WORLD WIDE WEB SITES

http://www.janegoodall.org/study-corner-biography

http://www.wic.org/bio/jgoodall.htm

Hatshepsut

Egyptian Pharaoh
Ruled Egypt from c. 1478 B.C.E. to 1458 B.C.E.
First Important Female Ruler in History

HATSHEPSUT WAS BORN around 1,500 B. C. E. Her name is pronounced hat-SHEP-soot. She was the oldest daughter of Pharaoh Thutmose I and his Great Royal Wife, Queen Ahmose. She was probably the granddaughter of Ahmose, who was the founder of Egypt's 18th Dynasty.

THE 18TH DYNASTY–THE NEW KINGDOM: The ancient dynasties of Egypt began more than 5,000 years ago, about 3,100 B. C. E. For more than 3,000 years the country was ruled by different family dynasties. Hatshelpsut was part of the 18th Dynasty, known as the "New Kingdom."

It was the custom among the royalty of Egypt to have members of the same family intermarry. So when her father Thutmose I died, Hatshepsut married her half-brother, Thutmose II, and became queen. When Thutmose II died around 1478 B. C. E., Hatshepsut became "co-regent," ruling Egypt with her stepson, Thutmose III. He was a young boy at the time, and co-regencies were a traditional way for the royal line to continue, while a young male heir grew up.

A WOMAN PHARAOH: What Hatshepsut did next was decidedly *not* traditional. She declared herself Pharaoh, a title traditionally used only by male kings of Egypt. She was one of only three women to be Pharaoh during all of Egyptian history. (One of them was **Cleopatra**, the last Pharaoh of all).

The people of Egypt rejected her at first. To win them over, she declared that she had the right to be Pharaoh because of her royal ancestry. She also claimed that her father had chosen her to be the leader of Egypt. She even claimed to be the descendent of the god Amun, the most important Egyptian god. She said this made her both the mortal and immortal heir to the throne of Egypt.

Hatshepsut also decided to dress as a man. Although the early statues and other images of Hatshepsut show her to be a woman, she appears dressed as a male Pharaoh in later images of her. For example, there are statues and paintings of her wearing the traditional male headdress and kilt of a pharaoh. They show her with a man's body, and with a beard.

To make sure she could stay in power, Hatshepsut had to control the army. Her stepson, Thutmose III, was being raised to

Sphinx statue of Hatshepsut.

lead the army. She had to make sure that he, and the army, would stay loyal to her. She decided how to accomplish that. Rather than send them into battle, she would send them on a peaceful mission.

THE TRIP TO PUNT:

Hatshepsut sent her army on a mission to Punt, a city to the south that hadn't been visited by the Egyptians for more than 500 years. The trip was very successful, and through it Egypt gained an important trading partner.

Hatshepsut also developed trading relations with the Greeks to the north, and with Asia to the east. Exotic goods, including ivory and incense, became available in Egypt. The additional trade brought money and stability to her reign.

Hatshepsut also commissioned works of art. During her reign, she had new temples built, and ruined ones repaired. She also had beautiful monuments and shrines built, including her own temple and tomb at Deir el-Bahri. Another temple, to the god Amun at Karnak, is considered one of the most majestic ever built. Many works of sculpture and pottery also date from her time.

THE DEATH OF HATSHEPSUT: When Hatshepsut died around 1458 B. C. E., Egypt was a peaceful, prosperous country. She had ruled for 20 years, developing the country through trade and allowing the arts to flourish. She should have gone down in history as a great ruler. But her true accomplishments were to be buried for thousands of years.

THUTMOSE III: After Hatshepsut died, Thutmose III reigned alone as Pharaoh. He was a powerful leader, and during his rule Egypt developed into a great military force.

But Thutmose III is most famous for what he did to his predecessor's memory. He had Hatshepsut wiped out, literally, from the history of Egypt. Thutmose III ordered that all images of Hatshepsut be destroyed.

Hieroglyphics depicting Hatshepsut on a wall in her burial tomb.

Hatshepsut's burial tomb in Deir-el-Bahri, Egypt.

He had workers erase her image wherever it appeared. Monuments, statues, and obelisks were destroyed, and images of her were chiseled out of the surfaces on which they appeared. No one is sure why Thutmose III did what he did. It could have been an act of revenge against the woman who kept him from power for 20 years. Whatever the reason, it was thousands of years before Hatshepsut's story, and achievements, came to light.

DISCOVERING THE TOMB OF HATSHEPSUT: Hatshepsut had created three different sarcophaguses—burial tombs—before her death. One was discovered in 1903 by the famous archeologist Howard Carter. He had become renowned for finding the tomb of King Tutankamun.

193

When Carter discovered Hatshepsut's tomb, her story became known to the world. But Carter couldn't find Hatshepsut's mummy. That great discovery wasn't made until 2007, when archeologists found it on the floor of a minor tomb. Next, a team of specialists led by Egyptian archeologist Zahi Hawass used the latest technology, including CT scanners, to determine whether the mummy was indeed Hatshepsut.

It turned out that the mummy, abandoned without a coffin, was indeed the great Pharaoh Hatshepsut. Her remains now rest in the Royal Mummy Rooms in Cairo's Egyptian Museum. Nearby are plaques that describe her achievements.

HER LEGACY: Hatshepsut was one of the greatest of the Egyptian Pharaohs. She was a great leader and built some of the finest monuments in Egypt. She was one of only three females every to reign as Pharaoh, and was the most powerful and accomplished of them all. Why she chose to reign as a king, rather than a queen, and why her stepson, Thutmose III, destroyed all record of her after her death, is one of the great mysteries that surround this fascinating ruler.

WORLD WIDE WEB SITES

http://ngm.nationalgeographic.com/2009/04/hatshepsut/brown-text.html

http://www.pbs.org/empires/egypt/newkingdom/hatshelpsut/

Elizabeth Lee Hazen

1885 – 1975
American Scientist and Co-Creator of the
First Anti-Fungal Antibiotic

ELIZABETH LEE HAZEN WAS BORN on August 24, 1885, in Rich, Mississippi. Her parents, William and Maggie Hazen, were farmers. They died when Elizabeth was three. She had one sister named Annis. Elizabeth and Annis were raised by an aunt and uncle, Laura and Robert Hazen.

ELIZABETH LEE HAZEN GREW UP in her aunt and uncle's house in Mississippi.

ELIZABETH LEE HAZEN WENT TO SCHOOL at the local public schools. She was an excellent student, and her relatives encouraged her to go to college. She attended what is now Mississippi University for Women. She graduated with a bachelor of science degree.

After teaching high school science, Hazen went back to school. She took classes at the Universities of Tennessee and Virginia, and Columbia University in New York City. She got her master's degree in biology from Columbia, then began working on her PhD.

SCHOOL AND MEDICAL RESEARCH: Hazen interrupted her studies during World War I (1914 - 1918). She left Columbia and served in an army lab. After the war ended, she headed a lab in a West Virginia hospital.

Hazen returned to Columbia in 1923 to continue her studies. In 1927, she received her PhD in microbiology. Microbiology is the study of living things on the smallest—microscopic—level.

In 1931, Hazen took a job with the New York Department of Health. She headed up the Bacterial Diagnostic Lab. She spent most of the next ten years studying infectious diseases. At that time, Alexander Fleming had discovered penicillin. The medical world became committed to finding more antibiotics to treat bacterial diseases.

STUDYING FUNGI: Hazen became fascinated with fungi (plural of "fungus"). Fungi are found everywhere, especially in soil and plants. Like bacteria and viruses, fungi can cause serious, life-threatening infections. Fungi cause infections of the skin, mouth, throat, digestive system, and other areas of the body.

Scientists were just learning that antibiotics could actually do harm as well as good. That's because antibiotics kill the "good" bacteria in the body that help fight infection. A patient taking an antibiotic could develop a fungal infection. And at that time, there was no treatment.

In 1944, Hazen became head of an investigation into fungi that caused disease. In a few years, she'd identified anitfungal agents that occurred in soil. These natural agents could kill fungi. Now she needed to find a chemist to test the antifungal agents.

WORKING WITH RACHEL FULLER BROWN: In 1948, a very important working relationship began. Hazen was working in New York City identifying antifungal chemicals. **Rachel Fuller Brown**, a chemist in Albany, New York, was chosen as her partner to develop the first antibiotic to fight fungal infections.

Over the span of two years, the two conducted long-distance research. Hazen collected samples of antifungal agents found in soil. She grew cultures in her New York City lab. Then, she sent them to Brown in Albany in mason jars. In her Albany lab, Brown conducted experiments to determine the chemical agents that killed fungi in the samples. She'd identify the agents, then send them back to Hazen. Hazen would retest the sample, to see if the agent killed the fungi. If it did, she'd test the sample on animals to see if it was toxic.

The scientists faced a difficult problem. If a chemical agent was effective against fungi, it could also be toxic to animals. To be safely used in humans, it first had to pass this important test.

Dr. Brown (left) and Dr. Hazen (right) in the lab.

Finally, in 1950, the scientists found an agent that killed fungi, but was safe on animals. They named the drug Nystatin. (Named for "New York State.") Soon, it was tested on humans. It was a success. Hazen and Brown had done it. They'd invented the first antibiotic drug that successfully treated fungal infections.

Hazen and Brown received the patent for Nystatin in 1957. The drug made more than $13 million dollars in its first years. It is important to note that neither scientist ever earned money from their discovery. Instead, Hazen and Brown invested the money in a nonprofit research foundation. That foundation still provides funding for medical research.

Nystatin proved to be effective in other areas, too. It was used to fight infections in plants, like Dutch Elm Disease. Nystatin was also used to kill mold in old paintings and other artwork.

After their work with Nystatin, Hazen and Brown continued to work together. They discovered two more antibiotics. Hazen also returned to teaching at Columbia. She continued doing medical research until she was 87.

ELIZABETH LEE HAZEN'S HOME AND FAMILY: Hazen never married or had children. She retired to Seattle, Washington, in 1973, to be near her sister. She was in frail health, and died on June 24, 1975. She was 89 years old.

THEIR LEGACY: Hazen and Brown's invention of Nystatin is considered one of the major breakthroughs in 20th century medicine. Nystatin has been used to treat fungal infections worldwide. The two scientists received many honors and awards, including the Chemical Pioneer Award. Hazen and Brown also inspired young women to become scientists.

In 1994, Hazen and Brown became the second and third women to enter the National Inventors Hall of Fame. They followed **Gertrude Elion**, who created many important and life-saving medicines.

WORLD WIDE WEB SITES
http://web.mit.edu/invent/iow/HazenBrown.html
http://www.chemheritage.org/EducationalServices/pharm/
http://www.invent.org/hall_of_fame/75.html

Isabella I

1451-1504
Spanish Monarch Who Helped Unify Spain
Sponsor of Christopher Columbus's Explorations

ISABELLA I WAS BORN on April 22, 1451, in Madrigal de las Altas Torres, Spain. Her father was King Juan II of Castille and her mother was Isabel of Portugal. When Isabella was born, there was not a unified country called Spain. So she was born in what is now one of Spain's provinces, Castile. She had a half-brother, Henry, and a younger brother, Alphonso.

ISABELLA I GREW UP at the court of her father, King Juan II, until she was three years old. When her father died in 1454, Isabella's half-brother, Henry, became the new king. She and her mother and younger brother moved to the city of Arevalo, where Isabella lived for the next several years. Isabella did not receive a formal education.

Isabella grew up at a time of war and instability. At that time, the Spanish province of Granada was ruled by people of the Islamic faith. Her brother, King Henry, declared war against the Muslim leaders of Granada, in the name of Christianity. But Henry was a weak king, and soon Castile was involved in civil war.

Isabella remained loyal to King Henry, and he named her his heir. But she defied him when she decided to marry.

MARRIAGE TO FERDINAND: Isabella proved herself to be intelligent and politically savvy in her choice of a husband. Against King Henry's wishes, she chose Ferdinand, prince of the Spanish kingdom of Aragon. It was a marriage that helped determine the future of Spain.

When Henry died in 1474, Castile was involved in a civil war. Isabella was Henry's heir, but had to muster support to gain control of the country. In 1476, she was declared queen of Castile, and she and Ferdinand began their reign. By this time, she had given birth to a daughter, Isabella, and had an heir of her own to strengthen her control.

In 1479, Ferdinand became king of Aragon. Isabella and Ferdinand ruled Castile and Aragon jointly. This became the first move toward a unification of the provinces that would eventually become the nation of Spain. The two monarchs also began a plan to take back land and power from wealthy nobles, to gain control of even more territory.

Painting that depicts the conquest of Granada by Ferdinand and Isabella.

THE RECONQUEST OF GRANADA: Isabella was a devout Catholic, and her religious beliefs led her to do things that many today find difficult to understand. One was the reconquest of Granada, a province that had been under Muslim control for 700 years.

Granada had been a center of science, learning, and art for hundreds of years. But because it was Muslim rather than Catholic, Isabella waged war against Granada. She was determined to reconquer it and make it Christian again. After a decade of warfare, in January 1, 1492, she and Ferdinand rode into Granada, declaring it their own.

THE SPANISH INQUISITION: As part of her efforts, Isabella instituted the Spanish Inquisition. It was a crusade to find and punish anyone who would not swear allegiance to the Catholic faith.

Its methods included trials, torture, and imprisonment, and it is believed that between 3,000 and 5,000 people were put to death during the Inquisition. Many of the people tried and killed during the Inquisition were Jews who had converted to Christianity, but whose beliefs Isabella suspected.

EXPELLING THE JEWS FROM SPAIN: In 1492, Isabella and Ferdinand demanded that all the Jews in Castile be baptized as Christians or leave the country. She believed that anyone who was not Christian had to be removed from her lands. She thought it was in fulfillment of a Biblical prophecy. Many Jews did indeed convert; many others left Spain forever.

Although Isabella had promised the Muslims of Granada that they could practice their faith after their land was reconquered, she changed her mind. In 1501, they, too, were expelled from their homeland, and the rest of Castile.

SPONSORING COLUMBUS: Isabella is perhaps best known as the sponsor of Christopher Columbus on his voyages to the New World. He asked Isabella and Ferdinand to provide the money for his journey to what he called the "Indies." At that time, no one knew the continent of North America existed. Columbus thought he was sailing west to Asia, in search of gold and spices.

In 1492, Isabella agreed to fund his voyage. She provided most of the money for his ships and crew. She and Ferdinand also agreed that Columbus would be governor of all the land he discovered, and he would receive 10% of all the wealth he brought back. They were all devout Christians, so as part of his mission he agreed to spread the word of Christianity to all the people he met on his journey.

On October 12, 1492, Columbus made landfall in the New World.

Chistopher Columbus kneeling before Ferdinand and Isabella.

He probably landed somewhere in the Bahamas. He called it "San Salvador," meaning Holy Savior. He was convinced he had landed in India, so called the local Arawak tribe "Indians."

In 1493, Columbus returned to Spain in glory. Isabella and Ferdinand were delighted with his successes. They wanted to pay for additional voyages. Word of Columbus's bravery and accomplishment spread all over Europe. He was a famous explorer, and Isabella was considered a great patron of exploration, and of spreading the Catholic faith.

Isabella and Ferdinand funded three more voyages for Columbus. He brought back gold, exotic foods and plants that Europeans had never seen, and slaves. Isabella had said that he should try to convert the native peoples, and if they resisted, they could be taken as slaves.

Columbus did not fare as well on his later voyages. In 1500, Isabella and Ferdinand sent a new governor to the New World. They had heard reports that Columbus had lost control of the Spanish colonies. He was forced to return to Spain as a prisoner in chains. He pled his case before Isabella and Ferdinand. They believed him, and he was freed. On his final journey, he faced hostile Indians and was marooned. When he returned to Spain, he was old and ill, as was Isabella.

FINAL YEARS: Isabella lived to see her children marry into several of the major families of Europe. This helped Spain become even more powerful. Yet she faced great personal losses. She had five children, Isabella, Juana, Maria, Catherine, and Juan. Juan, who was her heir, died in 1497. Isabella, who was next in line to the throne, died in childbirth in 1498. Isabella feared for the fate of her next daughter and heir, Juana, who was called "Juana la Loca," or the mad one. Yet Juana married a member of European royalty, Phillip, heir to the Hapsburg throne, whose son Charles V, became Holy Roman Emperor. And her youngest daughter, Catherine of Aragon, married King Henry VIII of England.

By the time of Isabella's death in 1504, Spain was a rising power, and her children and grandchildren had spread her influence throughout Europe.

HER LEGACY: Isabella I unified and established the country of Spain. She is best known today as the patron of Columbus, who founded the first colonies in the New World in the name of Spain.

Isabella's legacy also includes the policies of eradicating non-Christian peoples from Spain that many people today find barbaric and cruel. Her place in history is now examined in light of those policies, and her achievements for Spain are, in many people's estimation, diminished by the suffering she inflicted in the name of religion.

WORLD WIDE WEB SITE

http://www.pbs.org/kcet/when-worlds-collide/people/queen-isabella-and-king-ferdinand-i.html

Mae Jemison

1956–
African-American Scientist and Doctor
First African-American Woman to Travel in Space

MAE JEMISON WAS BORN October 17, 1956, in Decatur, Alabama. Her parents are Charlie and Dorothy Jemison. Mae's dad was a maintenance supervisor and her mom was a teacher. Mae has a sister, Ada, and a brother, Charles.

MAE JEMISON GREW UP in Chicago, where her family moved when she was four. Growing up, she had lots of friends and activities. She liked dance and sports and also loved to read and draw.

EARLY INTEREST IN SPACE: Jemison always knew she wanted to be an astronaut. She remembers watching the early space missions on TV. She knew she'd be a part of it. "It was something I knew I wanted to do," she says. "I read lots of books about space. I don't remember the time I said, 'I want to be an astronaut'. It's just always been there."

"When I was about five or six years old, I used to look at the stars with my uncle. He would tell me they were just like the sun except they were millions of miles away. That was why they were so small. I have always been interested in astronomy and what goes on in the world. So I guess you could say I've been interested in space travel ever since I can remember."

MAE JEMISON WENT TO SCHOOL at the public schools in Chicago. The name of her grade school was Alexander Dumas Elementary School. She says she wasn't a straight-A student, although she did very well. "Maybe the reason I didn't get straight As was that I did stuff because I enjoyed it."

Jemison went on to high school at Morgan Park High. She did very well in math and science. She also enjoyed dancing and cheer-leading. Jemison graduated a year early, at age 16, and went on to college.

Jemison attended Stanford University in California. She studied both engineering and African studies and graduated in 1977. Then, she went to medical school at Cornell University, getting her degree in 1981. As a medical student, she traveled to Kenya and Thailand and provided medical care to people there.

Jemison holding miniature space shuttle.

MAE JEMISON'S FIRST JOBS: After her travels, Jemison knew she wanted to help out in poor countries. She joined the Peace Corps in 1983. That is a group that sends U.S. citizens to countries around the world to help out in many ways. Peace Corps volunteers use their skills to help people grow food, build homes, or fight disease. Jemison worked as a doctor in the African countries of Liberia (lie-BEER-ee-ah) and Sierra Leone (see-ER-uh lee-OHN) as a Peace Corps member.

BECOMING AN ASTRONAUT: After two years in the Peace Corps, Jemison came back to the U.S. and began to work as a doctor. She was working in Los Angeles when she decided to apply to NASA — the National Aeronautics and Space Administration. NASA plans all the U.S. space missions and hires astronauts.

Jemison knew it might be tough to get into the space program. She was one of 2,000 people who applied to be an astronaut. Still, she wanted to fulfill her childhood dream.

In June 1987, she finally got the call she had been waiting for. She had been chosen to be an astronaut. She studied many different things to get ready. She learned how to fly an airplane. She also used her training in medicine and engineering to understand how the body responds to space travel. As a scientist, she prepared for experiments in space.

BLAST OFF: It was five years before Jemison actually went into space. On September 12, 1992, Jemison and a crew of six blasted off. She spent eight days orbiting the Earth. While in space she studied motion sickness and took part in an experiment hatching frog eggs. Those little tadpoles became the first creatures to develop in space.

After her space flight, Jemison became famous all over the world. She was the first black woman ever to be an astronaut. Children wrote to her from all over the world. In Detroit, a school

Jemison with the crew of the Endeavor. Front row, left to right, Jerome Apt and Curtis Brown; back row, N. Jan Davis, Mark C. Lee, Robert Gibson, Jemison, and Mamoru Mohri.

was named for her. The Mae C. Jemison Academy is a grade school that specializes in math and science.

In 1993, Jemison left NASA. She started her own company, The Jemison Group. Her company brings medical help and money to poor countries around the world. She also runs a science camp for kids 12 to 16. "The whole idea of understanding the world around you is important to everyone," she says.

Jemison continues to work to bring new technology and scientific advances to people all around the world. At her science camp, students work together to answer tough questions that affect all of us. Some of their topics have included "How Many People Can the Earth Hold" and "What to Do with All This Garbage."

MAE JEMISON'S HOME AND FAMILY: Jemison is single and lives in Houston, Texas. She has a cat named Sneeze that she got while working in Africa. She still has a lot of hobbies, including reading and dancing. She also likes to travel and she loves art. She still draws and takes photographs, and she collects African art.

HER LEGACY: Jemison is remembered as the first African-American women to travel in space. She is also known for her commitment to science, and to getting young people and other African-Americans involved in science.

WORLD WIDE WEB SITES

http://starchild.gsfc.nasa.gov/docs/StarChild/whos_who_level2/
  jemison.html

http://www.drmae.com

http://www.quest.arc.nasa.gov/women/TODTWD/jemison.bio.html

Joan of Arc

c. 1412-1431
French National Heroine and Catholic Saint
Led French Soldiers Against the English
in the Hundred Years War

JOAN OF ARC WAS BORN around 1412 in Domremy, France. Her father was named Jacques d'Arc, and her mother was named Isabelle Ramie. Jacques was a farmer and landowner. Isabelle was a homemaker.

Joan did not receive any formal education. She learned domestic duties, like spinning and sewing, at home. She was a very religious girl, and was devoted to her Catholic faith.

Joan was so devout, in fact, that she didn't want to get married. She wanted to become a nun, and dedicate herself to her faith. So when her parents arranged a marriage for her, she refused.

THE HUNDRED YEARS WAR: Joan grew up during the Hundred Years War. That was a conflict between England and France that began in 1377 when King Edward III of England declared that he was King of France, too. The two countries began a war that dragged on for nearly a century.

When Joan was born, the king of France was Charles VI. He was unstable, and suffered from mental illness. During his reign, Henry V of England invaded France and scored decisive victories. To try to stay in power, Charles VI declared that his own son, Charles VII, was no longer his heir. Instead, he arranged a marriage between Henry V and his daughter, Catherine. Their son, Henry VI, was declared King of both England and France when Henry V died.

CHARLES VII: But Charles VII would not give up his right to the throne. He decided to challenge the English and fight them for the right to be King of France.

That was the political scene when Joan of Arc was growing up. Her family and the people of her town were loyal supporters of Charles VII.

HEARING VOICES: One day, when she was 13 years old, Joan was standing in her father's garden when she heard voices. She thought the voices came from God. Joan claimed that she was also visited by the Archangel Michael, Saint Catherine, and Saint Margaret. They told her that she had to help Charles fight the English. She was to help him win back the throne of France and become King.

Portrait of Joan of Arc wearing a suit of armor.

The voices told Joan that she had to meet Charles in person. So she traveled to where he lived, in the French city of Chinon.

MEETING CHARLES VII: Joan of Arc met Charles VII in March 1429. They talked, and Charles became convinced that Joan was telling the truth. He consulted leaders of the Catholic Church. They questioned Joan, and asked if she could prove she had heard the voice of God. "Lead me to Orleans," she said. "And I will show you the sign." The religious leaders told Charles that Joan should be sent to the city of Orleans, where the French were fighting the English, to prove herself.

LEADING MEN IN BATTLE: When she arrived in Orleans, Joan of Arc, clad in armor, led French soldiers against the English. Under her command, the French won that battle. With Joan at his side, Charles was crowned King of France in Reims, in 1429.

CAPTURED BY THE ENGLISH: Then, the tide began to turn against the French. They lost several battles. In 1430, Joan was captured by the English troops. They put her on trial.

TRIAL AND DEATH: Joan was put on trial for "heresy." That is having beliefs that are against the Church. She was also accused of being a witch, and doing the work of the devil. Joan was also condemned for wearing men's clothes, which was considered an offense against the Church.

The English wanted Joan to be found guilty. It would prove that she was a witch, and that Charles was not the rightful King of France.

Statue of Joan of Arc in Notre Dame cathedral in Paris.

At her trial, Joan showed herself to be courageous and devout. She spoke to her accusers in court, telling them what the voice of God had told her to do. But it was not enough to save her. She was found guilty. She was sentenced to death by burning, as a witch. She died on May 30, 1431; she was 19 years old.

SAINTHOOD: Joan of Arc died in 1431, but the legend of her deeds lived on long after. In 1456, the Catholic Church investigated her trial and conviction. They declared that she was not guilty of any charges.

The people of France loved Joan of Arc, and shared the legend of her courage and achievements for generations. She became a folk heroine. Many Catholics believed she should be named a saint. That is a special designation in the Catholic Church for someone who has shown, through their words and deeds, to be righteous and virtuous. In the 20th century, the Catholic Church did indeed name her a saint. She is now known as Saint Joan and venerated for her deep faith and service to France.

HER LEGACY: Joan of Arc is a famous and revered woman in French history. She was devout and brave. She believed she was directed by God to save France and her King from the English. She was always courageous, in battle and facing death. These traits have made her a legendary figure, not just for the French or for Catholics, but for people of all countries and faiths.

WORLD WIDE WEB SITE

http://www.notablebiographies.com/Ho-Jo/Joan-of-Arc.html

Jackie Joyner-Kersee

1962-
African-American Athlete, Activist, and
Olympic Gold Medalist
Named Greatest Female Athlete of the 20th Century

JACKIE JOYNER-KERSEE WAS BORN on March 3, 1962, in East St. Louis, Illinois. Her parents were Alfred and Mary Joyner. Jackie is the second of four children. She has an older brother named Al and two younger sisters named Angela and Debra.

Jackie was named by her grandmother for Jacqueline Kennedy. She was the wife of President John Kennedy and the First Lady. Jackie Joyner's grandmother said that little Jackie was sure to "be first lady of something" when she grew up.

JACKIE JOYNER-KERSEE GREW UP in East St. Louis in a poor, rough neighborhood. The Joyner family was poor. Jackie's father worked for the railroad and didn't make much money. Her mother worked as a nurse's assistant, and she didn't make much, either. Sometimes the family had only mayonnaise sandwiches to eat. Sometimes they couldn't afford to pay for heat, and they slept around the stove to keep warm.

Even though they were poor, the Joyners raised their kids to have strong values. They expected their children to do well in school and to treat everyone with respect. And they taught their children the importance of family.

JACKIE JOYNER-KERSEE'S EARLY LIFE: Jackie's house was near a youth center and she spent a lot of time there. She wanted to take part in the track and field games at the center. A local coach named Nino Fennoy gave Jackie a lot of encouragement. She told him she wanted to compete, and he helped her to become one of the greatest athletes of all time.

Coach Fennoy remembered how hard she worked and how much she loved to race. When she ran her first race, she finished last. But she wasn't discouraged. She had a big smile on her face. Coach Fennoy remembered "her pigtails, the little skinny legs, the knees, and smile."

Within a short time, Jackie was showing the determination and willingness to work hard that made her a champion. Soon, she was

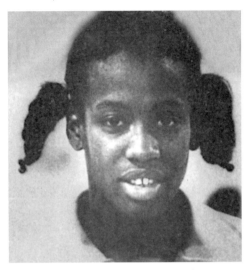

Jackie around age 10.

winning all her races. Her little sisters helped out, too. They brought sand into the Joyner backyard in potato chip bags to make Jackie a sand pit for long jump practice. She began to compete in the pentathlon. That's a five-event competition that includes running, jumping, and hurdles. By the time she was 14, she was National Junior Pentathlon Champion. She won the title for four years straight.

JACKIE JOYNER-KERSEE WENT TO SCHOOL at the public schools in East St. Louis. She always did well in school, and she was great in sports. She also took dance and acting classes and was a cheerleader. At Lincoln High School, she was a star of the basketball and volleyball teams. After high school, she went to the University of California at Los Angeles, called UCLA.

During her first year of college, Jackie's mother got very sick and died. Jackie had a very hard time dealing with her mother's death. She was training with a new coach, Bob Kersee. Bob had also lost his mother when he was a teenager. He gave Jackie support and understanding. As he helped her get over her sadness, Bob also helped her to focus on her school work and sports. They fell in love, and married in 1986.

Jackie went on to have a terrific college sports career. She was named Most Valuable Player (MVP) of the basketball and track teams. She graduated with a degree in history in 1986.

ASTHMA: In the 1980s, Jackie discovered she had exercise-induced asthma. The disease causes the air pathways in the lungs to swell and prevent breathing. It can even be fatal. Jackie continued to battle asthma throughout her career. But she refused to let it ruin her chance to become an athletic champion.

BECOMING A GREAT ATHLETE: Jackie competed in a very tough event called the "heptathlon" (hep-TATH-lon). It is made up of seven different events. They are the 200-meter run, the 100-meter hurdles, the high jump, the long jump, the shot put, the javelin throw, and the 800-meter run. The athlete with the highest combined score for these events is the winner.

OLYMPIC AND WORLD TITLES: In 1984, Joyner-Kersee made the Olympic team in the heptathlon. It was a dream come true for her. Even though she had trained hard and many people thought she would place first, Joyner-Kersee had an injury just before the Olympics. She placed second, winning the silver medal.

In 1988, Jackie competed again in the heptathlon at the Olympics. This time, she won two gold medals: one in the heptathlon and another in the long jump. She continued to train and compete. In addition to the Olympics, she also competed in national and world championships. She won championships and broke records all over the world. She still holds the World Record for total accumulated points in the heptathlon.

In the 1992 Olympics, Jackie won another gold medal in the heptathlon. She also won a bronze medal in the long jump. Joyner-Kersee kept training, with her eyes on the what would be her final Olympics, in 1996. Sadly, she had to withdraw from the heptathlon because of an injured thigh. But she wouldn't give up. She competed in the long jump that year, and through sheer determination, she won a bronze. All together, she has six Olympic medals, won in four Olympics.

In 1998, Joyner-Kersee competed in her final meet. At the Goodwill Games, she finished her last heptathlon, and she went out in style, with a first-place finish. "I can't believe it's over," she said. "I can't believe the time went so quickly."

Joyner-Kersee's track accomplishments are incredible. But she was also a fine basketball player. In college, she was an all-conference player for UCLA. And after she'd retired from track in 1996, she played for the women's team in Richmond.

Joyner-Kersee competes in the high jump for UCLA, 1986.

A ROLE MODEL FOR A GENERATION: This quiet, modest woman's achievements spoke volumes to an entire generation of young girls. Soccer great Mia Hamm was only 12 when she watched Joyner-Kersee competing in her first Olympics. What impressed Hamm wasn't her silver medal, but her determination and spirit. "You could see that she loved everything she did and that she invested every ounce of strength she had in it," Hamm recalls. "You saw her and you got the idea of what a woman athlete should be. At the time it seemed almost like she wasn't responsible for just her sport, but for all women's sports."

LIFE AFTER SPORTS: Joyner-Kersee is retired from sports, but busier than ever. She runs a sports marketing business and a sports medicine business. She also devotes her time to her foundation, the Jackie Joyner-Kersee Foundation, based in East St. Louis.

She opened the Jackie Joyner-Kersee Center in East St. Louis in 2000. The Center is a community resource used by thousands of residents each year. It's a place where they can come together to learn and to play. There's classes for everybody, from kids to seniors. Jackie suffers from asthma, so she's made asthma awareness and healthy lifestyles a priority for the center.

JACKIE JOYNER-KERSEE'S HOME AND FAMILY: Jackie married her coach, Bob Kersee, in 1986. They live in East St. Louis. Jackie's still close to her family, including brother Al, who was an Olympic champion and coach. He was married to the late track champion Florence Griffith-Joyner.

HER LEGACY: Jackie Joyner-Kersee is considered by many to be the finest female athlete ever. In 2000, *Sports Illustrated for Women* named her the "Greatest Female Athlete of the 20th Century." This is what they said about her: "In every revolution there is a leader. Whether vocal or silent, whether by purpose or happenstance, there is a figure whose shadow falls across an era and whose footprints mark the path for others to follow. In ways that could be measured, Jackie Joyner-Kersee was one of the greatest Olympic athletes in history. And in ways that could not, she was a rare combination of courage and grace."

Always humble, Joyner-Kersee sums up her contribution this way: "I realize that I've been blessed to do well in athletics. And I have had a lot of opportunities and a lot of doors have been

Joyner-Kersee competes in the long jump at the 1986 Olympics.

opened for me. I think being able to share that with someone else is a great satisfaction like winning the gold, being able to give back."

WORLD WIDE WEB SITES

http://www.jackiejoyner-kerseefoundation.org

http://sportsillustrated.cnn.com/sifor women/top_100/1/

http://www.espn.go.com/sportscentury/features/

Helen Keller

1880-1968
American Author, Speaker, Humanitarian, and Disability Activist

HELEN ADAMS KELLER WAS BORN on June 27, 1880, in Tuscumbia, Alabama. Her parents were Arthur Henley Keller and Kate Adams Keller. Her father had been an officer for the Confederate Army in the Civil War. While Helen was growing up, he was a newspaper editor and ran a cotton plantation. Her mother was a homemaker. Helen was the oldest of two girls.

BECOMING BLIND: Helen had been born with full sight and hearing. When she was 19 months old, she came down with an illness

224

Childhood portrait of Helen Keller, 1887.

that left her blind and deaf. No one was ever sure what the illness was, but she never regained her sight or hearing.

Unable to communicate, Helen became out of control. She had terrible tantrums. In her rages, she would break lamps and furniture. Her parents were desperate to find a way to reach out to their daughter and help her.

ALEXANDER GRAHAM BELL: The Kellers contacted Alexander Graham Bell, the famous inventor of the telephone. Bell was also a specialist on deafness. He put the Kellers in touch with Michael Anagnos, who was the director of the Perkins Institution for the Blind. Through Anagnos, the Kellers found Annie Sullivan, the teacher who changed Helen's life forever.

ANNIE SULLIVAN: Annie Sullivan was a graduate of the Perkins Institution. She had once been blind, but had regained her sight through several operations. She knew what it was like to be blind. She also knew American Sign Language, the language of the deaf.

Sullivan arrived at the Keller's home in March 1887, when Helen was about seven years old. She brought with her a doll that was made by the children of Perkins for Helen. She placed the doll in one of Helen's hands. In her other hand, Sullivan spelled "d-o-l-l" in American Sign Language.

Helen learned to repeat the letters formed in her hand. But she didn't really understand the meaning of the hand movements. She had never learned written language, and didn't know how to connect words with the objects they describe.

W-A-T-E-R: Then, one day, Helen understood. Sullivan took her to the water pump outside. She pumped water into one of Helen's hands. In the other, she spelled "w-a-t-e-r." Suddenly, Helen knew what Sullivan meant. The material flowing in her hand was "water." The word meant the thing.

Helen was overjoyed. She later wrote, "I knew then that 'w-a-t-e-r' meant the wonderful cool something that was flowing over my hand. That living word awakened my soul, gave it light, hope, joy, set it free!"

Helen touched the earth around the pump. Sullivan signed it. Helen learned 30 words that day; she would go on to learn thousands more.

Helen eagerly reached out to the world around her. With Sullivan as her guide, she learned the American Sign Language alphabet, then the words for everything inside and outside the house.

Helen Keller with Annie Sullivan, 1893.

Sullivan knew Helen wanted to learn even more, and taught her to read and write Braille. That is the system of raised letters that is used by blind people to read.

EDUCATION: Helen wanted to learn everything. And in Annie Sullivan, she had the most perfect, and patient, teacher. Helen learned of a Norwegian child who was deaf and blind who had learned to speak. She decided she had to learn, too.

Hellen Keller with Alexander Graham Bell and Annie Sullivan, 1894.

Sullivan took her pupil to meet an accomplished teacher named Sarah Fuller. She taught at the Horace Mann School for the Deaf. Helen was tireless in her attempt to learn to speak. Soon, she was speaking English, and also French and German.

Keller continued her education at the Wright-Humanson School for the Deaf and at Cambridge School for Young Ladies. She was an excellent student, and studied a wide range of subjects, including history, math, literature, and physics. Her hard work was in preparation for a lifelong dream: to attend college.

COLLEGE: Keller applied, and was accepted, to Radcliffe College, one of the finest schools in the United States. She graduated with honors in 1904. All of this was possible due to Helen's own intelligence and ambition, but also to the tireless efforts of Annie

Sullivan. Sullivan attended all of Helen's classes. She signed all of the lectures, and all of the books for Helen.

CAREER: While Keller was still in college, she began to write about her life and experiences. Her first book, *The Story of My Life*, appeared in 1903. It was a huge success. People everywhere were moved by her story. They were amazed at the achievements of a young woman who was deaf and blind, yet had accomplished so much. Keller proved to the world that the disabled could be educated and could achieve. Perhaps most importantly, Keller showed that the disabled deserved dignity and respect.

ADVOCATE FOR THE DISABLED: It is important to remember that Keller grew up at a time when many thought that people with disabilities like deafness and blindness could not be educated.

Helen Keller at her graduation from Radcliffe College, 1904.

Many thought that the disabled should be put away in asylums. Helen Keller was living proof that there were no limits to the achievements of people with disabilities.

In addition to becoming a best-selling author, Keller became a speaker and advocate for the disabled. She traveled all over the U.S., and then the world, spreading her message.

Keller advocated for social reforms for the disabled. She helped found schools for deaf

Helen Keller examines a talking book machine, 1955.

and blind children. She helped pass laws that allowed people with disabilities to receive access to education. She raised money for educational and rehabilitation facilities for the disabled.

AMERICAN FOUNDATION FOR THE BLIND: In 1921, Keller helped establish the American Foundation for the Blind. It is still in existence today, and is a clearinghouse for information for people with blindness, as well as their families. She served on its staff from 1924 until her death, and helped formulate its policies.

Throughout all Keller's efforts, she relied on the help of Annie Sullivan. Even after Sullivan married, she continued to help Keller in her traveling and speaking. Keller even lived with Sullivan and her husband until Sullivan's death in 1936. After Sullivan died, Keller built her own home, in Connecticut. She had additional aid from caregivers, who helped her in her work.

TRAVELING THE WORLD ON BEHALF OF THE BLIND: Keller continued her busy traveling and lecture schedule into her later years. She visited 35 countries from 1946 to 1957. In 1955, at the age of 75, she traveled 40,000 miles, helping to improve the lives of disabled people around the world.

THE MIRACLE WORKER: The story of Helen Keller's remarkable life reached even more people in the 1960s. Playwright William

Gibson wrote a play, *The Miracle Worker*, that was based on her life, and became a Broadway hit. When it was adapted as a film in 1962, millions of viewers came to know, and love, Helen Keller and her devoted teacher. Anne Bancroft played Annie Sullivan, and Patty Duke played Helen Keller. Their performances were remarkable, and they both won Academy Awards for their roles.

LATER YEARS: After Keller suffered a stroke in 1961, she could no longer travel. She continued to be a beloved icon to the world, but was limited in her daily tasks. When President Lyndon Baines Johnson awarded her the Presidential Medal of Freedom in 1964, she was too ill to attend the ceremony.

Helen Keller died in her sleep on June 1, 1968, at the age of 87. Thousands attended her funeral at the National Cathedral in Washington, D.C. She is buried there.

HER LEGACY: Helen Keller is revered as an author, speaker, and humanitarian who helped improve the lives of people with disabilities around the world. Her life was an inspiration to all. To the disabled, she offered hope, in access to education, equal treatment, and especially dignity and respect. Her achievements and advocacy were the first steps in ending centuries of discrimination, ignorance, and indifference in the treatment of the disabled.

WORLD WIDE WEB SITES

http://www.afb.org/

http://www.rnib.org.uk/aboutus/aboutsightloss/famous/Pages/
  helenkeller.asp

Coretta Scott King

1927 – 2006
African-American Civil Rights Leader

CORETTA SCOTT KING WAS BORN on April 27, 1927, in Heiberger, Alabama. Her parents were Bernice and Obadiah Scott. They were farmers. Obadiah also ran a country store and worked as a barber. Bernice drove a school bus. Coretta was one of three children. She had an older sister named Edythe and a younger brother named Obie.

CORETTA SCOTT KING GREW UP in a poor, hardworking family. Coretta and the other children worked on the farm, picking cotton and taking care of the animals and the garden.

GROWING UP BLACK IN THE SEGREGATED SOUTH — JIM CROW:
Coretta grew up at a time when black people did not have the same rights as white people. Blacks could not buy houses or find jobs where they wanted. In the South, they couldn't use the same buildings as white people. Blacks had to use separate restaurants, movie theaters, even drinking fountains. They went to segregated schools.

CORETTA SCOTT KING WENT TO SCHOOL at a one-room public school for black children. It was five miles away from her home. There were no buses for black children; she walked all the way. Most days, the bus for white children, whose school was much closer to her house, would pass her on her walk. It was the kind of injustice she, and all blacks, lived with every day.

Coretta was an excellent student. She was also an outstanding musician. She could play piano, and had a beautiful singing voice. For high school, she attended the private Lincoln School. She graduated first in her class in 1945.

Coretta went on to Antioch College in Ohio, on a full scholarship. She majored in music and education. She graduated from Antioch in 1949. She continued to study music at the New England Conservatory in Boston. That's one of the finest music schools in the country. It was while studying there that she met Martin Luther King Jr.

GETTING INVOLVED IN THE CIVIL RIGHTS MOVEMENT: By the time she was in college, Coretta Scott had become involved in the Civil Rights Movement. People in the movement fought for equal rights for blacks. They wanted equal education, health care, housing, and jobs. She joined groups like the NAACP (National Association for the Advancement of Colored People) who were

Coretta Scott King and husband, Martin Luther King, Jr., sit with three of their four children—Martin III, Dexter, and Yolanda— in their Atlanta, Ga. home, on March 17, 1963.

fighting for freedom.

DR. MARTIN LUTHER KING JR.: When Coretta Scott met Martin Luther King Jr., he was studying for his Ph.D. in theology. That's the study of religion. They fell in love and married in 1953. After that, they moved to Montgomery, Alabama. There, Dr. King became

233

minister of the Dexter Avenue Baptist Church.

King was deeply committed to the fight for Civil Rights. His focus was simple and clear. He believed that it was only through nonviolent demonstrations that equality for blacks could be won. He also fought for peace and the end of poverty for all people. He was already emerging as a major leader in the movement when he married Coretta.

THE MONTGOMERY BUS BOYCOTT: In 1955, a courageous woman named **Rosa Parks** refused to give up her seat in the "whites only" section of a Montgomery bus. She was arrested for refusing to give up her seat. That led to a famous action of the Civil Rights movement.

Parks challenged her arrest in court. Civil Rights groups used her case to plan the Montgomery Bus Boycott. They asked black people not to ride the buses in Montgomery until the laws were changed.

One of the leaders of the boycott was Dr. Martin Luther King Jr. He was arrested and sent to jail for his work on the boycott. Yet through his actions, people all over the country, and the world, could see how unfair the segregation laws were.

The boycott changed the laws in the U.S. It led to a Supreme Court ruling in 1956 outlawing segregation on buses. The movement for Civil Rights had won a great victory. But there was still much to do.

Over the next decade, Coretta Scott King actively worked with her husband in the movement. She had many other duties besides, including raising the couple's four children. But she remained

Coretta Scott King and her husband, Dr. Martin Luther King, Jr., marching for voting rights for blacks, Montgomery, Alabama, on March 25, 1965.

devoted to Civil Rights.

She said that, at first, Dr. King had a more "traditional" view of women. "He'd say, 'I have no choice, I have to do this, but you haven't been called.' And I said, 'Can't you understand? You know I have an urge to serve just like you have'."

Yet he did understand, and value, his wife's commitment. "I wish I could say, to satisfy my male ego, that I led her down this path," King said. "But I must say we went down together. She was as actively involved and concerned when we met as she is now."

During these years, Coretta Scott King also planned and produced Freedom Concerts. These were fund raisers, in which she would read and sing, spreading the word of Civil Rights.

But fighting for equality was dangerous work. The Kings' lives were threatened. Their home was firebombed. They faced violence and racial hatred. That hatred led to Dr. King's death.

THE ASSASSINATION OF MARTIN LUTHER KING: Dr. Martin Luther King Jr. was shot to death on April 4, 1968, in Memphis, Tennessee. It was a devastating loss, for Coretta Scott King as a wife and mother. For the nation, it meant the passing of perhaps the most important Civil Rights leader in history.

CONTINUING THE FIGHT FOR CIVIL RIGHTS: Coretta Scott King showed her courage and her commitment to her husband's legacy immediately. Dr. King had gone to Memphis to take part in a march for justice for sanitation workers. Coretta marched with the workers, as plans went on for her husband's funeral.

That set the tone for the rest of her life. For the next 38 years, she devoted herself to keeping the fight for Civil Rights alive. She fought for legislation to end discrimination. She fought against injustice everywhere, in the U.S. and abroad. She fought against poverty, violence, and for the rights of women and children. She became an outspoken critic of the racist system in South Africa.

Most importantly, King dedicated her life to two important goals. She wanted the country to create a national holiday in honor of her husband. And she wanted to create a center built in his honor. She managed to complete both.

THE MARTIN LUTHER KING JR. HOLIDAY: In 1983, after 15 years of work, Coretta Scott King accomplished one of her goals. Congress approved a law making the third Monday in January "Martin Luther King Jr. Day." It is a federal holiday. Each year, people around the country celebrate the life and work of this great man.

Coretta Scott King speaking at the commemoration of her husband Martin Luther King, Jr.'s "I Have a Dream" speech in 2003.

THE KING CENTER: Coretta Scott King also worked for nearly 30 years to build the King Center. It is a 23-acre national historic park in Atlanta, Georgia. It includes Dr. King's tomb, a library, museum, and exhibits devoted to education and history. It is also a center for study and learning about Dr. King's life and the movement for Civil Rights. A few years ago, Coretta turned the direction of the center over to her son Dexter.

CORETTA SCOTT KING'S HOME AND FAMILY: Coretta Scott married Martin Luther King, Jr. on June 18, 1953. They had four children, Yolanda, Martin III, Dexter, and Bernice.

King suffered a stroke and heart attack in August 2005. She also had cancer. In January 2006, she went to Mexico for treatment. She died there on January 30, 2006. She was 78 years old.

HER LEGACY: At the time of her death, tributes to this courageous Civil Rights leader poured in from all over the world. "She wore her grief with grace. She exerted her leadership with dignity," said the Reverend Joseph Lowery. "She was a woman born to struggle," said Andrew Young. "She has struggled and she has overcome."

WORLD WIDE WEB SITES

http://www.achievement.org/

http://www.npr.org/

http://www/kingcenter.org/csk/bio.html

Maya Lin

1959-
American Artist and Architect
Creator of the Vietnam Veterans War Memorial

MAYA LIN WAS BORN on October 5, 1959, in Athens, Ohio. Her parents were Henry Huan Lin and Julia Chang Lin. They were both professors at Ohio University. Henry taught art and Julia taught literature. They were also both artists. Henry was a ceramic artist and Julia was a poet. Maya has one brother, Tan.

MAYA LIN GREW UP in Athens, Ohio, the college town where her parents worked. Their home was a glass-walled house filled with books and art. A big window looked out on woods and a stream. "Our playground was the creek," remembers Lin. "We spent hours damming and undamming it, chipping away at the sandstone ledges."

Maya loved spending time at home. She worked with clay in her father's art studio. She built little towns with paper. She also loved to read. Even though she spent most of her time by herself, she wasn't lonely.

Maya wasn't a typical little girl. She says she "didn't play with dolls, didn't do a lot of traditional girl stuff." In fact, she says she did "nerd stuff." "I was very, very serious. Even as a kid, I worried about the environment."

MAYA LIN WENT TO SCHOOL at a special school that was part of Ohio University. The teachers were young and willing to try new things. Maya loved her school.

Lin then attended Athens High School, a local public school. She did very well, and she loved math, biology, and her courses in environmental science. But she didn't feel she fit in socially. "I never socialized in high school," she said. "I didn't go to prom. And I didn't wear makeup. High school was really miserable."

After graduating in 1977, Lin went to Yale University in Connecticut. She loved it. She called it "the first place I felt comfortable." She took all kinds of courses, from literature to science. Later, she studied architecture. That combined two areas she loved, math and art.

Lin spent her third year of college studying in Denmark. She visited cities in Europe. She studied their buildings, parks, and monuments. Lin graduated from Yale in 1981. But before she gradu-

Lin's Vietnam Memorial, known as "The Wall," with the Washington Monument in the background.

ated, she became designed a work that would make her famous.

THE VIETNAM VETERANS WAR MEMORIAL: In her senior year at Yale, Lin began to work on a special art project. She entered a contest to design a memorial to honor Americans who served in the Vietnam War. It was to be located on the National Mall in Washington D.C. That's a grassy park that extends from the Capitol Building to the Lincoln Memorial.

Much to her surprise, Lin, just 21 years old, won the contest. She had been chosen over 1,400 other artists, most of them well-known. The memorial, known as "The Wall," would become her best-known work.

Lin's winning design was done in remembrance of one of the most unpopular wars in U.S. history. In 1981, when she won the contest, the war was over, but not forgotten.

VIETNAM WAR: The U.S. became involved in the war between North and South Vietnam in the early 1960s. Over 500,000 U.S. soldiers served in the war. More than 57,000 died before U.S. troops left Vietnam in 1975.

Many Americans had opposed the war. And many soldiers who'd

fought in the war felt they had been forgotten or ignored. These feelings were still strong when Lin's design won the competition.

THE WALL: Lin's design came to her as she viewed the place where the memorial was to be built. She "thought about what death is and what loss is–a sharp pain that lessens with time but can never quite heal over. A scar. The idea occurred to me there on the site."

"I saw the Vietnam Veterans Memorial not as an object placed in the earth but as a cut in the earth that has then been polished," she said. She saw "the memorial going into the ground, then emerging from it, symbolizing death and calling for remembrance."

The memorial is made up of two walls of black granite. Each is over 245 feet long. The walls form a "V." At the center, they rise up to a height of 10 feet. They taper off to just eight inches high at the two ends. Carved in gold on the walls are the names of over 58,000 Vietnam veterans. These are the men and women who died or who are missing in action.

The judges who chose Lin's design described it as "a place of quiet reflection, and a tribute to those who served their nation in difficult times. All who come here can find it a place of healing."

Today, "The Wall" is one of the most popular memorials in the country. But when it was in the design stage, people argued about what it meant. Some Americans were very moved. They thought it was a beautiful tribute. Others were very angry. They thought that Lin had disgraced the soldiers who'd lost their lives.

Lin had to defend her design. It was a difficult time for her. She couldn't imagine how people could misunderstand her message. But she defended her idea with courage and simple strength. Once

"The Wall"

the memorial was completed in 1982, the arguing stopped. People loved the monument.

Now, the Vietnam memorial is one of the most popular and cherished sites in Washington. Millions of people have visited the monument. The Wall moves them with its simple power. Veterans and family members leave things in front of the names of their loved ones. They leave flowers, pictures, and other mementos tucked into and under the panels. They stand in silence. Many of them weep. Some touch the names on the Wall. It is a work of art that people interact with. It helps them understand the Vietnam War and the meaning of the lives lost.

After "The Wall," Lin was a famous artist. But she didn't really like all the attention, so she focused on other things. She went back to Yale and studied for a master's degree in architecture. Then, she received a request to create another memorial.

THE CIVIL RIGHTS MEMORIAL: In 1988 Lin began work on a memorial about the Civil Rights movement. The movement took place in the 1950s and 60s. People in the movement fought for equal rights for blacks. They wanted equal education, health care, housing, and jobs.

The Southern Poverty Law Center was the group who asked Lin to create the memorial. They are an organization that works to protect the rights of the poor and minorities. In creating her design, she was inspired by a line from a speech by Martin Luther King Jr.

The memorial, located in Montomery, Alabama, is made up of black and white granite. On a black granite wall are inscribed King's words: "until justice rolls down like waters and righteousness like a mighty stream." A steady stream of water spills over the words on the wall. Water also falls on a slab of granite inscribed with important dates of the movement. It also lists names of people who died in the struggle for Civil Rights.

The granite, the words, and the water work together in the memorial. "The water is as slow as I could get it," says Lin. "It remains very still until you touch it. Your hand causes ripples, which transform and alter the piece, just like reading the words completes the piece."

Like the Vietnam Memorial, Lin's Civil Rights Memorial has become a well-known and much-loved work of art.

The Civil Rights Memorial.

OTHER WORKS: Lin has done many other works besides her famous memorials. She designed a chapel for a college in Pennsylvania. She also created a monument called the Women's Table at Yale. That piece honors the contributions of women to the University.

Recently, she designed a fountain for a reading garden at the Cleveland Public Library. The garden has a pool with falling water. It also includes words etched on stones. They are poems written by her brother, Tan, who is a poet and teacher.

Lin creates art and architecture for many uses. She enjoys working on several different things at the same time. So she'll work on designing a house while she also designs furniture and sculpture.

Lin continues to be concerned with the environment. She likes to use recycled materials in her work. And she often gets her ideas from nature, like the curve of a landscape, or the way the horizon looks at sunset.

She has a dream of creating a memorial that will be about the environment and extinction. She says "I really care about the environment. It has been my love since I was a child. This work will probably take my lifetime to do, and it won't be a monument in a traditional sense. We are the one species that has rapidly caused the extinction of so many other species, and that is unique. We have to stop. We have to begin to understand that we cannot continue to overuse. Again, for me it is about teaching. I don't know how it will manifest itself, but this is my dream."

MAYA LIN'S HOME AND FAMILY: Lin married Daniel Wolf, a photography art dealer, in 1996. They have two daughters and live in New York City.

HER LEGACY: Mia Lin continues to create works of lasting value and beauty. She is considered one of the finest and most important artists of the current era.

WORLD WIDE WEB SITE
http://150.252.8.92/www.iawm/pages/lin/lin.html
http://web.mit.edu/invent/www/inventorsI-Q/mayalin.html

Barbara McClintock

1902-1992
American Biologist and Winner of the Nobel Prize in Medicine for Her Work in Genetics

BARBARA MCCLINTOCK WAS BORN on June 16, 1902, in Hartford, Connecticut. Her parents were Thomas Henry and Sarah Handy McClintock. Thomas was a doctor and Sarah was a homemaker. Barbara was the third of four children. She had two sisters, Marjorie and Mignon, and a brother, Malcolm.

BARBARA MCCLINTOCK GREW UP with parents who encouraged their children to be independent. They wanted them to do well in school, but also believed that there was much to learn outside the classroom.

Thomas McClintock told his children's teachers that Barbara and her siblings would not do homework. He thought they needed to get outdoors and explore. Barbara could miss school whenever she wished. Sometimes she took off a day, sometimes she missed weeks of school at a time.

Barbara took advantage of this freedom to explore her world, inside and out. She loved being outdoors, and enjoyed running, skating, and spending time in nature. She also loved to read, and to spend time "just thinking about things." She was often alone, but wasn't lonely. She was happy exploring what most interested her, and she thrived in that atmosphere of independence.

Barbara was unconventional in other ways, too. She didn't like long hair or long dresses, which were the fashions of the time. So she cut her hair short, and had her mother make her pants, so she could play, climb trees, and run free.

BARBARA MCCLINTOCK WENT TO SCHOOL at the public schools. Her family moved to New York City when she was six. She attended P.S. 139 and Erasmus High School. Even though she missed a lot of school, she was an excellent student. She graduated from high school at 16, with honors.

When McClintock was growing up, girls were expected to become wives and mothers. Very few of them went to college. But McClintock wanted to continue her education.

Her family didn't have a lot of money, so she found a college that had free tuition: Cornell University in Ithaca, New York.

McClintock as a student at Cornell University in the 1920s.

McClintock began her studies at Cornell in 1919. She loved it. "I was entranced at the very first lecture I went to," she said. "I was doing now what I really wanted to do. I never lost that joy, all the way through college."

STUDYING GENETICS: McClintock focused her studies on "genetics." That is the study of genes, the parts of cells that carry hereditary material.

All living things are made up of cells, and all living things reproduce. When they do, they pass on information on inherited traits like hair and eye color in humans, through the parts of cells called "genes."

McClintock was facinated by the study of genes. She was such an outstanding student that she was allowed to take graduate-level courses before she finished her undergraduate degree.

Yet after completing her bachelor of science degree in 1923, she wasn't able to attend Cornell's graduate school in her chosen field. At that time, the school did not admit women to its graduate program in genetics. So McClintock continued her studies in botany—the study of plants. Within botany, she studied "cytogenetics." That is the study of plant genes. It remained the center of her studies for the rest of her life.

FIRST JOBS: After she had finished her Ph.D. in 1927, McClintock began to work as a researcher at Cornell. She was an excellent researcher, and received several grants to continue her studies at other universities.

In the 1930s, she conducted research at the California Institute of Technology and the University of Missouri. She received a very special scholarship, a Guggenheim, and studied in Germany in 1933. But Germany was politically unstable, and the rise of the Nazi political party appalled her. She returned to the U. S. and to Cornell. After several years there, and at other universities, McClintock got an offer to conduct research at the Carnegie Institute's Cold Spring Harbor Laboratory.

COLD SPRING HARBOR: McClintock joined the research staff of

Mclintock at Cold Spring Harbor, 1960.

the Department of Genetics at Cold Spring Harbor, on Long Island, New York, in 1941. She would remain there for the rest of her life, doing groundbreaking research in the field of genetics.

THE GENETICS OF CORN: McClintock's studies focused on the genetics of corn, specifically maize. Maize is also called "Indian corn." It is the multicolored corn that is often used in Thanksgiving and harvest celebrations.

The color, shape, and size of

McClintock in the lab at Cold Spring Harbor, 1963.

the kernels of maize are based on inherited traits. McClintock studied how those traits are handed down from one generation of corn to the next. While still at Cornell, she had developed a method for identifying the 10 different "chromosomes" of maize. Chromosomes are the parts of the gene that contain the inherited information.

"JUMPING GENES": At that time, scientists believed that all genetic information was passed on in an orderly, predictable way. McClintock's research challenged that. She discovered that in maize the genes appeared to move randomly. They "jumped" during cell division, as they passed on their genetic material.

BREAKTHROUGHS IN UNDERSTANDING GENETICS: McClintock's research offered a groundbreaking look at the behavior of genes. She showed how certain genes could turn "off" or "on" in determining traits, like color or shape in corn kernels. She developed theories about how this happened, and was immediately challenged by many other scientists for going against the accepted explanation of the time.

McClintock had previously published her findings in scientific journals, but after her new research was challenged and rejected, she stopped publishing. But she didn't stop her research. With colleagues at Cold Spring Harbor, McClintock continued her study of the genetics of corn.

McClintock was a woman of great strength and intelligence. She didn't mind that other scientists didn't agree with her. Instead, she waited for them to catch up. She continued her work with the same determination and scientific precision. She raised the corn she used in her studies herself, planting, pollinating, and harvesting it.

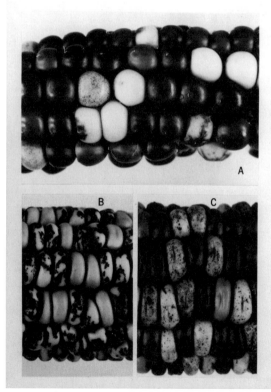

Corn kernel specimens from McClintock's experiments that show the variety of the size and shape of kernels.

Not all the country's scientists turned against her. She was elected to the National Academy of Sciences, and was only the third woman to be so honored. She was also the first woman president of the Genetics Society of America.

In 1957, McClintock received grants from the National Science Foundation and the Rockefeller Foundation to continue her study of maize.

*McClintock, third from the left in the front row, with staff at the
Cold Spring Harbor Laboratory.*

She began regular research trips to South and Central America to
study even more varieties of corn. She and her colleagues collected
a great amount of data that they finally published, in 1981, as *The
Chromosomal Constitution of Races of Maize.*

In the 1970s and 1980s, the scientific world finally did "catch
up" to Barbara McClintock. Molecular biologists, who study life on
the level of molecules, discovered that some bacteria behaved the
way that corn did in McClintock's studies. Their findings proved
that she had been right all along: genes did indeed pass their information on randomly, not in predictable patterns.

Finally, McClintock began to receive the recognition and honors
she deserved. In 1981, she received two major prizes. The first
was the MacArthur Award, called a "genius" grant, for her work in

genetics. The second was the Lasker Medical Research Award, one of the most important honors in science.

THE NOBEL PRIZE: In 1983, McClintock received one of the most prestigious awards in the world. At 81, she won the Nobel Prize in Medicine. She was the first woman to win the prize in Medicine that was not shared with another person. Only two other women, including **Marie Curie,** had won unshared Nobel Prizes, and those were both in Chemistry.

The Nobel committee noted McClintock's "discovery that genes can move from one spot to another on the chromosomes of plants and change the future generations of plants." The recognition came nearly 60 years after her first discoveries regarding the behavior of genes.

McClintock giving a speech at the Nobel Conference, 1983.

McClintock was pleased to be recognized for her work, but it didn't change her in any way. "When you know you're right, you're right. You don't care. You can't be hurt. You just know that sooner or later it will come out in the wash."

HOME AND FAMILY: McClintock never married or had children. She said that she never really felt the need for it. "There was not a strong necessity for a personal attachment to anybody. I just didn't feel it."

She devoted her life to her work, and was very happy in her career. She worked seven days a week, often 12 hours a day, well into her 80s. She lived a simple life, too. Her apartment was above her lab for many years. In the 1980s, after winning awards like the Nobel that came with cash prizes, she bought a car, and got a phone, for the first time. Barbara McClintock died on September 3, 1992, at the age of 90.

HER LEGACY: McClintock is one of the most important geneticists of the 20th century. Her work transformed the understanding of how genes pass on information. Medical researchers have used her work to understand bacteria, viruses, and how cancers grow. Her work has also led to some of the first studies in genetic engineering. She was a brilliant, determined, and focused scientist. Those characteristics guided her as she broke barriers in research and academics, to achieve scientific breakthroughs still important today.

WORLD WIDE WEB SITES

http://nobelprize.org/nobel_prizes/medicine/laureates/1983/mcclintock-autobio.html

http://profiles.nlm.nih.gov/LL/Views/Exhibit/narrative/biographical.html

Margaret Mead

1901-1978
American Anthropologist, Author, and Lecturer
Introduced the Field of Anthropology to Americans

MARGARET MEAD WAS BORN on December 16, 1901, in Philadelphia, Pennsylvania. Her parents were Emily Fogg Mead and Edward Sherwood Mead. Emily was a sociologist and teacher. Edward was a professor of economics. Margaret was the oldest of four children, and had one brother, Richard, and two sisters, Elizabeth and Priscilla.

MARGARET MEAD GREW UP in a family that valued independent thinking. She was very close to her mother and grandmother. They had both gone to college, which was very rare at the time. They encouraged Margaret and her siblings to read, explore the natural world, and have a broad range of friends.

Margaret flourished in this atmosphere. When she was just eight years old, she started keeping a journal. She loved to observe people, and write down her thoughts. It was the beginning of a lifelong pursuit of observation and study.

AN UNUSUAL EDUCATION:

Margaret's parents and grand-mother rejected traditional schooling for her and her

Margaret and her brother Richard in Nantucket, 1911.

siblings. They thought that having students sit in classrooms all day memorizing facts wasn't learning. Instead, Margaret's grand-mother tutored the Mead children at home one hour each day. Then, they were sent outside to study nature first-hand. They also made regular trips to the library and to museums. Their parents invited local artists and carpenters to their home to teach the children how to paint and work with wood and clay.

This way of learning stimulated Margaret's mind. It made her eager to learn as much as she could, in every area. When it came time for college, she looked forward to sharing her joy of learning with other students.

COLLEGE: Mead's first college experience was a disappointment. She started school at DePauw University in Indiana. The students and lifestyle at DePauw were very conventional, and she didn't fit in, socially or intellectually. Most of the students lived in sororities or fraternities. One sorority invited Mead to join, then rejected her. They thought she was too studious, and they didn't like her unfashionable clothes.

Mead was hurt by the rejection. She and a handful of other students—an African-American, a Catholic, and a Jewish student—formed their own group. They called themselves "The Minority."

Mead faced rejection in class, too. She was an excellent student, and her fellow students, especially the boys, taunted and bullied her for it. She later observed that "bright girls could do better than bright boys," but "would suffer for it."

Miserable at DePauw, Mead decided to make a change. She transferred to Barnard College in New York City. She finally felt at home there, and took classes in many areas, including a course with Frank Boas and Ruth Benedict that would change her life.

FRANK BOAS AND RUTH BENEDICT: Frank Boas and Ruth Benedict were professors of anthropology (an-throw-POL-oh-gee). That is the scientific study of cultures. It was a new field when Mead began to study it. Boas and Benedict were two of the most famous anthropologists in the world.

FIELD WORK: In their anthropology courses, Boas and Benedict stressed the importance of "field work." That is the close observation of cultures, especially primitive cultures. Boas and Benedict thought that anthropologists should study primitive cultures, especially in areas of the world not yet touched by modern civilization.

Boas and Benedict wanted to make observations about human behavior that had not been influenced by the outside world. They were especially interested in studying everyday life. So they focused on families, roles for men and women, and the raising of children.

Mead loved her courses with Boas and Benedict. She found what she wanted to do with the rest of her life. She finished her bachelor's degree in anthropology at Barnard in 1923, and her master's in 1924. She began her Ph.D. in 1925, and, as part of that program, began her first field work.

Margaret Mead standing between two Samoan girls, 1926.

Mead decided she wanted to study cultures in the South Pacific. When she made her plans known, she received intense criticism from male anthropologists. They told her she should be "having babies" and following traditional female pursuits. As she had always done, Mead ignored the insults. She followed her own path, breaking barriers and making history

SAMOA: In 1925, Mead left the U.S. and traveled to the Samoan Islands, in the South Pacific. She knew what she wanted to study.

She wanted to observe the behavior of adolescent girls in Samoan culture. She wanted to understand how girls in Samoa grew from childhood to adulthood, and how it was different from growing up in the U.S.

Mead wanted to live with the Samoans to closely observe them, and also to be part of their culture. When she first arrived, she spent several weeks learning the language and customs. After that, her real field work began. For eight months, she lived with three different tribes of people in villages on the Samoan island of Tau.

Mead developed her own research methods. She lived the way they did, "speaking their language, eating their food, sitting on the floor." The Samoans welcomed their guest. They began to treat her as one of the tribe.

COMING OF AGE IN SAMOA: Mead kept careful notes of all her observations. She turned these observations into a groundbreaking book, *Coming of Age in Samoa*, published in 1928. In the book, she described the Samoan way of growing up as peaceful and unpressured. She contrasted it with the way most American youth were raised. She wrote that the stress and unhappiness many American teenagers experienced was based on American *culture*. This was very different from the thinking of the time. In the 1920s, most anthropologists thought that teenagers' emotional lives were based on their background from birth, not the culture they grew up in.

Mead's book soared to the top of the bestseller lists. It was widely read, and introduced many Americans to the field of anthropology. It was translated into many languages and was an international success. Many young people considered becoming anthropologists for the first time. But Mead's book also drew harsh

Margaret Mead sitting on a canoe in Samoa, 1926.

criticism. Some critics rejected her findings and her portrait of Samoan life. But the importance of *Coming of Age in Samoa* was undeniable. Margaret Mead became a famous scientist and author. She introduced Americans to a way of looking at other cultures, and understanding their own.

AMERICAN MUSEUM OF NATURAL HISTORY: In 1926, Mead joined the staff of the American Museum of Natural History in New York. She worked there for the next 50 years. She helped create its collection of art and artifacts from cultures all over the world. These pieces formed the Museum's famed Hall of Pacific Peoples.

NEW GUINEA: Mead also went back to the South Pacific and continued her field work. From the 1930s through the 1960s, she visited and observed native peoples in New Guinea, Bali, and Samoa. She also became an excellent photographer and used these images in her field work.

Mead wrote many more best-selling books based on her studies, including *Growing Up in New Guinea*. That book focused on the lives of the children of Manus Island. She returned to Manus in 1953, after the people had been exposed to the outside world for the first time. She chronicled the changes she observed in *New Lives for Old*.

LATER YEARS: Mead's later years were devoted to writing and lecturing. She continued to write books, and also contributed a regular column for *Redbook* magazine. She had an ability to reach general readers, not just anthropologists, with her thoughts on human nature.

A view from Margaret Mead's room in Samoa, 1926.

Mead also became involved in the anti-nuclear movement and the environmental movement. She saw the build-up of nuclear weapons as a tremendous danger to humankind. In the growing trends of pollution and destruction of natural habitats for humans and animals, she foresaw a worldwide environmental crisis. She spoke out on these issues, too.

HOME AND FAMILY: Mead was married three times. Her first husband was Luther Cressman, whom she married in 1923. They were often apart, and divorced in

1929. That year she married Reo Fortune, a fellow anthropologist who did field work with her. They divorced in 1936. Mead married Gregory Bateson in 1936, and the two became well-known for their field work in the South Pacific. Mead and Bateson had one daughter, Mary Catherine. They divorced in 1950.

Mead continued to write and lecture into her 70s. In 1978, she learned she had pancreatic cancer. She died of the disease on November 15, 1978. She was mourned the world over, in the U.S., and among the people of the South Pacific whose cultures she had shared. Shortly after her death, she was honored with the Presidential Medal of Freedom.

HER LEGACY: Through her field work among the native people of the South Pacific, Margaret Mead opened up the world of anthropology to Americans. She shared her insights into human nature through her books and lectures. She hoped that people would have a better understanding of themselves if they could see the ways that others lived. She said, "I have spent most of my life studying the lives of other peoples—faraway peoples—so that Americans might better understand themselves."

Mead was optimistic about humankind's ability to change, too. One of her most famous quotes shows this: "Never doubt that a small group of thoughtful, committed citizens can change the world."

WORLD WIDE WEB SITES

http://www.amnh.org/exhibitions/expeditions/treasure_fossil/
  Treasures/Margaret_Mead/mead.html

http://www.interculturalstudies.org/Mead/index.html

Toni Morrison

1931 –
African-American Writer
First Black Woman to Win the
Nobel Prize in Literature

TONI MORRISON WAS BORN on February 18, 1931, in Lorain, Ohio. Her name when she was born was Chloe Anthony Wofford. (She changed her name from "Chloe" to "Toni" when she was older.) Her parents were Ramah and George Wofford. She was the second of four children.

TONI MORRISON GREW UP in a loving, hard-working family. She was born during the Great Depression. That was a time in the 1930s when up to 25% of Americans couldn't find work. Toni's father sometimes worked three jobs to keep his family fed and clothed.

Lorain was an integrated, working-class town. Morrison remembered that it was "an escape from stereotyped black settings. Neither plantation nor ghetto." Still, she faced racial discrimination as a child. She was raised among children of immigrants, and they always made her feel inferior.

A FAMILY OF STORYTELLERS: The Morrison family was close. They loved to entertain one another with stories. Many of them were based on African-American folk tales. Toni loved her father's stories, particularly his ghost stories. "We were always begging him to repeat the stories that terrified us the most," she remembered. These tales would influence her finest work.

TONI MORRISON WENT TO SCHOOL at the local public schools. She was always an outstanding student. She loved to read and explore the meaning of literature of all kinds. "Those books were not written for a little black girl in Lorain, Ohio," she recalled. "But they were so magnificently done that I got them anyway. They spoke to me directly."

Morrison graduated with honors and went on to college at Howard University. That is one of the finest traditional black colleges in the country. She majored in English. She enjoyed performing in the college theater group, the Howard University Players.

Morrison graduated from Howard in 1953. She went on to graduate school at Cornell University. She received her Master's degree in English in 1955.

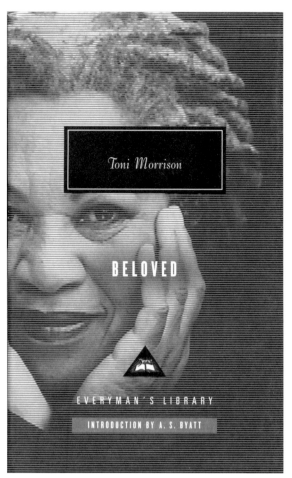

TEACHING, WRITING, AND WORKING: Morrison's first teaching job was at Texas Southern University. She worked there for two years, then accepted a teaching position at Howard, her former college. In 1958, she married an architect named Harold Morrison. They soon had two sons.

In 1964, Morrison's marriage ended. With her young sons, she took a job in Syracuse, New York, as an editor for Random House. She worked as a book editor for the next 25 years, editing during the day, and writing at night. "I had two small children in a strange place and was very lonely," she recalled. "Writing was something for me to do in the evenings, after the children were asleep." After working in Syracuse for several years, she moved to New York City. Still working full time, she managed to finish, and publish, her first novel.

FIRST NOVELS: Morrison's first novel is called *The Bluest Eye*. It was published in 1969. Like all of her books, it deals with racism and its effect on African-Americans. And like most of her books, it is a very adult story, though its main character is a child. It is the story of a little girl who desperately wants what black children rarely have—blue eyes. The book explores the humiliations blacks suffer in white-dominated society.

Morrison kept up her busy schedule of editing books and writing book reviews, while writing more novels. Her novels from this time include *Sula* and *Song of Soloman*. In her editorial work, she edited the work of many African-American writers, including Muhammad Ali.

BELOVED: Morrison was working on an African-American history book when she came across a real-life story. It was about a runaway female slave during the Civil War. The woman was caught, with her infant daughter, fleeing to freedom. The woman knew she and her baby would be forced to return to slavery. Rather than see her daughter raised a slave, the mother kills her baby.

That tragic, horrifying story became the basis for Morrison's best-known book, *Beloved*. In her novel, the mother, Sethe, is haunted by her murdered daughter, who returns as a ghost. Morrison says she wrote the book to remember the lives of the millions of slaves who died in this country. Slavery and its legacy is the curse that, like Beloved, haunts the novel, and American history.

In 1989, Morrison accepted a teaching position at Princeton University. From that point on, she has devoted her time to teaching and writing.

THE NOBEL PRIZE: In 1993, Morrison received the Nobel Prize in Literature. That is the greatest honor an author can receive. She was the first black woman to receive the award. The Nobel committee praised her "richly expressive depictions of Black America." Morrison was honored and overwhelmed by the prize. She gave a moving speech when she accepted the award. Soon, she was back at work, publishing more novels.

REMEMBER: In 2004, Morrison published another powerful book, this time for children. It's called *Remember: The Journey to School Integration.* It's the story of Brown V. The Board of Education and the integration of the public schools.

That landmark case, argued by Thurgood Marshall before the U.S. Supreme Court, ended legalized segregation. Morrison's book is a moving tribute to the courage of those who fought for the end of segregation. But it also shows the courage of the children, many of them elementary age, who bravely confronted the racist people who didn't believe they were equal. It is a powerful and wonderful book.

Morrison continues to write and teach. She takes both very seriously. When she's writing, she likes to get up early "before there is light," she says. "I write with pencil, yellow pads, words, scratchings out."

She says that the planning process behind a book takes a long time. "I've spent a couple of years, just thinking about these people, the circumstances, the whole architecture of the book. I sort of feel so intimately connected with the place and the people and the events that when language does arrive, I'm pretty much ready."

TONI MORRISON'S HOME AND FAMILY: Toni Morrison married her husband, Harold Morrison, in 1958. They had two sons,

Harold and Slade. They divorced in 1964. Harold and Slade are grown up now, and have children of their own.

HER LEGACY: Morrison is considered one of the finest writers of her generation, black or white, male or female. In 2006, *Beloved* was chosen as the best novel of the last 25 years. The power and beauty of her work isn't defined by race, although that is often her theme. Instead, she writes about the love, hope, and beauty of life, for all people.

WORLD WIDE WEB SITES

http://nobelprize.org/

http://voices.cla.umn.edu/vg/Bios/entires/morrison_toni.html

Lucretia Mott

1793-1880
American Abolitionist and Champion of Women's Rights
Led the Movement for Women's Suffrage

LUCRETIA MOTT WAS BORN on January 3, 1793, on Nantucket Island, Massachusetts. Mott became her last name when she married. Her name when she was born was Lucretia Coffin. Her parents were Thomas and Anna Folger Coffin. Thomas was a sea-captain when Lucretia was born. Anna was a shopkeeper. Lucretia was the second of five children.

THE QUAKER FAITH: The Coffin family were devout Quakers. Its beliefs were important to Lucretia's upbringing and to her life's work. The official name of the Quakers is the Society of Friends. It was founded in England in the 1600s.

The Quaker faith was centered on a "God of Love and Light." They believed that each person was capable of being saved by "the inner light." Unlike other faiths, the Quakers celebrated equal roles for women and men. They believed in equality for women in religion, education, employment, and all areas of social and political life.

EDUCATION: Lucretia Coffin and her sister were educated at Nine Partners, a Quaker school in Dutchess County, New York. She attended Nine Partners from the age of 13 to 18. After she graduated, she stayed on as an assistant teacher.

MARRIAGE: At Nine Partners, she met James Mott, a teacher and the grandson of the school's founder. They fell in love and married on April 10, 1811. They had six children. Five of them lived to be adults: Anna, Maria, Thomas, Elizabeth, and Martha.

A Marriage of Equals: Lucretia and James Mott's marriage was based on love, respect, and equality. She wrote that "In a true marriage relation the independence of the husband and the wife is equal, their dependence mutual, and their obligations reciprocal." James valued his wife's intellectual gifts and shared her fervent beliefs in social reforms, especially abolition.

ABOLITION: The abolitionist movement began in the 1780s in the United States and Europe. Abolitionists wanted to "abolish," or end, slavery, as well as the slave trade. In the 1830s, William Lloyd Garrison started the American Anti-Slavery Society. He called for the freeing of all slaves throughout the nation. **Susan B. Anthony,**

Portrait of James and Lucretia Mott.

Elizabeth Cady Stanton, Sojourner Truth, and **Harriet Tubman** were also early and ardent advocates of abolition.

Lucretia and James Mott were devoted to the abolitionist cause in all aspects of life. James made his living as the owner of a trading business. True to his Quaker principals, he refused to sell cotton, which was grown using slave labor. Instead, he sold wool, which was produced without the taint of slavery.

Yet within the abolitionist movement, Lucretia Mott and other women faced prejudice. She was gaining a reputation as a powerful speaker against slavery, but was not allowed to join formal abolitionist groups. When the American Anti-Slavery Society refused to let her join, she decided to form her own organization.

THE PHILADELPHIA FEMALE ANTI-SLAVERY SOCIETY: In 1833, Mott helped found the Philadelphia Female Anti-Slavery Society. She began a series of lectures and public speaking tours. Sometimes, her audiences cheered her. Other times, she was openly criticized, especially by men. They thought that women had no business speaking in public, about any subject.

Mott was never silenced by criticism. Instead, it made her even more fervent in her beliefs and in her speeches. Her husband,

James, was always supportive of her. In fact, he thought she was a more powerful speaker and leader than he was.

In 1837, Mott attended the Anti-Slavery Convention of American Women. It was the first meeting of the group, and was held in New York City. Once again, she spoke out against abolition. Once again, she faced criticism, especially for speaking to "mixed" groups, of men and women.

WOMEN'S RIGHTS AND ABOLITION: Mott spoke about how the fight for women's rights and abolition were intertwined. Denying equal rights to women and blacks was based solely on prejudice, she claimed, and the belief that women and blacks were inferior to white males was wrong on every level. Her powerful words again met with strong resistance. She was even threatened with physical harm. But she kept speaking.

WORLD ANTI-SLAVERY CONVENTION: In 1840, James and Lucretia Mott were named delegates to the World Anti-Slavery Convention in London. They both traveled to England for the conference. The members of the conference voted on whether or not women should be allowed to attend. Ninety percent of the delegates didn't want them. So, Lucretia attended the convention as a "visitor."

MEETING ELIZABETH CADY STANTON: At the convention, Mott met **Elizabeth Cady Stanton**. Like Mott, Stanton was a fervent abolitionist. She had also become equally committed to women's rights. They agreed to meet after returning to the U.S. to fight for the rights of women.

SENECA FALLS AND THE DECLARATION OF SENTIMENTS: In July 1848, Mott and Stanton organized the first, and one of the most important, conventions ever held on women's rights. At

DECLARATION AND PROTEST

OF THE

WOMEN OF THE UNITED STATES

BY THE

NATIONAL WOMAN SUFFRAGE ASSOCIATION,

JULY 4th, 1876.

WHILE the Nation is buoyant with patriotism, and all hearts are attuned to praise, it is with sorrow we come to strike the one discordant note, on this hundredth anniversary of our country's birth. When subjects of Kings, Emperors, and Czars, from the Old World, join in our National Jubilee, shall the women of the Republic refuse to lay their hands with benedictions on the nation's head? Surveying America's Exposition, surpassing in magnificence those of London, Paris, and Vienna, shall we not rejoice at the success of the youngest rival among the nations of the earth? May not our hearts, in unison with all, swell with pride at our great achievements as a people; our free speech, free press, free schools, free church, and the rapid progress we have made in material wealth, trade, commerce, and the inventive arts? And we do rejoice, in the success thus far, of our experiment of self-government. Our faith is firm and unwavering in the broad principles of human rights, proclaimed in 1776, not only as abstract truths, but as the corner stones of a republic. Yet, we cannot forget, even in this glad hour, that while all men of every race, and clime, and condition, have been invested with the full rights of citizenship, under our hospitable flag, all women still suffer the degradation of disfranchisement.

Our history, the past hundred years, has been a series of assumptions and usurpations of power over woman, in direct opposition to the principles of just government, acknowledged by the United States at its foundation, which are:

First. The natural rights of each individual to self-government.

Second. The exact equality of these rights.

Third. That these rights, when not delegated by the individual, are retained by the individual.

Fourth. That no person can exercise the rights of others without delegated authority.

Fifth. That the non-use of these rights does not destroy them.

And for the violation of these fundamental principles of our Government, we arraign our rulers on this 4th day of July, 1876,—and these are our

ARTICLES OF IMPEACHMENT.

BILLS OF ATTAINDER have been passed by the introduction of the word "male" into all the State constitutions, denying to woman the right of suffrage, and thereby making sex a crime—an exercise of power clearly forbidden in Article 1st, Sections 9th and 10th of the United States Constitution.

First page of the Declaration and Protest of the Women of the United States, July 4, 1876.

274

Seneca Falls, New York, they established the first women's rights convention.

They presented to the world their "Declaration of Sentiments." Its language and fervent message were based on the U.S. Declaration of Independence. "We hold these truths to be self-evident: that all men and women are created equal," it proclaimed. Mott was the first to sign the document.

Mott continued to speak out on women's rights. In 1849, she delivered an important speech, "Discourse on Woman," outlining her beliefs. In 1850, she attended the first National Woman's Rights Convention, and 1852, became president of the group. That same year, she met abolitionist and women's rights advocate **Susan B. Anthony**.

As the country moved toward Civil War, Mott continued her abolitionist efforts, but did not support war. As a Quaker, she was a pacifist and opposed to all acts of violence. During the Civil War (1861-1865), she continued to work to end slavery, and often spoke to groups of African-American soldiers.

THE FOURTEENTH AMENDMENT: When the Civil War ended, slavery ended as well. Mott and other supporters of women's rights were then faced with a dilemma. The proposed Fourteenth Amendment guaranteed equal rights to all American men, regardless of race. Mott and others thought it should be changed to extend equal rights to women as well.

In all her work for social reform, Mott was dedicated to achieving equal rights for all. She believed in the natural equality of all—of women, African-Americans, Native Americans—and from all walks of life.

In 1866, Mott was chosen as the first president of the Equal Rights Association. Mott then joined **Susan B. Anthony** and **Elizabeth Cady Stanton** in creating the National Woman Suffrage Association. Their goal was an amendment guaranteeing women the right to vote.

Marble statue of Elizabeth Cady Stanton, Susan B. Anthony, and Lucrecia Mott in the U.S. Capitol, Washington D.C.

276

After her husband's death in 1868, Mott continued her efforts to gain equal rights for women. She and her husband had both been involved in the formation of Swarthmore College in Philadelphia, a Quaker school. She remained committed to making sure it admitted both women and men.

NATIONAL WOMAN SUFFRAGE ASSOCIATION: In 1876, as the country celebrated the 100th anniversary of the Declaration of Independence, Mott led the National Woman Suffrage Association's convention. The group published its Declaration and Protest of the Women of the United States by the National Woman Suffrage Association. It said, in part:

"Our faith is firm and unwavering in the broad principles of human rights, proclaimed in 1776, not only as abstract truths, but as the cornerstones of the republic. Yet, we cannot forget, even in this glad hour, that while all men of every race, and clime, and condition, have been invested with the full rights of citizenship, under our hospitable flag, all women still suffer the degradation of disfranchisement."

This stirring defense of women's right to vote was read to the convention by Mott, who was then in her 80s. In 1878, she appeared in public for the last time, giving a speech at the 30th anniversary of the **Seneca Falls** convention. Lucretia Mott died on November 11, 1880, at a family farm near Philadelphia. She was 87 years old.

HER LEGACY: Lucretia Mott was one of the most important figures in women's history. She was a fervent believer in the equality of women, and just as committed to the cause of abolition. She used her intellectual and speaking powers to persuade her fellow Americans, and paved the way for equality for all. Although she did not live to see the passage of the **NINETEENTH AMENDMENT**, which finally guaranteed women the right to vote, her importance to the history of women's rights and the fight for equality is incomparable.

WORLD WIDE WEB SITES

http://www.anb.org/articles/15/15-00494

http://www.mott.pomona.edu/mott1.htm

Florence Nightingale

1820-1910
English Nurse and Health Care Advocate
Founder of Professional Nursing

FLORENCE NIGHTINGALE WAS BORN on May 12, 1820, in Florence, Italy. She was named for the city of her birth by her parents, William and Edward Nightingale. They were a wealthy, upper-middle class family from England, where Florence grew up. She had an older sister, Parthenope.

FLORENCE NIGHTINGALE GREW UP in her family's two homes, one in Derbyshire, in northern England, and one in Hampshire, in southern England. She was educated at home, by a governess and by her father. She was an excellent student, and learned French, German, Italian, history, and philosophy. Her father was a mathematician, and Florence shared his love for statistics. That is the study and analysis of numbers and data. She also studied music and art.

A CALLING FROM GOD: Florence was a deeply religious person. When she was 16, she believed that she heard the voice of God calling her. He was telling her to be a nurse.

When she shared the news with her family, they were shocked. Women of Florence's class were not supposed to work. They were supposed to enjoy parties and social gatherings. They were expected to get married, have children, and live lives solely within their family's class.

At that time, there were no professional nurses. There weren't nursing schools, or specific training programs. There were nurses, but they were generally uneducated, and from the lower classes.

WANTING TO STUDY NURSING: Florence knew what she wanted to be. Even though her parents refused to allow her to become a nurse, she began to study in secret.

Nightingale decided she never wanted to marry. Instead, she would devote her life to nursing the less fortunate. This, too, disappointed her family. But she persevered.

In 1845, at the age of 25, Nightingale met **Elizabeth Blackwell** in London. Blackwell was the first woman to receive a medical degree in the U.S. Nightingale told Blackwell of her plans. Blackwell told her she would face prejudice, but that she should be true to her calling.

Finally in 1851, Nightingale's father gave her permission to study nursing. She traveled to Germany, where she studied at a religious community that included a hospital, a college, and an orphanage. Nightingale loved the work. "Now I know what it is to love life," she wrote. She learned about medicine, wound dressing, and caring for sick people.

Returning to England in 1853, Nightingale got her first nursing job. It was at the Hospital for Invalid Gentlewomen in London. An epidemic of cholera broke out, and she used her skills to help victims, especially those from the poor areas of the city.

THE CRIMEAN WAR: In 1854, England came to the aid of Turkey, which was fighting against Russia in the Crimean War. Soon, news was coming back to England about the horrible conditions in the military hospitals. Hundreds of English soldiers were dying every day, but not from their wounds. Instead, they were dying of diseases that spread like wildfire through the hospitals. Nightingale knew she was needed, and she went to the Turkish city of Scutari to do whatever she could. She brought 38 women to help her.

What she found was horrifying. The men didn't have food, medicine, clothing, or blankets. The hospitals were filthy, and that helped the rapid spread of disease. Nightingale went to work analyzing the problems and coming up with solutions.

When she met with the doctors in charge of the hospital, they didn't want her help. They felt insulted when she told them of the horrible conditions. So she appealed directly to the English people.

Nightingale took her story to *The Times* of London, one of the biggest newspapers in England. The people read about the horrible conditions. They responded immediately. They demanded that the

The hospital at Scutari, Turkey, where Nightingale worked in 1854.

government do something to improve the hospitals. English citizens collected money and sent it to help. Nightingale was put in charge of cleaning up the hospitals, and making them run properly.

She immediately established rules for cleanliness in the hospitals, and improved the food and sanitary conditions throughout. Using her own money, she bought scrub brushes and buckets, and organized the cleanup. She bought beds, linens, and operating tables, and made sure they were clean and used properly.

The results of her methods were immediate. Within one year, the death rate of the wounded patients fell from 40 percent to 2 percent.

THE LADY WITH THE LAMP: Nightingale was the only nurse allowed in the patient wards at night. Lamp in hand, she visited the wounded soldiers, taking care of their medical needs and giving them comfort. Henry Wadsworth Longfellow celebrated her achievements in a poem called "The Lady with the Lamp."

A WORLD-FAMOUS NURSE: When Nightingale returned from the Crimean War, she was a famous woman. She even had to travel under a false name to avoid crowds.

Nightingale used her fame to continue to press for change in medical care for all. She met with Queen Victoria, who supported her requests for reform in hospitals. Based in large part on her writings and recommendations, the British government established an army medical college.

A SCHOOL OF NURSING: The English people wanted to give something to Nightingale to express their gratitude. She wanted only one thing in recognition of her efforts: a nursing school. In 1860, the Nightingale School and Home for Nurses opened in London at St. Thomas Hospital.

But by this time, Nightingale was often ill and limited in what she could do. She had become sick in Turkey with a disease they called "Crimean Fever." It was probably a food-borne infection, and it affected her for the rest of her life. She was often weak and in pain, and spent much of her later life as an invalid.

Nightingale was able to stay involved with the nursing school, however. She met with students and faculty, and many of her graduates went on to train other nurses all over the world.

Nightingale also wrote an important book, *Notes on Nursing*, to share her philosophy. In addition to talking about the importance of observing patients and proper treatments, she outlined what might be called a "holistic" approach today. She believed firmly in the benefits of fresh air, light, and good nutrition in patient care. The book became a bestseller all over the world, and helped spread her influence and methods.

ADVOCATE FOR HEALTH CARE: Despite her frequent illnesses, Nightingale continued to advocate for health care. She studied the design of hospitals and made recommendations for how they should be built. She investigated the health care available to the poor. She made recommendations to improve hospital and health care for people of all economic and social backgrounds. Based on her recommendations, health facilities for the poor became available for the first time.

It is interesting to note that Nightingale, like many people in medicine at the time, did not believe that germs carried disease.

Nightingale caring for wounded soldiers at Scutari.

She believe instead that disease was carried by "miasma," a kind of fog or cloud of infection.

In 1867, surgeon Joseph Lister showed that it was bacteria, not miasma, that caused infection. He used that information to develop antiseptic techniques in surgery, a change that saved thousands of lives. Nightingale accepted Lister's findings, and in some ways, Nightingale's methods of cleanliness were similar to his. They both knew that infection could be prevented through cleanliness, before, during, and after medical treatment.

LATER YEARS: In her later years, Nightingale received honors and awards from around the world. She received the Royal Red Cross from Queen Victoria in 1883, and in 1907 became the first woman ever to receive the Order of Merit. Continuing to suffer from her illness, Nightingale died at her home on August 13, 1910. She was 90 years old.

HER LEGACY: Nightingale is a major figure in the history of medicine. She developed nursing as a profession, established the first nursing school, and wrote medical manuals used around the world. She also broke barriers for women, becoming a medical professional when women were generally banned from working at all. She championed the importance of clean and sanitary conditions in medical treatment, and advocated health care for people of all economic and social backgrounds. Her work helped save thousands of lives, in England and around the world.

WORLD WIDE WEB SITES
http://www.florence-nightingale.co.uk/
http://www.victoriaweb.org/history/crimea/florrie.html

Sandra Day O'Connor

1930-
American Judge
First Woman to Serve on the U.S. Supreme Court

SANDRA DAY O'CONNOR WAS BORN on March 26, 1930, in El Paso, Texas. Her name when she was born was Sandra Day. Her parents were Harry A. Day and Ada Mae Wilkey Day. They owned a cattle ranch, the Lazy B, on the border of Arizona and New Mexico. Sandra was the oldest of three children, with a sister, Ann, and a brother, Alan.

GROWING UP: Sandra loved growing up on the ranch. She didn't have other children to play with, but she wasn't lonely. She was involved in all the work around the ranch. She helped out with the cattle and with repairs. She rode horses, and learned to take care of them, too.

O'Connor remembers it fondly and vividly. "When you grow up on a ranch, you tend to participate along with everyone else in whatever the activity is going on around you. If there's a roundup, then everyone gets involved. If there's a fence to be fixed, or if there's a gate or a well to be repaired, then everybody participates."

She also enjoyed playing with dolls and learning to cook. She learned to read when she was four, and was soon an avid reader, too. It was a wonderful childhood. O'Connor wrote a children's book a few years ago, called "Finding Susie," based on those memories.

GOING TO SCHOOL: The nearest public schools were far away from the Day's ranch. Sandra's parents knew she was very bright and needed to go to a good school. They decided to send her to live with her grandparents in El Paso, Texas. There, she attended a private school, Radford School for Girls. She missed her parents terribly, and they missed her, too. She spent every summer back on the ranch, and it was always hard to say goodbye in the fall. But she did very well in school, and actually skipped a grade in high school. She graduated from Austin High School at 16, and went on to college.

COLLEGE AND LAW SCHOOL: Sandra went to Stanford University, one of the best colleges in the country. She was an excellent student. She majored in economics, and also took courses in business law. She enjoyed her law classes especially, and decided to apply to Stanford's law school.

Stanford had a special program for students who wanted to get both undergraduate and law degrees. Sandra took part in the "three-three" program. She finished her bachelor's degree in three years, graduating in 1950, then went right on to Stanford's law school.

Sandra was an outstanding law student, too. She was chosen to be on the Stanford Law Review. That is a high honor reserved for the best students. Students on the law review select and edit articles by outstanding law professors.

MARRIAGE: On the staff of the law review was another excellent student, John Jay O'Connor. They worked together, and fell in love. They married at the Lazy B ranch in December 1952, right after Sandra Day O'Connor had graduated from law school. John graduated the following spring.

FINDING A JOB AS A LAWYER: Sandra Day O'Connor had graduated third in her class from Stanford Law School. But she couldn't find a job as a lawyer. At that time, because of discrimination, very few law firms had female attorneys. She interviewed with law firms in Los Angeles and San Francisco, and got only one job offer, as a legal secretary.

O'Connor wouldn't give up. She got an interview with a county attorney's office in San Mateo, California, where she offered to work for free. She got the job, but had to sit with the legal secretaries, not the lawyers.

O'Connor worked for San Mateo county for one year, then left when her husband was drafted into the army. They moved to

Germany, where she found a job as a lawyer for a government agency. She worked there from 1953 to 1956.

A GROWING FAMILY: When her husband's army service was completed, the family moved back to the U.S. They settled in Phoenix, Arizona, where O'Connor started a law firm. Their first child, Scott, was born there in 1957.

O'Connor was delighted to be a parent, and worked out a schedule so she could both work and raise Scott. "There was never a doubt in my mind about wanting to have a career as well as a family," she says. "Life is just more interesting if one is engaged in intellectually stimulating work."

By 1962, the O'Connor family had grown to include two more boys, Brian and Jay. O'Connor decided to take a few years off from work to raise her sons. She also became involved in volunteer activities and the local Republican Party.

In 1965, O'Connor went back to work. She got a job as an assistant attorney general for Arizona, a job she held until 1969. That year, she was appointed to the Arizona state senate as a representative of the Republican Party.

GOING INTO POLITICS: O'Connor had been appointed to the senate position when the previous senator had left office. She enjoyed being a state senator, and decided to run on her own in 1970. She won, and was reelected in 1972. She brought her thorough knowledge of the law to her work in the senate, and was a well-respected member of the legislature.

While working in the senate, O'Connor focused on laws that were prejudicial against women. "I examined every single statute in the state of Arizona to pick out the ones that discriminated against women and get them changed," she recalled.

THE "FIRST" OF MANY "FIRSTS": In 1973, O'Connor was elected the majority leader of the Arizona senate. She was the first woman in the U.S. ever to hold that position in a state legislature. Once again, she won wide praise and respect for her work.

BECOMING A JUDGE: In 1974, O'Connor decided to return to the law, this time as a judge. She ran for a position on the Arizona Superior Court, and she won. She served on that court until 1979. That year, she was appointed to the Arizona Court of Appeals. She served on the Appeals Court for two years. She gained a reputation as a judge who was always well prepared, and who was tough, but fair.

NOMINATED FOR THE SUPREME COURT: On July 7, 1981, Sandra Day O'Connor made history. She became the first woman ever

Sandra Day O'Connor and the other Supreme Court Justices with President Reagan in the Supreme Court Conference Room, 1981.

nominated to the U.S. Supreme Court. She was nominated by President Ronald Reagan.

Supreme Court nominees must be approved by the U.S. Senate. O'Connor went to Washington, D.C. where members of the Senate questioned her about her background and her decisions as a judge. When she finished her testimony, the Senate voted, 99-0, to confirm her as an associate justice of the Supreme Court.

O'Connor's appointment and confirmation were history-making. For the first time, a woman was joining the highest court in the land. Americans of all political backgrounds followed the story, and were delighted in the outcome.

O'Connor herself was surprised at the outpouring of support she received. "I had no idea when I was appointed how *much* it would mean to many people around the country. It affected them in a very personal way. People saw the appointment as a signal that there are virtually unlimited opportunities for women. It's important to mothers for their daughters and to daughters for themselves."

THE U. S. SUPREME COURT: The purpose and powers of the Supreme Court are outlined in the Constitution. The Constitution is a document that contains the plan for the national government. It divides power between three branches. The Executive Branch is made up of the President and the Cabinet. The Legislative Branch, or Congress, is made up of the House of Representatives and the Senate. They make the laws for the country. The Judicial Branch is made up of the U.S. Court system, including the Supreme Court.

The Court is made up of nine justices and is headed by the Chief Justice. The Supreme Court hears cases involving the

Constitution. The justices determine whether laws or decisions made in lower courts—of the state or federal system—are true to the meaning of the Constitution and the rights it guarantees.

SERVING ON THE COURT: O'Connor began serving on the Supreme Court in September 1981. Over 25 years, she developed a reputation as an independently minded judge, neither conservative nor liberal in her voting. She was noted for her close analysis of cases, her open-mindedness, and her insightful questioning of lawyers arguing before the Court.

O'Connor was involved in some of the most significant and controversial decisions of the past 25 years. One of the most important involved "affirmative action" programs in college admissions. The case involved the University of Michigan's programs that were designed to allow more minority students into its undergraduate and law schools to achieve greater diversity.

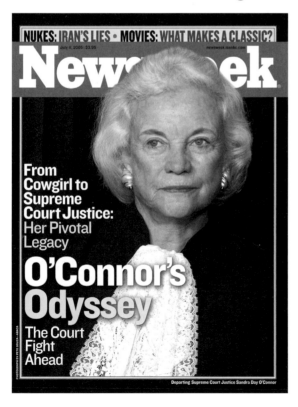

NUKES: IRAN'S LIES • MOVIES: WHAT MAKES A CLASSIC?

July 11, 2005; $3.95   newsweek.msnbc.com

Newsweek

From Cowgirl to Supreme Court Justice: Her Pivotal Legacy

O'Connor's Odyssey

The Court Fight Ahead

Departing Supreme Court Justice Sandra Day O'Connor

The Court ruled against the undergraduate program, but found in favor of the law school's program to achieve diversity. O'Connor cast the deciding vote in the case, and wrote the opinion outlining the Court's reasoning. She noted that the original purpose of affirmative action—to overcome the prejudice that had kept women and minorities from equal access to education, employment, and other aspects of life—had not yet been fulfilled. "We expect that 25 years from now, the use of racial preferences will no longer be necessary to further the interest approved today," she wrote. Her writings in the case reflected her careful, centrist approach to the law.

RETIREMENT: In 2006, O'Connor announced she would retire from the Supreme Court. Her husband, John, was ill with Alzheimer's Disease. That disease slowly takes away the brain's ability to function properly. She wanted to take care of him in his later years. John O'Connor died of Alzheimer's Disease in November, 2009.

STARTING A WEB SITE FOR CIVICS EDUCATION: In 2009, O'Connor began a new role in public life. She started a web site for middle school students to explain "civics." That's the role of government in the lives of Americans. She was stunned at the findings that most citizens didn't know about or understand the workings of government in the U.S. So she worked with a group of educators and law professors to develop the site, named icivics.org.

The site has information on all the branches of government, including what each does. It is "designed to teach students civics and inspire them to be active participants in our democracy," she says. It also offers special materials for teachers.

A JUDGE AGAIN: O'Connor is once again serving as a judge. She hears cases as a visiting judge for the federal appeals court in Arizona.

HER LEGACY: As the first woman to serve on the U.S. Supreme Court, Sandra Day O'Connor has earned her place in history. There are now three more women on the Court, Ruth Bader Ginsberg, Sonia Sotomayor, and Elena Kagan. These accomplished women have followed in the footsteps of a woman who served with distinction for 25 years. She broke barriers, and always rejected any efforts to label her, preferring to be remembered as "a fair judge and a hard worker."

WORLD WIDE WEB SITES

http://www.icivics.org/About

http://www.oyez.org/justices/sandra_day_oconnor

http://www.supremecourt.gov/about/biographies.aspx

Georgia O'Keeffe
1887-1986
American Artist

GEORGIA O'KEEFFE WAS BORN on November 15, 1887, in Sun Prairie, Wisconsin. Her parents, Francis and Ida O'Keeffe, were farmers. Georgia was the second of seven children. She had two brothers, Francis and Alexis, and four sisters, Ida, Anita, Katherine, and Claudia.

GROWING UP: Georgia grew up on her family's farm on the Wisconsin prairie. Several members of her family were artistic: two of her sisters were painters, and her brother became an archik private art lessons at home. She knew early on

n career would be. "I'm going to be an artist," she

ien she was in the eighth grade.

SCHOOL: Georgia attended the Sacred Heart Academy in Mac n, Wisconsin, for elementary and middle school. When she was 14, her family moved to Williamsburg, Virginia. There, she attended Chatham Protestant Episcopal Institute. When she graduated in 1904, she was sure what she would do. "I am going to live a different life from the rest of you girls," she told her classmates. "I am going to give up everything for my art."

STUDYING ART: In 1905, O'Keeffe moved to Chicago, where she studied at the Art Institute. But she became ill with typhoid fever, and had to leave school. By 1907, she was better, and ready for a new challenge.

O'Keeffe moved to New York, where she studied at the Art Students League. It was a well-known school, and O'Keeffe experimented with the approach they taught, called "imitative realism." While O'Keeffe could create paintings using that approach, she knew it wasn't the direction she wanted to follow.

In 1912, she decided to move to Texas, where she found a teaching job in the Amarillo public schools. In the summer of 1912, she took an art class at the University of Virginia. There, she was introduced to the art theories of Arthur Dow.

Arthur Dow: Dow believed that art was an expression of an artist's personal vision. He taught an approach to painting that stressed line, color, and "notan." (That is a Japanese word for the interaction of light and dark elements in art).

O'Keeffe returned to New York and took classes at Columbia University with Dow. He became an important teacher and mentor to her. She later stated that he "helped me to find something of my own." More confident in her abilities, O'Keeffe returned to Texas to teach, paint, and draw.

O'Keeffe produced a series of charcoal drawings, using Dow's methods. She sent them to a friend from art school, Anita Pollitzer. Pollitzer showed them to Alfred Stieglitz, one of the most important people in modern art.

ALFRED STIEGLITZ: Alfred Stieglitz was a giant in the world of art. He was a famous photographer in his own right. He was also the owner of an influential art gallery in New York, called "291." Through his gallery, he introduced Americans to the masterpieces of modern artists like Pablo Picasso.

Stieglitz saw genius in O'Keeffe's charcoal drawings. "Finally, a woman on paper!" he said of them. In 1916, she became the first woman artist to be displayed at his gallery.

Stieglitz was so struck by O'Keeffe's talent that he offered to support her while she established herself as an artist. She moved to New York, and soon was exhibiting and selling her art. She and Stieglitz fell in love. For the next 30 years, their professional and personal lives would be entwined.

MARRIAGE: O'Keeffe and Stieglitz married in 1924. They divided their time between New York City and a summer home in upstate New York. Both landscapes appear in her paintings from the time.

A FAMOUS PAINTER: O'Keeffe became a famous painter during her New York years. Her works of the time show a freshness and originality not seen before in American art. They were eagerly purchased by museums and collectors.

O'Keeffe's work from the 1920s reflects two major subjects: New York City landscapes and flowers. Her flowers especially became a signature subject for her. She depicted them in bright, vivid colors, often showing single blooms in full flower, large enough to fill an entire canvas. Stieglitz organized exhibitions to display her work, and her fame increased nationwide.

In 1929, O'Keeffe traveled to the American west and visited New Mexico for the first time. She was instantly drawn to the place, especially to the quality of light and the landscape. She began to spend summers there painting.

"Calla Lily for Alfred," 1927.

MOVING TO NEW MEXICO: Drawn by its stark beauty, O'Keeffe moved to New Mexico permanently in 1946, after Stieglitz died. It would be the inspiration for some of her most famous work. She had two homes there. One she called her Ghost Ranch House, where she spent the summer and fall. The other was an adobe-brick home she called "Abiquiu," where she spent the winter and spring.

O'Keeffe loved the areas south and west of Taos, and she would roam the land, soaking in the colors and shapes. She loved the red and yellow hills of the Ghost Ranch area. The village near Abiquiu had white cliffs; west of Ghost Ranch were the black hills that marked the ancient home of the Navajo.

O'Keeffe's later work reflects these singular landscapes. She found in their natural beauty an endless source of inspiration. She worked in oils, pencil, and watercolors, showing the wide, open sky saturated in brilliant light.

Many of her paintings contain her signature flowers, especially calla lilies, irises, and the wildflowers of the Southwest. She painted the mountains that loomed in the distance from her home. Another

"Black Mesa Landscape, New Mexico," 1930.

element in many of these paintings are animal skulls. These sun-bleached bones, often of cattle, seem to symbolize the stark yet beautiful nature of desert life to her. These works became so close-ly related to the New Mexican desert that the region became known as "O'Keeffe Country."

LATER YEARS: O'Keeffe continued to paint into her later years, and also started to travel. She toured Europe and Asia, and, in her 70s, went rafting on the Colorado River.

O'Keeffe's artistic powers stayed with her well into old age. At 90, she claimed she "could read the tiniest type. Or see the tiniest tree on the mountain." But that acute vision began to fade, and by her mid-90s, she was blind. Yet O'Keeffe could not stop producing art. Unable to see to paint, she began to sculpt clay. These would be her last works of art. Georgia O'Keeffe died in Santa Fe, New Mexico, on March 6, 1986. She was 98 years old.

HER LEGACY: O'Keeffe is considered one of the most important artists of the 20th century. She never thought of herself as a "woman artist," nor let the term define her. Yet she is one of the most success-ful women artists of all time. She was incredibly productive, creating more than 2,000 paintings in her career. These hang in more than 100 museums and collections throughout the world, a testament to this brilliant artist's vision and accomplishments. She created a singular style of art whose complexity and richness have inspired the admira-tion of generations of art lovers.

WORLD WIDE WEB SITES

http://www.okeeffemuseum.org/

http://www.pbs.org/wnet/americanmasters/episodes/georgia-okeef-fe/about-the-painter/55/

Emmeline Pankhurst

1858-1928
British Political Activist and Suffragette
Led the Movement for Voting Rights for
Women in England

EMMELINE PANKHURST WAS BORN on July 4, 1858, in Manchester, England. Her name when she was born was Emmeline Goulden. She was one of 10 children born to Robert and Jane Goulden. Robert was the owner of a textile business. Jane was a homemaker, and both were very involved in social and political reform.

GROWING UP: Emmeline's parents were involved in two of the most important movements of their times: **ABOLITION**—ending slavery–and **WOMEN'S SUFFRAGE**—the right of women to vote. **Harriet Beecher Stowe's** father, the avid abolitionist Lyman Beecher, was a guest in their home. Her mother started taking Emmeline to suffrage meetings when she was young, and she heard **Elizabeth Cady Stanton** speak.

EDUCATION: Emmeline went to a local school in Manchester for several years, then to a boarding school in Paris. She returned to Manchester in 1878, where she met Richard Pankhurst.

Richard Pankhurst was a prominent lawyer and advocate for women's rights. By the time they met, he had drafted several laws expanding women's rights. One allowed unmarried women to vote in local elections. Another allowed women to own property.

VOTING RIGHTS IN ENGLAND: In England, the right to vote had been limited to landowning men for centuries. It took Reform Acts in 1832, 1867, and 1884 to finally grant full voting rights to all men.

Advocates for women's suffrage tried to gain the vote for women as the Reform Acts were passed, but they were unsuccessful. From their earliest years together, the Pankhursts committed themselves to fight for the right of women to vote.

MARRIAGE AND FAMILY: Emmeline Goulden married Richard Pankhurst in 1879. They continued to work for social reform, while they started a family. Emmeline had four children in five years: daughters Christabel, Sylvia, and Adela, and a son, Frank. Tragically, Frank died of diptheria when he was four years old. Another son, Harry, was born in 1889.

The Pankhursts remained committed to social reform, and Richard ran for Parliament (the British legislature). He did not win, but that didn't stop his fervor for reform.

THE FIGHT FOR VOTING RIGHTS: In 1889, Emmeline Pankhurst founded the Women's Franchise League. ("Franchise" is another word for the right to vote.) She ran the organization out of her home, aided by her husband and other social reformers. In 1894, they won the right for married women to vote in elections for local offices. They continued to fight for full voting rights.

When a recession caused high unemployment in Manchester, the Pankhursts started a Relief Committee. They ran soup kitchens and Emmeline became a Poor Law Guardian. In that role, she saw first-hand the conditions of "workhouses." Those were "homes" for the poor that were overcrowded, filthy, unsafe, and full of disease. Pankhurst began a campaign to reform then.

Pankhurst's two eldest daughters, Christabel and Sylvia, joined their parents in the fight for women's rights. Both became active in the movement, and wrote and spoke on the issues.

In 1898, Richard Pankhurst died suddenly. His family was left in debt, and Emmeline found work as a registrar of births and deaths. In that job, she again confronted the plight of poor people, especially women. She saw them as victims of a system in which they had few legal rights. She continued to focus on voting rights as a means to address social and political inequality.

THE WOMEN'S SOCIAL AND POLITICAL UNION: In 1903, Pankhurst founded another organization for women. The Women's Social and Political Union had one cause: voting rights for women.

Pankhurst being arrested during a rally, 1914.

Pankhurst tried to form a political alliance with the powerful Labor Party to promote women's right to vote, but they weren't interested. Her approaches to other political groups had the same result. In frustration, she took her message to the people.

RALLIES, SPEECHES, AND VIOLENCE: Pankhurst became a fiery and moving speaker, taking part in rallies for her cause. She was met with police brutality and shoving, jeering crowds.

It is hard for modern readers to understand the brutality and violence faced by British women as they sought the right to vote. But Emmeline Pankhurst and her followers faced threats, violence, and imprisonment in pursuit of their goal.

In 1905, her daughter Christabel and fellow-activist Annie Besant attended a Liberal Party rally, and asked about women's right to vote. For simply asking a question, they were arrested by police and fined. When they refused to pay the fine, they were jailed. When the British public found out, they were outraged. Many women became involved in the movement for voting rights.

In 1906, Pankhurst and her followers tried to disrupt a government meeting. The press called them "suffragettes," trying to make fun of them. But they liked the name, and took it as their own.

In 1907, Pankhurst called a "Women's Parliament" to address the issue of voting rights. She led a group of women to the House of Commons, where the British government meets. They were met by policeman, who fought them. They tried again in 1908, and the government revived an ancient law banning such groups. Pankhurst and her followers were arrested and put in jail. It was the first of many imprisonments she would face for her cause.

In 1909, Pankhurst's youngest child, Harry, became ill with polio. She left for the U.S., to raise money on a speaking tour. Harry died shortly after she returned.

On November 18, 1910, Pankhurst again led a group of women to the House of Commons. They wanted to talk to the Prime Minister, Henry Asquith. That year, a new bill that would have granted women the right to vote had been cancelled. They wanted to know why.

The police wouldn't let the women in. A riot started. At its end, more than 100 women had been arrested.

VIOLENCE, IMPRISONMENT, AND HUNGER STRIKES: In 1912, the movement for voting rights took on new tactics, becoming more militant and violent. Women began a campaign of smashing windows and setting fires to bring attention to their cause. Pankhurst personally threw a rock through a window of the Prime Minister's home. She was arrested and sentenced to nine months in prison.

Pankhurst, calling herself a political prisoner, decided to lead her fellow prisoners in a hunger strike. The prison responded by force-feeding the women with rubber tubes. The public was appalled at the treatment the women received.

*Pankhurst addressing a crowd at a Women's Suffrage rally
on Wall Street in New York City, 1911.*

Pankhurst was arrested 12 times in the next 12 months. Each time, she would begin a hunger strike. Each time, the prison staff would try to force feed her, and she would refuse. She would be released, only to be rearrested. Parkhurst remained undaunted. "We are here, not because we are lawbreakers," she said in court. "We are here in our efforts to become lawmakers."

Her actions caused the British government to create a new law, the Prisoners Temporary Discharge for Ill Health Law. Called the "Cat and Mouse Law," it allowed prisons to release a prisoner on a hunger strike. When the prisoner was stronger, she was rearrested, and forced to complete her sentence.

WORLD WAR I: The violence in support of voting rights continued until the outbreak of World War I, in 1914. Pankhurst thought that all British citizens needed to support the war effort, although some in the movement, including her daughter Sylvia, did not agree.

During the war, Pankhurst traveled to the United States and Canada, where she spoke about the movement for women's rights.

FIRST VICTORY: In 1918, as the war was ending, the British Parliament passed a Reform Bill that granted women over the age of 30 the right to vote. It was the first victory for voting rights for women, but there was still work to be done.

LAST YEARS: Pankhurst lived and worked briefly in France, returning to Britain in 1925. In 1926, she ran as a Conservative candidate for a seat in Parliament. But she became ill, and was unable to continue her campaign.

Pankhurst did live to see equal voting rights for women. In May 1928, the British Parliament finally passed the Representation of the People Act, which granted equal voting rights to all British women. Emmeline Pankhurst, the cause's greatest champion, died just a few weeks later, on June 14, 1928.

HER LEGACY: Emmeline Pankhurst was a tireless advocate for women's right to vote. She devoted her life to the cause, and faced imprisonment, starvation, and violence on its behalf. She had the courage of her convictions, and she lived them as well. British writer Rebecca West described her this way: "she put body and soul at the service of liberty, equality, and fraternity, and secured a triumph for them."

WORLD WIDE WEB SITES

http://www.bbc.co.uk/history/historic_figures/pankhurst_emmeline.shtml

http://www.time/time100/heroes/profile/pankhurst

Rosa Parks

1913 – 2005
African-American Civil Rights Leader

ROSA PARKS WAS BORN on February 4, 1913, in Tuskegee, Alabama. Her name when she was born was Rosa McCauley. Her mother, Leona McCauley, was a teacher. Her father, James McCauley, was a carpenter. She had one brother named Sylvester.

ROSA PARKS GREW UP in Pine Level, Alabama. She moved there with her mother and brother to live on her grandparents farm after her parents divorced. Rosa helped out on the farm, picking vegetables and cotton. The family was poor, but they always had enough to eat.

GROWING UP UNDER JIM CROW: Rosa grew up at a time when black people did not have the same rights as white people. Black people could not buy houses or find jobs where they wanted to. In the South, they couldn't use the same buildings as white people. Blacks had to use different restaurants, movie theaters, even drinking fountains.

Hate groups like the Ku Klux Klan could beat and even murder black people and not be punished. Rosa remembered lying in bed at night and listening to the Klan ride by. Her grandfather would sit up at night by the door with a shotgun to protect them.

ROSA PARKS WENT TO SCHOOL at the black elementary school in her town. Schools were segregated in the South. Black children did not go to school with white children. Black schools were poor and had fewer books and supplies than white schools. Many blacks could not go to high school because there were not high schools for blacks in many areas. That is what happened to Rosa. After she finished junior high, she couldn't go on to high school because there wasn't one in her town for black students.

Around this time, Rosa's grandfather died and her mother and grandmother became ill. Rosa needed to leave school and help out with the family. She finished her high school degree later, through a local college.

ROSA PARKS'S FIRST JOB was sewing clothes for other people. She was living in the city of Montgomery, Alabama, with her husband, Raymond. She and Raymond became active in the fight for Civil Rights for blacks. They joined the NAACP (National

Association for the Advancement of Colored People) to help in the fight for equality for African-Americans.

At that time, blacks could not sit in the same section of the bus as whites. A black person had to enter a bus at the front and pay the fare. Then they had to get out of the bus and get back in at the back. Rosa rode the bus to work each day. Each day she had to sit in an area for blacks only.

THE MONTGOMERY BUS BOYCOTT: Rosa Parks became a hero for challenging a law she found racist and intolerable. It happened on a bus in Montgomery, Alabama, on December 1, 1955. On that day,

Rosa Parks being fingerprinted after her arrest for refusing to move to the back of a bus in Montgomery, AL, in 1955.

Rosa Parks riding a bus in Montomery, AL.

Parks took a seat in the first row of the "blacks only" section of the bus. A white man got on and found that all the seats in the white section were taken. The bus driver told the people in Rosa's row to stand and give their seats to the white man. Park's wouldn't do it.

"I had had enough," she recalls. "I wanted to be treated like a human being." The driver told her she had to move. She wouldn't. He said he would call the police. She told him to go ahead. Rosa Parks was arrested that day for refusing to give her seat on the bus to a white man.

Black Civil Rights leaders asked Parks to challenge the law that allowed her to be arrested. She agreed, even though she knew she would be in danger. Civil Rights groups used her case to plan the Montgomery Bus Boycott. They asked black people not to ride the buses in Montgomery until the laws were changed.

It was a great sacrifice for most of the blacks in Montgomery. Many were poor and needed the bus to get to work. But they stood behind Rosa and the Civil Rights leaders. Almost all the blacks "boycotted," or did not use, the buses.

People all over the country became involved in the Montgomery Bus Boycott. They organized, raised money, and let people all over the country know how unfair the laws were. Some people in the Civil Rights movement were arrested and sent to jail for their work on the boycott. One of them was Dr. Martin Luther King Jr.

In 1956, the U.S. Supreme Court declared that Alabama's segregated bus system was unconstitutional. It was a great triumph for the Civil Rights movement.

Because of their work on the boycott, Parks and her husband lost their jobs. They received threats from people who hated them for what they did. They decided to move to Detroit, Michigan. For many years Parks worked in the office of a black congressman, John Conyers.

Parks was especially interested in working with young people. She wanted them to know about the fight for Civil Rights. She and Raymond set up the Rosa and Raymond Parks Institute for Self-Development. There young people could take courses in black history and learn about the Civil Rights movement.

ROSA PARKS'S HOME AND FAMILY: Rosa and Raymond Parks were married in 1932. They lived together in Detroit until his death in 1977. They never had children of their own. They devoted much of their time to the education and care of children through their Institute.

Parks lived in Detroit until her death in 2005. Her casket was placed in the rotunda of the U.S. Capitol for two days. Thousands of people paid their respects to this beloved Civil Rights leader. Her funeral in Detroit was attended by people from all over the country.

HER LEGACY: Parks is remembered for her courage in the face of racism, and for beginning one of the most important protests in the Civil Rights Movement. She was a humble woman who devoted her life to peace and justice. She said, "If I were to wish for anything at all, I would wish for peace, happiness, and justice and equality for all persons, regardless of race."

Rosa Parks with South African President Nelson Mandela.

WORLD WIDE WEB SITES

http://www.achievement.org/autodoc/page/par0bio-1

http://memory.loc.gov/ammem/today/dec01.html

http://montgomery.troy.edu/rosaparks/museum

http://www.rosaparks.org

http://www.time.com/time/time100/heroes/profile/parks01.html

Condoleezza Rice

1954 –
African-American Political Scientist and Academic
First African-American Woman to
Serve as Secretary of State

CONDOLEEZZA RICE WAS BORN on November 14, 1954, in Birmingham, Alabama. Her parents were John Rice and Angelena Rice. Her father was a college administrator and minister and her mother taught music and science. She is an only child.

Her mother created her unusual name. Condoleezza (kahn-dah-LEE-za) is taken from an Italian musical term, "con dolcezza," meaning "with sweetness." She's always been known as "Condi" to her friends.

CONDOLEEZZA RICE GREW UP in a loving family that expected much of her. She started piano at age three. She began studying French and Spanish a few years later. She says her parents put her in "every book club," so she read a lot, too.

GROWING UP IN THE SEGREGATED SOUTH: Rice grew up in a segregated world. She lived in an all-black neighborhood and went to an all-black school. It was a time in American history when black people did not have the same rights as white people. Blacks could not buy houses or find jobs where they wanted. In the South, they couldn't use the same buildings as white people. Blacks had to use different restaurants, movie theaters, even drinking fountains.

During the Civil Rights Movement of the 1960s, blacks became the targets of racial violence. And Birmingham, Alabama, was at the center of the struggle. In 1963, the 16th Avenue Baptist Church in Birmingham was bombed by white racists. Four girls died. One of them was a friend of Condi Rice. She recalled the tragedy later. "Birmingham was a violent place in 1963-64," she said. But Rice was taught to see beyond the violence born of racial hatred. "Our parents really did have us convinced that you couldn't have a hamburger at Woolworth's, but you could be President of the United States."

CONDOLEEZZA RICE WENT TO SCHOOL at the local public schools in Birmingham. She was an outstanding student. She skipped both first and seventh grades. When she was 14, the family moved to Denver. Her dad had gotten a job at the University of Denver.

315

Rice, George W. Bush, and adviser Paul Wolfowitz at Bush's ranch in Crawford, Texas, before the 2000 Presidential election.

Rice graduated from high school at age 14. She started college at the University of Denver at 15. At that time, she thought she would be a concert pianist. But she realized she didn't have the talent. "I was going to have to practice and practice and practice and was never going to be extraordinary," she says.

Then she took a class that changed her life. It was a course in international politics taught by a professor named Josef Korbel. He was a former diplomat from Czechoslovakia who had brought his family to the U.S. after World War II. Korbel was also the father of Madeleine Albright, who would go on to become the first woman Secretary of State. Rice was often a guest in the Korbel home.

Through Korbel, Rice discovered what would become her life's work. She took courses in Russian history, concentrating on the Soviet Union. After World War II, the Soviet Union and the U.S. became the two strongest nations in the world. They represented two very different political systems. The U.S. was a democracy. The Soviet Union was a Communist state. For more than 40 years, the hostilities between these two powers determined world politics.

It was this aspect of politics that fascinated Rice. She wanted to understand the nature of political power. "How it operates, how it's used," intrigued her, she says. She read all the books she could find on World War II, "and about war in general," she recalls.

Rice graduated with honors from the University of Denver in 1974. She went on to earn a master's degree from the University of Notre Dame in 1975. Rice returned to the University of Denver for her doctoral degree, which she completed in 1981. That same year, she became a professor at Stanford University.

FIRST JOBS: For the next 18 years, Rice rose within the ranks at Stanford. She worked as a professor of political science for several years. Her special areas were arms control and the Soviet Union.

Rice developed a reputation as a smart, hardworking scholar. She was considered brilliant and charming. But she also had "velvet-glove forcefulness," said Coit Blacker of Stanford. "She's a steel magnolia," he said. "She always knows what she wants and is extremely disciplined."

SERVING IN THE ADMINISTRATION OF GEORGE H.W. BUSH:
Rice's reputation brought her to the attention of President George H.W. Bush, who was president from 1989 to 1993. She joined his administration in 1989 as assistant for national security affairs. She was also senior director for Soviet Affairs in the National Security Council.

Rice talks with Secretary of State
Colin Powell, June 2001.

George Bush was President at a time of great change in the world. During his term, the Soviet Union abandoned Communism and broke up into many independent states. The former Communist nations of Eastern Europe became democracies. This was the end of the "Cold War," the hostilities between the U.S. and the Soviets.

Now, a "new world order," as Bush called it, was at hand. It was a thrilling time to be part of world politics. Rice helped develop the U.S. response to changes taking place in Europe. When Bush met with Soviet leader Mikhail Gorbachev, he introduced her. "This is Condoleezza Rice," he said. "She tells me everything I know about the Soviet Union." Gorbachev said to Rice, "I hope you know a lot."

As an aide to Bush, Rice wasn't afraid of showing her "steel magnolia" side. She once blocked Russian leader Boris Yeltsin from entering an area of the White House. Yeltsin wanted to see Bush.

Rice said no. Yeltsin backed down.

BACK TO STANFORD: After several years working for Bush, Rice returned to Stanford. In 1993, she became Provost of the university. A Provost is a high-ranking college administrator. Rice was the youngest person ever chosen for the job, as well as the first woman, and the first African-American. She determined budgets, developed curriculums, and handled a wide variety of issues.

SERVING IN THE ADMINISTRATION OF GEORGE W. BUSH: In 1999, Rice stepped down as Provost of Stanford. She became a close adviser of George W. Bush as he started his campaign for President.

Bush and Rice worked well together. Bush called her the person who "can explain to me foreign policy matters in a way I can understand." He said she was a "good manager and an honest broker of ideas." She also became a close friend of the President and his family.

Rice helped Bush develop his foreign policy strategy during the campaign. She traveled with him, met with the press, and answered questions about Bush's stance on international issues. After he won the election in 2000, Bush chose Rice to be his national security adviser.

THE NATIONAL SECURITY ADVISER: The national security adviser is the chief consultant to the President on foreign policy. Rice was the first woman ever to hold the post. She advised the President on issues relating to foreign policy. She also discussed treaties between the U.S. and other nations. And she gave him advice in her special areas of interest, nuclear weapons and missile defense systems.

A TERRORIST ATTACK ON THE UNITED STATES: On September

Rice meets with President Bush, Vice President Cheney, and other officials following the terrorist attacks, September 15, 2001.

11, 2001, terrorists attacked New York City and Washington. In her role as national security adviser, Rice played a pivotal role in determining U.S. policy after the attack. Together with the President, the Cabinet, and military officials, she helped plan America's response.

SECRETARY OF STATE: On January 26, 2005, Rice became Secretary of State. She became the first African-American woman ever to hold the job. She replaced Colin Powell, who stepped down from the position at the end of George W. Bush's first term.

As Secretary of State, Rice was the chief diplomat of the U.S. She worked to develop U.S. foreign policy. She traveled around the world, defining and carrying out that policy in other countries. She was also involved with programs to fight disease, such as stopping the spread of AIDS in Africa.

During the Bush presidency, Rice's major political focus was the Middle East. She was actively involved in U.S. foreign policy as it affected the war in Iraq. She brokered talks between Israel and the Palestinians, hoping to pave the way for peace in the region. She also oversaw talks between North Korea and other nations to stop pursuing nuclear power.

After leaving Washington in 2008, Rice moved back to California. She is now teaching political science at Stanford, and also a fellow at the Hoover Institution. She has also written a book about her parents, *Extraordinary, Ordinary People.*

CONDOLEEZZA RICE'S HOME AND FAMILY: Rice, who is single, lives in Palo Alto, California. She still takes time to play the piano. She especially likes to play in small chamber groups.

During her first years at Stanford, Rice founded the Center for a New Generation. It's an after-school academy for poor, under-privileged kids in East Palo Alto. It provides a positive atmosphere where kids can do homework and play safely.

Rice loves to exercise. "Exercise is a very high priority for me," she says. "I do some of my best thinking on the treadmill." She also loves to play tennis. After her years at Stanford, she's become a devoted fan of the school teams. She loves football especially, both college and pro. She's joked that someday she'd like to be head of the National Football League.

Rice is very religious. "I have a very, very, powerful faith in God," she says. "I'm a really religious person, and I don't believe that I was put on this earth to be sour, so I'm eternally optimistic about things."

HER LEGACY: It is too early to define Condoleezza Rice's legacy. As the first African-American woman to be Secretary of State, she is already a person of historical importance. *Forbes* magazine has called her the most powerful woman in the world. *Time* magazine named her one of the Top 100 world leaders. She will most likely add to her distinguished list of accomplishments for years to come.

WORLD WIDE WEB SITES

http://www.forbes.com/lists/2005/

http://www.state.gov/secretary

http://www.time.com/time/

http://www.whitehouse.gov/nsc/ricebio.html

Sally Ride

1951 –
American Astronaut and Scientist
First American Woman to Travel in Space

SALLY RIDE WAS BORN on May 26, 1951, in Los Angeles, California. Her full name is Sally Kirsten Ride. Her parents are Dale and Carol Ride. She has one younger sister, Karen.

SALLY RIDE GREW UP in Encino, near Los Angeles. She was an active and curious child. Her parents gave Sally and Karen the freedom to choose activities they loved. "We might have encouraged, but mostly we let them explore," her father said.

Sally loved to play sports with the neighborhood boys. Her sister remembers that "when the boys chose up sides, she was always first." At one point, she wanted to be a professional football player. She was especially good at tennis. She was offered a scholarship to a private school to play on their team.

SALLY RIDE WENT TO SCHOOL at the local public schools until high school. She went to a private school, Westlake School for Girls, where she got an excellent education. She remembers in particular a science teacher who encouraged her abilities. Ride did very well in school and continued to improve at tennis.

By the time she graduated from Westlake in 1968, she was a national champion tennis player. She went to Swarthmore College for just three semesters. Then she decided to drop out and try to become a professional tennis player. But after several months she decided that she wasn't really good enough. She went back to college, this time to Stanford University.

At Stanford, Ride had a double major in physics and English Literature. She was fascinated by the world of science, but also by the beauty of Shakespeare's plays. She completed her bachelor's degree in 1973. Ride stayed on at Stanford to study astrophysics. She received her Master's degree in 1975 and Doctorate in 1978.

APPLYING TO THE SPACE PROGRAM: Ride entered the space program right after graduation. She saw a newspaper ad saying that NASA (the National Aeronautics and Space Administration) was looking for scientists to fly in space. She applied, and she was accepted.

WORKING FOR NASA: So in 1978, Ride moved to Texas. She was part of a new group of 34 astronaut trainees. And she was one

Ride aboard the Challenger, June 1983.

of the first six women ever chosen to be part of the astronaut program.

Ride spent the next four years training at the Johnson Space Center in Houston. She learned how to fly an airplane, and then a space shuttle. She studied the communication systems on the shuttle, mastering the role of the CAPCOM, or capsule communicator. She helped to develop a robotic arm that was used to launch and retrieve satellites. Ride recently recalled her training. She said the hardest part was "learning everything that you need so that you are an expert on every detail of the space shuttle and the experiments."

MAKING HISTORY—FIRST AMERICAN WOMAN IN SPACE: On June 18, 1983, Ride flew into space—and into history—as the first American woman astronaut. The Soviet Union had sent two women earlier, **Valentina Tereshkova** in 1963, and Svetlana Savitskaya in 1982. But Ride was the first American woman.

She flew aboard the space shuttle *Challenger* with a crew of five. Her job on the flight was as a mission specialist. On the mission, she conducted experiments and launched satellites. When she returned to Earth on June 24, 1983, Sally Ride was famous.

Ride flew again on October 5, 1984. This time, she was part of a crew of seven. On the mission Dr. Kathryn Sullivan became the first woman to walk in space. Ride conducted experiments and also served as the flight engineer. In that role, she was involved with the launch and re-entry of the shuttle.

In June 1985, Ride was chosen to fly on another shuttle mission. But then a tragedy occurred that changed her career, and the space program, for years.

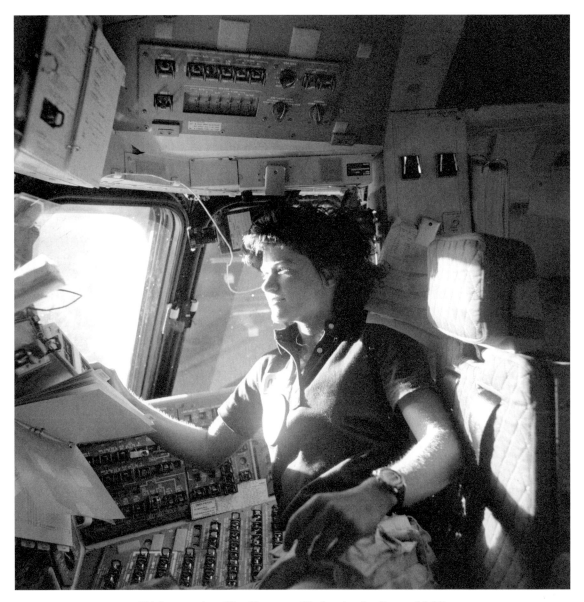

Ride on the Challenger flight deck, June 1983.

THE *CHALLENGER* CRASH: In January 1986, the *Challenger* crashed after takeoff. All the astronauts on board died. Ride became a member of the commission investigating what happened in the accident. She stopped her training to devote herself to the assignment.

After the *Challenger* accident, there were no space shuttle flights for three years. Ride decided to leave NASA and return to teaching and research. She taught at Stanford, then at the University of California at San Diego. She also became Director of the California Space Institute.

Today, Ride teaches physics and conducts research at the University of California at San Diego. She has also written a children's book about her experience in space, *To Space and Back*.

Recently, Ride has been involved with promoting science education to girls in elementary and middle school. She developed programs for girls, including science festivals, to introduce them to different fields of science. Thousands of young girls take part in the festivals, and are energized by the experience. "Working with the students is very rewarding," says Ride. "You can look the students in the eyes and see that sparkle, see those stars." "We need to make science cool again," she claims. Through her efforts, she's doing just that.

SALLY RIDE'S HOME AND FAMILY: Ride married Alan Hawley in 1982. They divorced in 1987. They didn't have children.

HER LEGACY: Ride is remembered as the first American woman to travel in space. She is also honored for her devotion to science education, especially for young girls.

WORLD WIDE WEB SITES
http://ltp.arc.nasa.gov/space/frontiers/chat_archives/ride03-23-99.
  html
http://starchild.gsfc.nasa.gov/docs/StarChild/shadow.whos_who_
  level2/ride.html
http://www.jsc.nasa.gov/Bios/htmlbios/ride-sk.html

Eleanor Roosevelt

1884-1962
American First Lady of the United States, 1933-1945
U.S. Delegate to the United Nations
Helped Create the Universal Declaration of Human Rights
"First Lady to the World"

ELEANOR ROOSEVELT WAS BORN on October 11, 1884, in New York City. Her full name was Anna Eleanor Roosevelt, and her parents were Anna and Elliott Roosevelt. They were prominent members of New York society. Anna was from a powerful, wealthy family. Elliott was the younger brother of Theodore Roosevelt, who was President from 1901 to 1909. Eleanor had two younger brothers, Elliott and Hall.

329

ELEANOR ROOSEVELT GREW UP as a very shy, insecure young girl. Her mother, who was beautiful, was rather cold toward her plain daughter. Her father was often ill, and he became an alcoholic.

Eleanor's mother died of diphtheria when she was eight. Just a few months later, Eleanor's brothers came down with scarlet fever. Elliott died, and Eleanor and her brother Hall were sent to live with their grandmother. Two years later, her father died.

Eleanor spent the next six years living with her grandmother in Tivoli, New York. It was an unhappy time for her. She often felt lonely and isolated.

SCHOOL: Eleanor studied at home with tutors until an aunt suggested she go away to school in England. So, at 15, Eleanor moved to London to attend Allenswood, a private school for girls.

It was a wonderful experience for her. She learned much under the care of the school's head, Marie Souvestre. Eleanor later said that her teacher gave her confidence, and was her first mentor. Eleanor did well in school, made many friends, and played field hockey on the school team.

RETURNING TO NEW YORK SOCIETY: When Eleanor returned to New York in 1902, she didn't go to college. She was from an upper-class family of wealth and privilege. At that time, many girls of her background didn't go to college. Instead, they became part of "society." They had "coming out" parties and spent much of their time socializing.

Eleanor called those kinds of social activities "utter agony." She preferred to help out at the Rivington Street Settlement House. There, she helped teach children from poor families. She also

Eleanor Roosevelt at age 14, 1898.

became involved in investigating "sweatshops." Those were factories where men, women, and children worked in dangerous conditions, for meager wages. Eleanor loved working to improve the lives of others. It was rewarding and deeply meaningful to her.

FRANKLIN DELANO ROOSEVELT: Around this time, Eleanor became reacquainted with Franklin Delano Roosevelt. They were distant cousins— fifth cousins once removed. They fell in love and married on March 17, 1905. Their wedding was quite famous. Her uncle, President Teddy Roosevelt, walked her down the aisle.

A GROWING FAMILY: Over the next 10 years, the Roosevelts had six children. Their first child, Anna, was born in 1906. Their son James was born in 1907, and Franklin in 1909. Sadly, Franklin died when he was a baby. Elliott was born in 1910, and another son, whom they also named Franklin, was born in 1914. The Roosevelt's final child, John, was born in 1916.

Those years were busy for the young mother. "For ten years, I was always just getting over having a baby or about to have one," she wrote later. For many of those years, she lived next door to her mother-in-law, Sara Roosevelt. She was a very powerful presence in the lives of Franklin and Eleanor.

FRANKLIN'S EARLY POLITICAL CAREER: In 1911, Franklin Delano Roosevelt was elected to the New York state senate. It was the beginning of a political career that would take him to the White House.

The family moved to the state capitol, Albany. There, Eleanor made new friends and raised her children. When Franklin was named Assistant Secretary of the Navy in 1913, the family moved to Washington, D.C

In 1920, Franklin ran for Vice President on the Democratic ticket. He and his running mate, James Cox, lost. Roosevelt wasn't ready to give up politics. But just one year after losing the Vice Presidential race, he faced the greatest crisis of his life.

POLIO: In 1921, when he was 39 years old, Franklin came down with polio. Polio is a disease that can cause crippling, paralysis, and death. Roosevelt's legs became paralyzed. He could not move his legs and was never able to walk again without leg braces and canes.

Franklin fought the disease with courage and determination. He swam and did exercises to regain his strength. Eleanor nursed him through his illness and helped him regain his confidence. She remembered his bravery. "I think probably the thing that took most courage in his life was his mastery of polio. I never heard him complain. He just accepted it as one of those things that was given you as discipline in life."

According to those close to him, having polio changed Franklin's outlook. Living with his own disability, he began to feel a greater compassion for those who were poor and in need.

Eleanor and Franklin, with Anna and James, 1908.

ELEANOR ROOSEVELT'S RISING POLITICAL VOICE: During the 1920s, Eleanor took a greater role in her husband's political career. She became an advisor to him, and became involved in politics herself. She became a leader in the Democratic Party, the National Consumers League, and the Women's Trade Union League.

She also headed the Civic League's City Planning Department. In that job, she worked to improve housing, transportation, child labor laws, and employment.

Despite his disability, Franklin's political career flourished. In 1924 he gave a rousing speech at the Democratic convention for Presidential candidate Alfred Smith. Eleanor served as Smith's contact with women voters. Smith didn't win, but he remembered both Roosevelts' political abilities.

GOVERNOR OF NEW YORK: In 1928 Alfred Smith encouraged Franklin Roosevelt to run for Governor of New York. He won the election and served as Governor for two terms.

THE GREAT DEPRESSION: During Roosevelt's years as Governor, the era known as the "Great Depression" began. It was a time from 1929 to 1939 when up to one-quarter of Americans were out of work. People who had jobs lost them. Those who wanted jobs couldn't find them. Banks closed all over the country. People who had their life savings in banks lost all their money. It was a terrible, frightening time for the entire nation.

Herbert Hoover was President when the Depression began. He did not believe that the federal government should provide large relief programs. Many people in the country disagreed with him. Roosevelt believed that the federal government should provide aid in extremely difficult economic times. He decided to run for President to promote his ideas.

Roosevelt won the Democratic nomination for President in 1932. He promised to bring relief to "the forgotten man." In his speech accepting the nomination, he said, "I pledge you, I pledge myself, to a new deal for the American people."

PRESIDENT OF THE UNITED STATES: Roosevelt beat Hoover in a landslide victory in 1932. As he took office, Roosevelt knew the country was in despair. In his inaugural address, he reassured the American people. "The only thing we have to fear is fear itself," he said.

Eleanor Roosevelt visits a WPA African-American nursery school in Des Moines, Iowa, 1936.

Throughout his Presidency, Roosevelt inspired Americans with his confidence. Eleanor said, "I have never known a man who gave one a greater sense of security. I never heard him say there was a problem that he thought it was impossible for human beings to solve."

ELEANOR ROOSEVELT'S WHITE HOUSE YEARS: Eleanor Roosevelt was unlike any First Lady the country had ever seen. She transformed the role, becoming very involved with the country's problems during her husband's presidency. She visited poor areas all over the U.S. She listened to her fellow Americans and gave the people hope.

President Roosevelt could not travel easily, because of his disability. Eleanor Roosevelt told the people of the country that she was her husband's "eyes and ears." In one year alone, she traveled 40,000 miles to see the economic conditions of the people firsthand. She answered more than 300,000 letters from those she called "forgotten Americans." She wrote a monthly column in the *Pictorial Review* outlining what she was hearing and seeing.

"MY DAY": In 1935, Eleanor Roosevelt began a daily column called "My Day." It was hugely successful and appeared in newspapers all over the country. In her columns, she wrote about the problems facing the nation, and how the government was responding.

She also wrote hundreds of articles for magazines, appeared on the radio, and gave lectures around the country. She became one of the most popular and respected women in the country. Some people disagreed with her and her political views. They felt she overstepped her role as First Lady. But most Americans loved the First Lady for her courage and compassion. And that compassion extended to all Americans, white and black, rich and poor, male and female.

In 1933, Eleanor Roosevelt became the first First Lady to give a press conference. And, because women reporters had been banned from Presidential press conferences, she made it open to women only.

MARIAN ANDERSON: In 1939, the D.A.R. (Daughters of the American Revolution), refused to allow the celebrated African-American singer **Marian Anderson** to perform at Constitution Hall, because she was black. Eleanor Roosevelt, a member of the D.A.R. was outraged. She quit the organization.

Harold Ickes, then Interior Secretary, arranged to have Anderson perform at the Lincoln Memorial. It was one of the most memorable concerts ever heard in the nation's capitol.

WORLD WAR II: On December 7, 1941, Japanese planes bombed the U.S. naval base at Pearl Harbor, in Honolulu, Hawaii. President Roosevelt immediately asked Congress to declare war. He called it a "day that will live in infamy." Congress approved the President's request, and the U.S. joined the Allies to fight the Axis powers.

Over the next four years, from 1941 to 1945, the U.S. and the

Eleanor Roosevelt visiting wounded soldiers, 1944.

Allies fought the Germans and Italians in Europe and Africa. In the Pacific, they fought the Japanese. Millions of American troops and millions of dollars in American-made weapons and supplies went to fight the war.

Once again, Eleanor Roosevelt traveled on behalf of her husband, speaking to Americans. Many American soldiers lost their lives in the war. At home, she offered comfort and concern to citizens dealing with frightening news about the war. Eleanor carried a poem with her to remind her of the sacrifices many were making on behalf of the country. It said, "Dear Lord, lest I continue in my complacent ways, help me to remember that somewhere someone died for me today and help me to remember to ask am I worth dying for."

THE DEATH OF PRESIDENT ROOSEVELT: By 1945, President Roosevelt was very ill with heart disease and high blood pressure.

He died of a stroke on April 12, 1945. Vice President Harry Truman became President. He valued Eleanor Roosevelt, and wanted her to continue to help the nation.

At first Eleanor told everyone "the story is over," and planned to retire from public life. But soon she was busier than ever. She continued to write her column, lecture, and also published books. She served on the board of the NAACP, and headed up the President's Commission on the Status of Women. She became involved in the Committee for a Sane Nuclear Policy to promote peace and control nuclear weapons.

DELEGATE TO THE UNITED NATIONS: In 1945, President Truman asked Eleanor to become the U.S. delegate to the United Nations. She accepted. Entering a new phase of her life, she committed herself to bettering the lives of people around the world.

THE UNIVERSAL DECLARATION OF HUMAN RIGHTS: At the U.N., Roosevelt was head of the Human Rights Commission. As part of her duties, she helped write the Universal Declaration of Human Rights. This document outlines the U. N's commitment to preserving the rights of the people of all nations. It says, in part: "All human beings are born free and equal in dignity and rights. They are endowed with reason and conscience and should treat one another in a spirit of brotherhood."

When the Universal Declaration was read to the U.N., Eleanor Roosevelt received a standing ovation. She regarded the document as her greatest achievement.

LATER YEARS: Eleanor Roosevelt served at the U.N. until 1956. She continued to write, lecture, and travel on behalf of her beliefs. Ill with anemia, tuberculosis, and heart failure, she died on November

Eleanor Roosevelt with the Universal Declaration of Human Rights, 1948.

7, 1962, in New York City. She was praised around the world for her efforts on behalf of social justice for all.

ELEANOR ROOSEVELT'S HOME AND FAMILY: Eleanor Roosevelt married Franklin Roosevelt in 1905. They had five children, Anna, James, Elliott, Franklin, and John. In her later life, she enjoyed spending time at her home in upstate New York, Val-Kil. It is now a national park.

HER LEGACY: Eleanor Roosevelt became known as the "First Lady of the World" for her tireless work to secure dignity, equality, and justice for all people. She considered her most important legacy to be the Universal Declaration of Human Rights. Writing on behalf of the document, she said this:

"Where, after all, do universal rights begin? In small places, close to home—so close and so small that they cannot be seen on any maps of the world. Yet they are the world of the individual person; the neighborhood he lives in; the school or college he attends; the factory, farm, or office where he works. Such are the places where every man, woman, and child seeks equal justice, equal opportunity, equal dignity without discrimination. Unless these rights have meaning there, they have little meaning anywhere. Without concerted citizen action to uphold them close to home, we shall look in vain for progress in the larger world."

WORLD WIDE WEB SITES

http://www.fdr.ibrary.marist.edu

http://www.greatwomen.org/

http://www.pbs.org/wgbh/amex/eleanor/

http://www.udhr.org/history/biographies/

http://www.whitehouse.gov/about/first-ladies/eleanorroosevelt/

Wilma Rudolph

1940 – 1994
African-American Track and Field Athlete
Winner of Three Olympic Gold Medals

WILMA RUDOLPH WAS BORN on June 23, 1940, in St. Bethlehem, Tennessee, about 50 miles from Nashville. Her full name was Wilma Glodean Rudolph. Her parents were Ed and Blanche Rudolph. Blanche worked as a maid. Ed worked as a porter for a railroad company, carrying suitcases for train passengers. He already had 11 children from his first marriage when he met Blanche. They had nine more children together. Wilma was one of the youngest members of this large family.

WILMA RUDOLPH GREW UP in the town of Clarksville, Tennessee. She was often sick as a child. When she was four years old, she caught polio. Polio is a virus that attacks the brain and spinal cord. It causes a high fever and sometimes paralysis (loss of movement). Polio damaged the nerves and muscles in Wilma's left leg. Her doctors worried that she might never be able to walk again.

Six-year-old Wilma Rudolph, right, poses with her older sister Yvonne.

Wilma wore a heavy metal brace on her leg for many years. Her mother and sisters rubbed her leg every day to make more blood flow to the muscles. One day each week, Wilma and her mother took a bus to Nashville. They went to a city hospital where Wilma learned exercises to strengthen her leg.

GROWING UP IN THE SEGREGATED SOUTH: During these weekly bus trips, Wilma saw the effects of segregation. At this time, segregation laws kept people in the South separated by race. Wilma and other African-Americans were forced to use different waiting areas, bathrooms, and drinking fountains than those used by white people. Black people also had to sit in the back of public buses.

When Wilma was nine years old, she shocked her doctors by walking without her leg brace. She wore special support shoes until she was 11. After that, she was completely healed. "By the time I was 12, I was challenging every boy in our neighborhood at running, jumping, everything," she remembered.

WILMA RUDOLPH WENT TO SCHOOL in Clarksville. Because of her illness, she did not start school until the second grade. She attended two all-black public schools, Cobb Elementary School and Burt High School. As she grew older, Wilma became a star basketball player. She averaged 32 points per game during her sophomore year of high school.

Wilma's speed on the court attracted the attention of Ed Temple. Temple was the women's track coach at Tennessee State University. He told Wilma that she had the talent to be a great runner. He invited her to train with his college team, the Tigerbelles, during the summer. The next year, Wilma joined her high school track team. She never lost a race in two seasons.

RUNNING IN THE 1956 OLYMPICS: Rudolph had never even heard of the Olympics until she met Ed Temple. She still managed to qualify for the 1956 Games in Melbourne, Australia. At 16, she was the youngest member of the U.S. team. Rudolph earned a bronze medal by helping the American women finish third in the 400–meter relay race. She knew at that time that she wanted to try for a gold medal in 1960.

In 1958 Rudolph enrolled at Tennessee State. She studied education and joined the Tigerbelles track team. She practiced hard and qualified for three events at the 1960 Olympic Games in Rome, Italy.

1960 OLYMPICS: Rudolph's first event was the 100–meter sprint race. She won the gold medal easily, finishing three meters ahead of her closest competitor. A writer for *Time* magazine said that

*Rudolph winning the women's 100–meter dash at the
Rome Olympics, September 2, 1960.*

Rudolph's long, flowing strides "made the rest of the pack seem to be churning on a treadmill." Rudolph earned a second gold medal by winning the 200-meter race.

Then Rudolph joined three of her Tigerbelle teamates — Martha Hudson, Barbara Jones, and Lucinda Williams — in the 400–meter relay race. Each woman ran 100 meters and then passed a baton to the next woman. Rudolph ran the fourth, or anchor, leg of the race. When her turn came, she dropped the baton on the ground. But she picked it up and passed three other runners to claim a third gold medal. Rudolph became the first American woman ever to win three Olympic gold medals in track and field.

*Rudolph wins a gold medal in the women's 400-meter relay
race at the Rome Olympics, September 8, 1960.*

BECOMING A STAR: Rudolph's amazing performance at the 1960
Olympics made her a star in Europe and the United States. Many
people were touched by the story of how she overcame illness,
poverty, and segregation to become the world's fastest woman.
Rudolph appeared in parades, gave interviews on television, and
even visited President John F. Kennedy at the White House.

When Rudolph returned home to Tennessee, Clarksville officials organized a rally in her honor. But the event they planned was segregated. Rudolph refused to participate if only white people were invited. Town officials were forced to allow black people to attend. The rally attracted 40,000 people. It was the first racially integrated event in the town's history.

Now that she was famous, Rudolph found it hard to go back to her old life. But she could not earn a living as a track star. American companies did not hire black athletes to advertise their products in those days. Rudolph decided that she had to finish her education and get a job. She retired from track in 1963. She earned her college degree and started working as a teacher and coach.

HELPING POOR CHILDREN ENJOY SPORTS: Rudolph learned many important lessons by competing in sports. She wanted to share her experiences with others. She also wanted to help more children from poor families get involved in sports. "My life wasn't like the average person who grew up and decided to enter the world of sports," she explained.

In 1977 Rudolph wrote a book about her life, called *Wilma*. It was turned into a TV movie starring Cicely Tyson and Denzel Washington. Rudolph also gave speeches and helped open sports clinics in cities across the country. In 1981 she started the Wilma Rudolph Foundation to promote amateur sports. Rudolph always taught children the value of working hard to overcome the obstacles in their lives.

WILMA RUDOLPH'S HOME AND FAMILY: Rudolph was married and divorced twice. She had four children: daughters Yolanda and Djuanna, and sons Robert Jr. and Xurry. Rudolph died of a cancerous brain tumor at her home in Brentwood, Tennessee, on November 12, 1994. She was 54 years old.

HER LEGACY: Rudolph is a symbol of courage and perseverance to generations of athletes, black and white, male and female. She received many awards over the years for her achievements on and off the track. She was a member of the U.S. Olympic Hall of Fame, the National Track and Field Hall of Fame, and the Black Athletes Hall of Fame. Rudolph's image appeared on a U.S. postage stamp, and Tennessee State University named its new track after her. The Women's Sports Foundation created the Wilma Rudolph Courage Award in her honor. It is presented each year to a female athlete who succeeds in the face of challenges. "The triumph can't be had without the struggle," she said. "And I know what struggle is. I have spent a lifetime trying to share what it has meant to be a woman first in the world of sports so that other young women have a chance to reach their dreams."

WORLD WIDE WEB SITES

http://www.wilmarudolph.net

http://www.lkwdpl.org/wihohio/rudo-wil.htm

http://espn.go.com/sportscentury/features/00016444.html

Sacagawea

c. 1778 –1812
Shoshone Indian Guide and Translator for the
Lewis and Clark Expedition

SACAGAWEA WAS BORN around 1778 in what is now Idaho. Her name is also spelled "Sacajawea" and "Sacakawea." It is pronounced many different ways, including "sah-CAH-guh-wee-ah," "sack-uh-guh-WAY-uh" and "sack-uh-juh-WAY-uh." She was a member of the Shoshone tribe.

KIDNAPPED: Around 1800, Sacagawea was kidnapped by Hidatsa Indians, who were enemies of the Shoshone. As a prisoner, she was taken to the Hidatsa village near Bismarck, North Dakota. She was later sold as a slave to a French-Canadian trader named Toussaint Charbonneau. Charbonneau claimed that Sacagawea and another young Indian woman were his "wives," but there is no evidence that he ever married them. Instead, Sacagawea served as his slave.

MEETING LEWIS AND CLARK: In 1804, Sacagawea met Meriwether Lewis and William Clark. She was to become the only woman on the most important American expedition to the West.

THE LEWIS AND CLARK EXPEDITION: In 1803, President Thomas Jefferson had chosen Lewis to put together an expedition to explore the American West. Jefferson was clear about what he expected of the expedition. They were to follow the Missouri River out of St. Louis, looking for a waterway to the Pacific Ocean. They knew the Missouri would lead them to a mountain range — the Rockies. They thought it would be similar in size and scope to the Appalachians. They also knew another river system, the Columbia, flowed into the Pacific on the west coast. Jefferson wanted to find a waterway that connected the two river systems.

The new American government also needed to know all about the western lands. They needed maps, with information about rivers, mountains, and terrain. They needed to know about the plants, animals, and opportunities for trade and settlement. They also needed to know about the many Indian tribes in the vast area. What were they like? Were they peaceful or warlike? And how would they feel about their new leader, Jefferson?

Lewis and Clark named their crew the Corps of Discovery. The

33 men who made up the Corps set out from St. Louis, Missouri, on May 14, 1804.

Fort Mandan: In October 1804, as winter neared, they stopped near what is now Bismarck, North Dakota. There, near the camps of the Mandan and Hidatsa tribes, they made their winter camp. It was there that they met Sacagawea.

When Sacagawea met Lewis and Clark, she was about 17 years old and pregnant with her first child. She and Charbonneau spoke several Indian languages, so the explorers thought they would be valuable as translators. And because the expedition was traveling through Shoshone territory, Sacagawea could help as a guide. So Lewis and Clark hired Sacagawea and Charbonneau. In February 1805, Sacagawea gave birth to a son, Jean Baptiste Charbonneau. Lewis helped in delivering her baby.

Starting Off Again—April 1805: When the Corps left Fort Mandan in April 1805, Sacagawea went with them, along with Charbonneau and her son. They traveled in two boats called pirogues and six canoes. Jean Baptiste traveled strapped to his mother's back during the long, difficult journey. The little boy grew to become a favorite of William Clark, who called the boy "Pompy."

The Corps crossed into Montana. They saw huge herds of buffalo, elk, and deer. They also saw a Grizzly bear for the first time. One chased a crewman up a tree. During a storm, the boat holding the maps and journals nearly capsized. Sacagawea calmly saved the precious documents. Lewis wrote that she was as brave as any man in handling the near-tragedy.

A Fork in the River: The crew reached a point where the Missouri divided into a northern and a southern route, or "fork." They chose

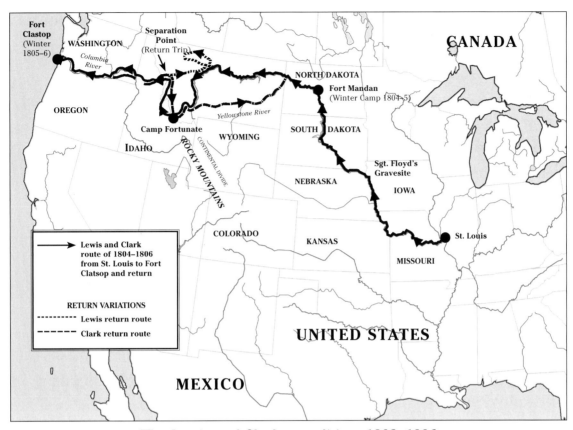

The Lewis and Clark expedition, 1803–1806.

the southern path, and they soon reached waterfalls. Lewis knew the path was the right one, because the Indians had told him to expect the waterfalls. They were near what is now Great Falls, Montana.

A Long Portage: The boats could not travel over waterfalls, so the crew had to make a long, difficult portage. That is, they had to carry their boats overland. They actually built wheels out of cotton-wood, which they attached to the boats. But the 18-mile trip still took them three weeks. Finally, they reached a point in the river where they could put the boats back in the water.

Three Forks of the Missouri: The next major landmark they came to was a place where the Missouri divided into three forks. They named them for three famous Americans. They named one the

351

"Madison," in honor of the Secretary of State (and later President) James Madison. Another was named the "Gallatin," for Secretary of the Treasury Albert Gallatin. And one they named for their President and sponsor, Jefferson. They followed the Jefferson west.

The Continental Divide: In August 1805, Lewis and Clark reached the Continental Divide. That is a point at the crest of the Rocky Mountains where rivers flow either eastward, toward the Mississippi River, or westward, toward the Pacific Ocean.

As Lewis walked to the top of the ridge, he expected to see on the other side plains leading to the Columbia River and to the ocean. Instead, he saw the Bitterroot Range of the Rockies. Their hopes to find the Northwest Passage were dashed. The Rockies were so much more vast, in size and scope, than they had ever imagined. Their route would be longer, and harder.

Sacagawea Reunited with her People: Continuing down the other side of the divide, Sacagawea began to recognize the land. She knew she was close to her home. Lewis decided to scout ahead and meet the Shoshone. He met several Shoshone women, then several men. He led them back to the crew, and to everyone's astonishment, Sacagawea recognized an old friend. It was a wonderful reunion. But the greatest surprise came when she recognized her brother, Cameahwait, now the chief. When she saw him, "she jumped up, ran, and embraced him," wrote Lewis. She "threw her blanket over him and cried profusely."

They named their camp, near the Lemhi Pass, "Camp Fortunate." Lewis and Clark traded with the Shoshone for horses. They knew that their canoes would be of no use in going over the mountains. They began the overland part of their journey. They hired a Shoshone guide named Old Toby. Then they began the difficult crossing over the Bitterroot Mountains.

They crossed from what is now Montana into Idaho. The weather was fierce, and they were near starvation. Once over the mountains, they met members of the Nez Perce tribe. This friendly group gave them food and shelter.

The crew left their horses with the Nez Perce, built new canoes, and proceeded on the Clearwater River. In October, they reached the Snake River, and from that, the Columbia. The river is fierce, with many rapids and waterfalls. Once again, they had to make difficult portages.

The Pacific Ocean: In November 1805, they reached the Pacific Ocean. Clark wrote in his journal of the "great joy in camp" as they reached "this great Pacific Ocean" they had "been so long anxious to see." They had traveled over 4,000 miles in 554 days.

The Corps spent the next four months on the Pacific coast, near what is now Astoria, Oregon. They built a fort, named Fort Clatsop after a local tribe. They hunted and fished, and built a salt-making camp. With salt, they could preserve meat and fish for the journey home.

The crew learned that a dead whale had washed up on shore near their camp. Sacagawea especially wanted to see it. Clark wrote that "she observed that she had traveled a long way with us to see the great waters, and that now that monstrous fish was also to be seen." She saw the whale, and was impressed.

The Journey Home: In March 1806, the Corps began the journey home. They canoed back up the Columbia, finally reaching the Nez

U.S. Mint Commemorative Coin Cover for Sacagawea Golden Dollar, Jan. 2000.

Perce. They got their horses back, and headed back across the Bitterroots. But their path was blocked with snow and ice. After the snow melted, they made their way across the mountains.

The Corps Divides: In July 1806, the Corps separated into two groups. Lewis wanted to explore possible northern routes that could be used by later settlers. He took a group north into the Marias River region. There, near the Canadian border, they had a run-in with a group of Blackfeet Indians. The groups exchanged gunfire, and two Indians were killed. They were the only Indian deaths of the expedition.

Clark chose a southern route, and Sacagawea went with him. His group crossed the Rockies, then took the Jefferson River as far as Three Forks. The Clark group divided again, and he explored the Yellowstone River region. Clark named an unusual sandstone formation "Pompy" for Sacagawea's son. He also wrote his name and the date on the rock. It can still be found, near Billings,

Montana.

All the groups came together where the Yellowstone and the Missouri Rivers meet, in August 1806. Lewis had been wounded in a hunting accident, but he was mending.

Sacagawea Leaves: The Corps reached Fort Mandan on August 17, 1806. Sacagawea's part of the expedition was over. As the Corps continued on to St. Louis and a heroes' welcome, she stayed in the area with Charbonneau and her son. Charbonneau was paid $500 and given 300 acres of land for his services to the expedition.

Statue of Sacagawea near Fort Mandan, North Dakota, where she joined Lewis and Clark.

Sacagawea received nothing.

Later, Clark wrote to Charbonneau. "Your woman who accompanied you that long dangerous and fatiguing route to the Pacific Ocean and back deserved a greater reward for her attention and services than we had in our power to give her." Sacagawea never knew the importance of her contribution to the Lewis and Clark Expedition.

SACAGAWEA'S HOME AND FAMILY: Several years after Sacagawea returned to the Hidatsa village, she had another child, a girl named Lisette. Sacagawea died in 1812, around the age of 25. Both of her children were adopted by William Clark after her death. Jean Baptiste grew up in St. Louis, where Clark paid for his education. There is no information about what happened to Lisette.

HER LEGACY: As a valued member of the Lewis and Clark expedition, Sacagawea is remembered as an excellent translator and brave guide. Sacagawea has become a legendary figure in American history. Even though no one is exactly sure what she looked like, there are many depictions of her, including statues and a golden dollar with her picture on it. More than 200 years after the Lewis and Clark expedition, Sacagawea continues to inspire and fascinate people of all ages.

WORLD WIDE WEB SITES

http://www.lewisandclark.org/

http://www.lewisandclarkeducationcenter.com/

http://www.loc.gov/exhibits/lewisandclark/lewisandclark.html

http://www.nps.gov/lecl/

http://nwrel.org/teachlewisandclark/home.html

http://www.pbs.org/lewisandclark/

Clara Schumann

1819-1896
German Musician and Composer
Wife of Robert Schumann

CLARA SCHUMANN WAS BORN on September 13, 1819, in Leipzig, Germany. Her name when she was born was Clara Josephine Wieck (VEEK). Her parents were Friedrich Wieck and Marianne Tromlitz Wieck. Friedrich was a music teacher and Marianne was a singer. Clara was the second of five children. Her mother left the family when she was five and her parents eventually divorced. Both of her parents remarried.

GROWING UP A MUSICAL PRODIGY: Clara Wieck was raised to be a musical prodigy by her father. She began piano lessons with him when she was five. Soon, she was also studying violin and singing.

Composing Music: Friedrich Wieck also taught Clara to compose music, including courses in music theory. In those courses, she studied the musical styles of composers of the "baroque" (bah-ROWK) era, such as Johann Sebastian Bach, as well as those of her own time. She learned how to write for solo piano, voice, for small ensembles, and for orchestra. She wrote her first piece, for piano, at age 11.

Performing Music: While she was learning to write music, Clara also began to perform. She gave her first public concert at the age of nine, at one of the most famous concert halls in Leipzig. Two years later, at the age of 11, she gave her first solo concert. Audiences loved her playing. Clara Wieck was becoming a famous musician.

Portrait of Clara Wieck at age eight.

MEETING ROBERT SCHUMANN: In 1830, when Clara was 11, the German musician Robert Schumann came to Leipzig to study with her father. At that point, he was still unknown, although he would become one of the greatest composers of the century.

COMPOSING AND PERFORMING: Clara and her father left Leipzig in 1830 for her first long concert tour. She played in Germany and France.

In the German city of Weimar, she played for the famous German poet Johann Wolfgang von Goethe.

Over the next five years, Clara and her father toured Europe. Although she was just a teenager, she played with brilliant technique and musicality. Audiences adored her. Major composers of the era, including Felix Mendelssohn and Frederic Chopin, praised her compositions and her playing.

Clara continued to compose, and she performed her own pieces at her concerts, including works for solo piano, for piano and orchestra, and songs, or "lieder," as they are known in German. She also played works of major composers, including Johann Sebastian Bach and Ludwig van Beethoven. She also began performing the works of Robert Schumann, her father's student.

When Clara was 17, she and Robert fell in love. They wanted to marry, and Schumann asked Clara's father for his permission. (At that time, a woman under 21 could not marry without her father's consent.)

Friedrich Wieck refused to allow the engagement. He thought that Clara was a far better musician than Schumann. He thought she would be throwing away an outstanding career as a composer and performer if she married him. He sent Clara on a concert tour, and tried to prevent her from seeing Robert.

Clara and Robert became secretly engaged. They wrote to each other in secret. They also took their case to court, so that they could marry. Their court fight dragged on for years. Finally, in 1840, they won their case, and were free to marry.

MARRIAGE, FAMILY, COMPOSING AND PERFORMING: Clara Wieck and Robert Schumann were married on September 12, 1840,

Clara and Robert Schumann, 1850.

the day before Clara's 21st birthday. They started their life together in Leipzig.

Their relationship was very close, both musically and emotionally. Shortly after their marriage, Robert bought Clara a diary. He wanted them to take turns writing in it, describing the music they wrote or heard, the people they met, and any personal thoughts. At the end of each week, they would exchange the diary, and keep up with each other's most personal thoughts. They kept the diary for years.

The couple began to compose music together, too. Their most famous works written together are songs, or lieder. Robert Schumann is one of the most famous lieder composers of all time. His lieder are most often set to words drawn from some of the best poetry of the era. They are close, intimate interpretations of those poems.

Robert wanted their musical compositions to be published together, with their individual pieces intermingled. One of these early works is Clara's composition, "Am Strande" (On the Bank), which she gave to Robert for their first Christmas together. Throughout the first year of their marriage, each composed several songs, using texts by the German poet Friedrich Rueckert. Robert had them published and gave them to Clara for their first wedding anniversary.

Clara also continued her performing career, now as Clara Schumann. She had the first of the couple's eight children, Marie, in September 1841. Over the next 13 years, Clara gave birth to Elise, Julie, Emil, Ludwig, Ferdinand, Eugenie, and Felix. Emil died as an infant, but the other children survived to adulthood.

Despite all her responsibilities as a mother, Clara Schumann continued to give concerts and compose. At a time when most women were limited to home and family, Clara continued to grow and develop as a musician, encouraged by Robert.

Clara Schumann was a champion of the composers of her era, especially of her husband, Robert. She was often the artist who premiered his major works for piano. Through her performance, Robert's music became widely known, and admired, throughout Europe.

Clara toured widely, and was a very successful concert performer.

During most of the years of their marriage, she was the main breadwinner in the family. Her concert schedule didn't leave a lot of time for her children, who were raised by family, friends, and governesses.

The family moved from Leipzig to Dresden in 1844, and to Duesseldorf in 1850. There, Robert became conductor of the orchestra.

Clara Schumann with her children, 1855.

In 1853, Clara's piano music was published, which helped to spread her fame. That same year, the composer Johannes Brahms visited the Schumanns. He became their friend, and was especially close to Clara in her later years. Some historians believe he was in love with her. Whether or not that is true, he was a good friend to her as she faced a difficult time in her life.

ROBERT SCHUMANN'S DEATH: Tragically, Robert Schumann began to show signs of mental illness. He tried to take his own life in 1854, and was sent to a mental hospital in Endenich. Thinking that he could be dangerous, Robert's doctors forbid Clara to visit him. She was only allowed to visit him once, on July 27, 1856. Robert died two days later, on July 29, 1856, at the age of 46. Clara was now a widow with seven children.

BACK TO THE CONCERT STAGE: With a large family to support, Clara Schumann began an even more active performing career. From 1856 to 1891, she traveled constantly, performing in England, Switzerland, Holland, Belgium, France, Russia, and other countries.

Schumann also began to edit her husband's complete works, and had them published from 1881 to 1893. In 1878, her 50th year of performing was celebrated with music festivals in Germany. That same year, she began teaching piano at a music conservatory in Germany.

LATER YEARS: Schumann's later years were full of sadness, too. Three of her children died, Julie in 1872, Felix in 1879, and Ferdinand in 1891.

Schumann continued to perform, and gave her final concert in Frankfurt in 1891. She did little composing in her later years, but continued to teach until her final illness. Clara Schumann suffered a stroke and died on May 20, 1896.

MUSICAL REPUTATION: After Clara Schumann died, her music was rarely performed. As her husband's musical reputation grew, hers diminished. She became known as a supportive wife, rather than as the major musical force she was.

Clara Schumann playing the piano, c. 1880.

Some of Clara's compositions, especially her songs, were mistakenly assigned to Robert. It took years for music historians to properly credit Clara's music to her. Only in the middle of the 20th century was her music played again in concerts. That brought back interest, and acclaim, to this musical genius of the 19th century.

HER LEGACY: Clara Schumann was one of the greatest pianists of her generation. Her playing and her compositions were praised by her fellow musicians, including Frederick Chopin and Felix Mendelssohn. For many years, her husband's reputation overshadowed her own. But in the past 50 years, Clara Schumann has become recognized as a musician in her own right. Today, she is admired and valued for her contributions as a performer and composer of great gifts.

WORLD WIDE WEB SITES

http://comminfo.rutgers.edu/~eversr/biogra1.html
http://www.geneva.edu/~dksmith/clara.bio

Margaret Chase Smith

1897-1995
American Political Leader
First Woman to Serve in both the U.S. House and Senate
First Woman to Run for President from a Major Party

MARGARET CHASE SMITH WAS BORN on December 14, 1897, in Skowhegan, Maine. Her name when she was born was Margaret Madeline Chase. Her parents were Carrie Murray and George Emery Chase. Carrie worked as a waitress and in a shoe factory, and George was a barber. Margaret was the oldest of six children.

GROWING UP: Margaret grew up in a family that valued hard work, and everyone pitched in when times were tough. Margaret learned to help her Dad at the barber shop. She worked at the Five and Dime store in high school to help makes ends meet.

EDUCATION: Margaret went to the local public schools in Skowhegan. She graduated from Skowhegan High School in 1916, but couldn't afford college. She went to work instead.

FIRST JOBS: Margaret's first job was as a teacher in a one-room schoolhouse in Skowhegan. She worked there for seven months, then got a job as a telephone operator. In 1919, she got a job with a local newspaper, the *Independent Reporter*. She worked at the paper for eight years, taking on a wide variety of jobs in the ad department, the editorial department, and circulation.

She became active in a number of organizations, and founded the local chapter of the Business and Professional Women's Club. She went on to serve as the president of the statewide organization.

MARRIAGE: In 1930, Margaret Chase married Clyde H. Smith. He was a wealthy and successful businessman, the owner of the *Independent Reporter*, and a very successful politician.

EARLY POLITICAL LIFE: Clyde Smith was very active in Republican politics in Maine, and Margaret joined him. When Clyde ran for the U.S. House of Representatives, Margaret ran his campaign. He won, and the couple moved to Washington, D.C.

Margaret Chase Smith served as her husband's secretary while he served in Congress. She handled his schedule, his correspondence, and researched current issues for him.

In April 1940, Clyde Smith died suddenly of a heart attack. It was often the custom for a wife to fill her husband's congressional seat in the event of his death. So Margaret Chase Smith filled her husband's position for two months, then in May 1940 ran in a special election to complete his term and won. That fall, she ran for re-election to the House on her own. She won again.

Representative Smith watches President Truman sign the Army-Navy Permanent Nurses Corp Bill, 1947.

THE U.S. HOUSE OF REPRESENTATIVES: Margaret Chase Smith served in the U.S. House for eight years. It was the beginning of a storied political career that lasted 33 years.

In her early days in Congress, Smith showed independence and intelligence. She didn't vote the way the Republican Party always suggested. She always followed her own conscience.

Smith was especially interested in military and defense. She joined the Congress just as the U.S. was getting involved in World War II (1939-1945). She became a member of the Armed Services Committee. In that role, she made sure that soldiers, arms, and supplies were delivered wherever they were needed, throughout the war. She traveled to where the soldiers were fighting, to make sure their needs were met.

A CHAMPION FOR WOMEN IN THE MILITARY: Smith was also an ardent advocate for women's roles in the armed services. She helped create the Women Accepted for Voluntary Emergency Service, called the WAVES. It sent women to Europe and the Pacific to perform non-combat jobs. That freed male servicemen to take part in combat.

In 1945, Smith introduced legislation that gave women permanent status in the armed forces. The Army-Navy Permanent Nurses Corps Bill became law in 1947. Perhaps even more important was the Women's Armed Services Integration Act of 1948. That act guaranteed that women would receive equal pay and equal rank with men in the military.

BECOMING A U.S. SENATOR: In 1948, after eight years in the House, Smith decided to run for the U.S. Senate from Maine. She challenged three powerful Republican men for the nomination.

To the amazement of many, Smith won, and went on to win the election as well, with 70% of the vote. In doing that, she became the first woman ever to serve in both the U.S. House and Senate. She also became the first woman ever to serve in the Senate in her own right. (Before Smith, the only women in the Senate had been appointed to serve out the terms of their husbands.)

TAKING ON JOSEPH MCCARTHY: By the end of World War II, the U.S. and the Soviet Union had emerged as the world's two superpowers. They represented two very different political systems. The U.S. was a democracy; the Soviet Union was a Communist state. The relationship between the two nations was very important. For more than 40 years, the hostilities between these two nations affected world politics.

Senator Smith meets with Prime Minister Winston Churchill and Foreign Minister Anthony Eden of Great Britain, 1954.

Smith had always been a staunch patriot and anti-Communist. In the late 1940s, Senator Joseph McCarthy from Wisconsin began a vicious smear campaign against members of the government and other public figures. He accused them of being Communists, and threatened them. At that point, many people in the country were fearful of the powerful Soviet regime. An accusation by McCarthy could ruin a person's career, whether or not there were any grounds to the charges. Some believed McCarthy; many in the Congress feared him. But Smith thought he was a dangerous bully.

She delivered her most famous speech, "A Declaration of Conscience," on June 1, 1950. In front of the full Senate, she condemned McCarthy for his methods and his false accusations. She showed the nation her courage and her commitment to fairness and justice. It made her an icon to the nation.

Smith later wrote, "If I am to be remembered in history, it will not be because of legislative accomplishments, but for an act I took in the U.S. Senate when on June 1, 1950, I spoke in condemnation of McCarthyism, when the junior Senator from Wisconsin had the Senate paralyzed with fear that he would purge any Senator who disagreed with him."

Smith next began a tour of the world, which she paid for herself. In 1954, she visited 23 countries to become aware of the changes that were happening worldwide. She met many world leaders, including the heads of Britain, France, Spain, and China. When she returned, she shared her travels with Americans on Edward R. Murrow's popular television show, *See It Now*. At the end of her trip, she returned to Washington just in time to vote for the "censure," or formal reprimand, of Joseph McCarthy.

RUNNING FOR PRESIDENT: In 1964, Smith decided to run for the Republican nomination for President. She announced her candidacy in January 1964, and took part in several presidential primaries. At the Republican Convention that summer, she became the first woman to be nominated by a major party for the Presidency. Barry Goldwater ultimately won the nomination, and Smith campaigned for him, then returned to the Senate.

Smith continued to work hard for the people of Maine, and for the country. She was tireless in her devotion to her work, and she encouraged her fellow Senators to be, too. Smith held a voting record in the Senate: she was there for every vote in the Senate for

*Rally for Senator Smith at the 1964
Republican National Convention.*

13 straight years—2,941 votes in all. (She broke her own record when she had to miss a vote because of hip surgery.)

In her 25 years in the Senate, Smith worked on several important committees, including Appropriations and Armed Services. She was also committed to funding medical research and space exploration. In fact, she was one of the first members of the Senate's committee on space.

Smith was also very frugal when it came to running for re-election. She refused to take campaign contributions, and never spent much on her re-election campaigns.

Smith was very popular in Maine, and ran for re-election successfully four times. Then, in 1972, she lost to Democratic challenger William D. Hathaway in a close race.

RETIREMENT: Smith retired from the Senate in 1973, after serving a total of 33 years in Congress. She returned to Maine, and became active as a speaker. She was named a Visiting Professor for the Woodrow Wilson National Fellowship Foundation. In that role, she spent three years touring colleges and universities and speaking to students.

LATER YEARS: In her later years, Smith was involved in the planning and building of her library. The Margaret Chase Smith Library is located next to her home in Skowhegan, Maine. It houses the papers from her public career, and presents programs for students, scholars, and the general public.

Smith received many awards and honors in her later years, including many honorary degrees. In 1973, when the National Women's Hall of Fame was founded, she was among the first to be inducted. In 1989, she received the Presidential Medal of Freedom, the highest honor a civilian can receive, from President George H. W. Bush.

Margaret Chase Smith died at her home in Skowhegan, Maine, on May 29, 1995. She was 97 years old.

HER LEGACY: Margaret Chase Smith is revered as a public servant of integrity, intelligence, and tenacity. She is the only women ever to serve in both the U.S. House of Representatives and the Senate, the first to be elected to the Senate in her own right, and the first woman to run for the presidency for a major party. Uncompromising in her ideals, she is considered one of the finest political leaders of the 20th century

WORLD WIDE WEB SITES

http://www.mcslibrary.org/index.html

http://bioguide.congress.gov/scripts/biodisplay.pl?index=s000590

Elizabeth Cady Stanton

1815-1902
American Activist and Champion for Women's Rights
Led the Fight for Women's Suffrage

ELIZABETH CADY STANTON WAS BORN on November 12, 1815, in Johnstown, New York. Her name when she was born was Elizabeth Cady. Her parents were Margaret Elizabeth Cady and Daniel Cady. Margaret was a homemaker and Daniel was a lawyer, judge, and congressman. Elizabeth was one of 11 children.

GROWING UP: Elizabeth grew up in a wealthy family and was outspoken and outgoing from a very young age. Very early on, she recognized that women were treated very differently under the law.

Women's Rights in the 19th Century: It is hard for young readers of the 21st century to imagine the condition of women in the 19th century. At that time, American women had none of the rights they have today. They did not have the right to an education or employment. They could not own property or control their own money. Married women had no rights. In cases of divorce, only men could get custody of children. If a woman made money in a job, the money was not hers. It belonged, by law, to her husband, or her father. Also, women made a fraction of a man's salary for the same job. Nor were women free to speak in public.

Most importantly, women could not vote. They had no voice in electing the government or making the laws that controlled them. Elizabeth Cady heard about these issues from her father. Once, in an effort to fight the injustice she felt, she found all the passages in her father's law books that mentioned the rights of men. She wanted to cut them out with scissors. Her father suggested a better idea. "When you are grown up and able to prepare a speech, you must go down to Albany [the state capitol] and talk to the legislators. And if you can persuade them to pass new laws, the old ones will be dead-letter."

Elizabeth took her father's advice to heart. Another memory of her father inspired her, too. All of her brothers died before reaching adulthood. At the funeral of her brother Eleazar, she climbed onto her father's lap to comfort him. "Oh my daughter, I wish you were a boy!" he said. "I will try to be all my brother was," she told him.

EDUCATION: Elizabeth received the finest education available to a girl at the time. She went to the Johnstown Academy, where she had classes with boys, and studied history, mathematics, Greek, and Latin. She continued her education at Emma Willard's Troy Female Seminary in New York, where she received the equivalent of a high school education. She was unable to go to college because women were not allowed to attend them.

ABOLITION: In 1833, Elizabeth finished her schooling and returned home. Soon, she became involved in one of the major social reforms of the day, **ABOLITION**. Abolitionists wanted to "abolish," or end, slavery, as well as the slave trade. In the 1830s, William Lloyd Garrison founded the American Anti-Slavery Society. He called for the freeing of all slaves throughout the nation. Many members of the fight for women's rights were also avid abolitionists, and Elizabeth Cady was among them.

Elizabeth Cady Stanton and daughter, Harriot, 1856.

Elizabeth had a cousin, Gerrit Smith, who was deeply involved in the Abolitionist movement. At his home, Elizabeth met many members of the movement, including Henry Stanton. They fell in love, and against her parents' wishes, married.

MARRIAGE AND FAMILY: Elizabeth Cady and Henry Stanton married in 1840. At that time, most traditional wedding vows included the wife promising to "love, honor, and obey" her husband. At her ceremony, Elizabeth refused to use the term "obey." She also insisted on using her full name, including her maiden name. Henry agreed.

The couple went on a honeymoon to London, to attend the World's Anti-Slavery Convention. There, Stanton met **Lucretia Mott**, a fervent abolitionist who was equally committed to women's rights. They were both denied participation in the Anti-Slavery Convention, because they were women. It infuriated them both. They agreed to meet after returning to the U.S. to speak out for the rights of women.

RAISING A FAMILY, COMMITTED TO WOMEN'S RIGHTS: Stanton returned to the U.S., where she and her husband lived in Boston. Over the next several years, she had seven children, and spent most of her time caring for them. She still remained committed to the cause of women's rights, attending meetings and reading all she could about reforms for women.

SENECA FALLS: In 1847, the Stanton family moved to Seneca Falls, New York. Together with Lucretia Mott, Stanton began to plan a meeting for women's rights.

In July 1848, Stanton and Mott presented the first, and one of the most important, conventions ever held on women's rights. At Seneca Falls, they established the first women's rights convention.

Stanton, a brilliant writer, presented the "Declaration of Rights and Sentiments." Its language and fervent message were based on the U.S. Declaration of Independence. "We hold these truths to be self-evident: that all men and women are created equal," it proclaimed. It outlined their demands for social and political equal-

Elizabeth Cady Stanton House in Seneca Falls, New York.

ity for all women, and the right to vote.

Although the right to vote was of central importance to Stanton, it was not her only concern. She wanted women to have the rights to equal education and employment, as well to own property, control money, to divorce, and to gain custody of their children.

In 1848, Stanton began to circulate petitions that would change the laws of New York regarding married women's rights to own property. It took 12 years, but it eventually was passed as the New York Married Women's Property Act. That law, in addition to allowing married women to own property, also gave them the rights to own a business, manage their money, and be named guardian of their children.

MEETING SUSAN B. ANTHONY: In 1851, Stanton met **Susan B. Anthony**, a fellow crusader for abolition, women's rights, and especially the right to vote. The two formed a close friendship that lasted 50 years and that was the main force behind the fight for women's rights. They complimented each other very well. Stanton was a great writer and speaker. Anthony had powerful organizational skills. Together, they changed the nation.

They began working together in the 1850s, although Stanton was limited because of her responsibilities as a mother. In 1856, Anthony was hired by the American Anti-slavery Society to run its New York operations. Until the Civil War began in 1861, Anthony, Stanton, and other abolitionists gave speeches against slavery all over the state.

THE RIGHT TO VOTE: In 1863, during the Civil War, Anthony and Stanton organized the Women's National Loyal League. It was the first national women's association. They fully supported the Thirteenth Amendment to the U.S. Constitution, which outlawed slavery. They also campaigned for the Fourteenth and Fifteenth Amendments, which granted African-American men citizenship, and the right to vote. They wanted those same rights given to women, too. They wanted an amendment to the Constitution that would make a woman's right to vote the law of the land.

When the Civil War ended in 1865, Anthony, Stanton, and other women's rights activists redoubled their campaign. In 1866, they founded the American Equal Rights Association. They hoped it would lead to women's right to vote. But most of the former abolitionists rejected that idea. They thought that the vote for black men should come first.

DECLARATION AND PROTEST
OF THE
WOMEN OF THE UNITED STATES
BY THE
NATIONAL WOMAN SUFFRAGE ASSOCIATION.
JULY 4th, 1876.

First page of the Declaration and Protest of the Women of the United States, July 4, 1876.

Anthony and Stanton founded the National Woman Suffrage Association in 1869, to continue the fight for an amendment. They started a newspaper, "The Revolution," calling for equal rights. Its goal was: "Men their rights, and nothing more; women, their rights, and nothing less."

On July 4, 1876, 100 years after the Declaration of Independence, Stanton, Anthony, Mott, and other members of their association published the "Declaration and Protest of the Women of the United States." It outlined their goals for equality for women, and called for the "impeachment" of U.S. government officials. They accused the officials of "taxation without representation," because women had to pay taxes, but were not allowed the right to vote to represent themselves.

In 1878, Stanton wrote and submitted the suffrage amendment to the U.S. Senate. It was brought before every Congress for the next 40 years.

To her surprise, Stanton found herself at odds with other women fighting for the vote. Some found her opinions too radical. They established a more conservative association, the American Woman Suffrage Association.

Marble statue of Elizabeth Cady Stanton, Susan B. Anthony, and Lucrecia Mott in the U.S. Capitol, Washington D.C.

In the 1880s, Stanton devoted most of her time to writing and giving speeches. She helped to write and edit *History of Woman Suffrage*, which documented the movement from its earliest days.

In 1890, the National Woman Suffrage Association and the American Woman Suffrage Association finally settled their differences and merged. They became the National American Woman Suffrage Association, and Stanton became their president.

"Solitude of Self": When she retired from the Association in 1892, Stanton gave what many consider her finest speech. It is called "Solitude of Self." In it, she talks about how women should be given education and opportunities, and freed of all the social customs that restrain them. Only then will each achieve "the solitude and personal responsibility of her own individual life."

LATER YEARS: In 1895, Stanton published her most controversial book, *The Woman's Bible*. She wrote it to show how organized religion demeans women. It was a bestseller, and also caused a great controversy. Many readers, in the general public and also in suffrage organizations, found her position too radical, and felt that she condemned Christianity unfairly.

In 1898, Stanton published her autobiography, *Eighty Years and More*. It was the final statement of her political and social beliefs. Elizabeth Cady Stanton died on October 26, 1902, of heart failure. She was 86.

HER LEGACY: Elizabeth Cady Stanton was a champion of women's rights. Although she died 17 years before the passage of the **NINETEENTH AMENDMENT**, which guaranteed women the right to vote, it is difficult to imagine it would have happened without her.

With Susan B. Anthony, she brought the issue of women's suffrage to the people. With her great gifts as a writer and speaker, she also outlined other social and political injustices faced by women. Through her efforts, American women won not only the right to vote, but also greater equality in education, employment, and legal rights, as well as a voice in determining their own lives.

WORLD WIDE WEB SITES

http://www.americaslibrary.gov/aa/stanton/aa_stanton_women_3. html

http://www.elizabethcadystanton.org/

http://memory.loc.gov/ammem/today/nov12.html

http://www.nps.gov/wori/historyculture/elizabeth-cady-stanton. htm

Gloria Steinem

1934-
American Writer, Editor, Lecturer, and Feminist
Political Activist and Leader of the Women's Movement

GLORIA STEINEM WAS BORN on March 25, 1934, in Toledo, Ohio. Her parents were Leo and Ruth Steinem. Leo was self-employed and worked at a number of jobs over the years. Ruth was a teacher. Gloria has one older sister, Susanne.

GROWING UP: Gloria had a very unhappy childhood. Her father's businesses weren't very successful. During the winter, he bought and sold antiques in Florida and California. The family lived out of a trailer, moving all the time. It was hard for Gloria to make friends, in the neighborhood or at school.

Leo Steinem also owned a resort in Michigan. When Gloria was 10, it failed. Soon after, her father left the family. Her parents later divorced.

Gloria and her mother moved first to Massachusetts to be with her sister, who was going to college there. After a year, they returned to Toledo, where they lived in a run-down house owned by her mother's family. They were very poor. Gloria's mother, Ruth, suffered from depression. Soon it was clear that she had developed a serious mental disorder. She was unable to work, and often could not even get out of bed. Gloria tried to do what she could for her mother, but she was just a child, and was unable to take care of her.

After several years, Gloria's sister, Susanne, got involved. She had Gloria move in with her, in Washington D.C. She also found caregivers for their mother.

EDUCATION: Gloria went to Western High School in Washington, D.C. She graduated in 1952, and went on to Smith College in Massachusetts. That is one of the finest schools in the country. When Gloria went there, it was an all-women's school.

Steinem loved college. She later wrote that she "couldn't understand the women who were not happy there. They gave you three meals a day to eat, and all the books you wanted to read. What more could you want?"

College was a wonderful experience for Steinem. She did well in school, and majored in government. She had time for social activities, and dates, too. Steinem graduated from Smith with high honors in 1956.

After graduation, Steinem went to India for two years to study and learn about the country. She was shocked at the poverty and living conditions of most of the people. She tried to help them, learning about the land and farming system. When she left, she knew that she wanted to do something to make a difference in people's lives.

FIRST JOBS: Steinem returned to the U.S. in 1958, and tried to make her living as a writer. She was especially interested in writing about politics. But the attitudes of the time were against her. It was difficult for a woman to get serious assignments at a newspaper or magazine. Instead, she got offers to write stories on fashion, make-up, or child care.

Steinem moved to Boston, where she became the co-director of the Independent Research Service. That is an organization that promotes democracy around the world.

NEW YORK: Steinem returned to New York in 1960, and kept writing serious pieces. She started to get published, and made a name for herself. In 1968, she co-founded *New York* magazine. It was a great success, and is still published today.

Steinem wrote a column for the magazine called "The City Politic." She was finally able to cover serious political stories, and show her strengths. And she found the path she would take in all her work.

Steinem went to a meeting of a women's political group, the Redstockings. As the women spoke about their lives, she was moved by one consistent theme: discrimination. Each of them had

Steinem on the cover of Ms., *which she edited from 1971 to 1987.*

a story about how she had been kept from achieving what she knew she could do, only because she was a woman. Steinem knew that she had to devote herself to fighting discrimination against women, in whatever form.

BECOMING A FEMINIST: The experience made Steinem a committed feminist. She wanted to find, expose, and fight discrimination against women. She became one of the most important leaders of the modern movement for women's rights.

Steinem knew that it was crucial that women gain political power, by getting elected to political office. She helped found the National Women's Political Conference, with fellow political leaders like **Shirley Chisholm**. That organization helps women who want to run for office. They help to raise money and establish the political organization necessary for women to run and get elected.

Steinem became a well-known advocate for women's rights. She was the face and voice of the women's movement. She spoke at public lectures, and she wrote newspaper and magazine articles. Women all over the country were drawn to her message. Steinem decided the time was right to begin a magazine focusing on women's issues.

MS. **MAGAZINE:** In 1971, Steinem created *Ms.* magazine. It was the first magazine created, owned, and operated by women. The first issue appeared as an insert in *New York* magazine. The response was immediate, and overwhelming.

In January 1972, Steinem published the second issue of *Ms.*, as a separate publication, not an insert. The response surprised everyone. The 300,000 copies they printed sold out in just 10 days. *Ms.* magazine was a huge success.

Gloria Steinem at Brighton High School, Brighton, Colorado, 2008.

Steinem edited *Ms.* for 15 years. During those years, she developed the magazine to become the most important platform for the continuing fight for equal rights. She continues to serve as a contributing editor.

CONTINUING TO WORK FOR CHANGE: Over the past 35 years, Steinem has continued to lecture and write about women and their place in society. She travels all over the world spreading her message.

She has helped found organizations that help women succeed. She helped establish the Women's Action Alliance. That is an organization devoted to educating children in a nonsexist, multiracial way. She continues to work with the Ms. Foundation. That group helps empower women and girls to achieve. It is also the organization that started "Take Our Daughters to Work Day," which is now an international event. Steinem also takes part in organizations that promote multiracial policies. Recently, she founded the Women's Media Center. That group helps advance opportunities for women in the media professions, including newspapers, magazines, television, and online sources.

Steinem is also devoted to the rights of children. She has

produced a documentary on child abuse. She has worked with organizations that stop child abuse and help victims. She has also worked with groups that fight child labor around the world.

Steinem also continues to write. She has published many books, and is working on a history of her work in the women's movement. It is called *Road to the Heart: America As if Everyone Mattered.*

HOME AND FAMILY: Steinem lives in New York City with her husband, David Bale. They have no children.

HER LEGACY: Gloria Steinem is one of the most important figures in the movement for women's rights and equality for all people. Her entire career has been devoted to bringing to light the injustices suffered by women, to fighting them, and correcting them. She has empowered and inspired generations of women as they, too, fight to achieve.

WORLD WIDE WEB SITES

http://www.gloriasteinem.com/

http://www.greatwomen.org/women.php?action=viewone&id=150

http://www.gale.cengage.com/free_resources/whm/bio/steinem_g.htm

Harriet Beecher Stowe

1811-1896
American Author and Abolitionist
Creator of *Uncle Tom's Cabin*

HARRIET BEECHER STOWE WAS BORN on June 14, 1811, in Litchfield, Connecticut. Her name when she was born was Harriet Elisabeth Beecher. Her parents were Lyman Beecher and Roxanna Foote Beecher. Lyman was a minister, and Roxanna was a homemaker. Harriet was the sixth of eight children born to Lyman and Roxanna.

When Harriet was five, her mother died. Her father remarried. He and his second wife, Harriet Porter Beecher, had three children together. So Harriet grew up with 10 siblings.

GROWING UP: Harriet grew up in a family that valued education and the importance of social reform. Her father was a famous Protestant minister, and an outspoken advocate for **ABOLITION**. Abolitionists wanted to end, or "abolish" slavery. For Lyman Beecher, it was a matter of conscience as a Christian to fight slavery.

The Beecher children were raised to believe that they could make a difference in the would. Lyman Beecher encouraged his children to debate the major issues of the day. Around the dinner table, they would outline and defend their arguments about social issues, including women's rights and slavery.

They were a close-knit family, and enjoyed working and playing together. All the children were encouraged to find what they loved to do. Harriet's seven brothers all followed their father's profession, and became ministers. Her older sister Catharine became one of the first advocates for women to be fully educated. She founded schools in Connecticut, Ohio, Iowa, Illinois, and Wisconsin.

Harriet had an early love of writing and painting. She started to write at an early age, and her family encouraged her. She won an essay contest when she was just seven years old.

EDUCATION: Harriet received an excellent education. Her father taught at the Litchfield Female Academy, which she attended. It was one of the first schools to have a strong academic curriculum for girls. They studied Greek, Latin, mathematics, and philosophy, the same courses given at boys' schools.

An early portrait of Harriet Beecher Stowe, 1853.

Unlike most girls of her time, Harriet continued her education beyond the eighth grade. She went on to get a high school-level education at the Hartford Female Seminary. It was an outstanding school, and had been founded by her sister Catharine. After she graduated in 1829, Harriet became a teacher at the school.

In 1832, the Beecher family moved to Cincinnati, Ohio, where Lyman Beecher became president of the Lane Theological Seminary. Harriet, then 21, moved with them.

BECOMING A WRITER: Harriet had always been a gifted writer. Her first book, written for young readers, was *Primary Geography for Children.* It was published in 1833. Two years later, she published a collection of short stories, *New England Sketches.*

MARRIAGE AND FAMILY: In Cincinnati, Harriet met Calvin Stowe, who taught at Lane Theological Seminary with her father. They fell in love and married in 1836. They had seven children.

In 1850, Calvin Stowe got a job teaching at Bowdoin College in Maine, and the family lived there for three years. During that time, Stowe was inspired to write *Uncle Tom's Cabin.* It was a book that would transform the nation, and make her one of the most famous authors in history.

The Fugitive Slave Act: In the 1850s, the country was locked in a furious debate over slavery. Most Northerners opposed slavery, but it was staunchly defended in the South. In 1850, the U.S. Congress passed the Fugitive Slave Act. It permitted any white person to accuse any black person, slave or free, of being a runaway. Any runaway, or "fugitive," could be captured and sent to the South, and into slavery.

The Fugitive Slave Act inspired abolitionists all over the country to action. One of Stowe's relatives said to her, "If I could use a pen as you can, Hattie, I would write something that would make this whole nation feel what an accursed thing slavery is." Stowe sat down and began to write.

UNCLE TOM'S CABIN: In 1851, the first chapters of Stowe's *Uncle Tom's Cabin* appeared in an abolitionist newspaper, *The National Era.* It tells the story of a group of slaves, focusing on a man named Tom. It traces Tom's life from the opening scene, when he is sold off to pay the debts of his owners, and is sent away from his beloved family. Later scenes describe Tom's degradation under three different owners. Every chapter outlines the brutality and indignity of life under slavery. In the final chapter, Tom, fighting for his family's freedom, loses his life to Simon Legree, a cruel slave master, because he will not give up his Christian faith, or reveal where fugitive slaves are hidden.

Stowe had originally planned for the work to be complete in four chapters. By the time she was done, it was 40 chapters long. Its publication was a sensation. When the novel version came out, it sold 10,000 copies in the first week. There were 300,000 copies sold in one year. In Britain, there were 1.5 million copies sold.

To depict slave life, Stowe relied on several sources. She had

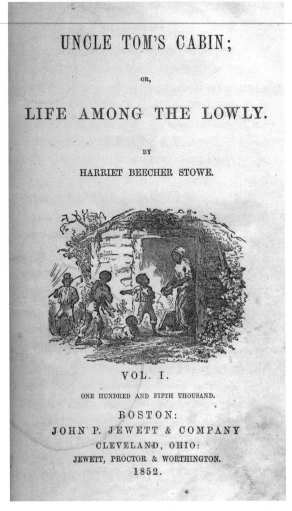

Title page of Uncle Tom's Cabin, *1852.*

vivid memories of living in Cincinnati, a free city across the Ohio River from the slave state of Kentucky. She knew runaway slaves, and saw what they faced first-hand. Stowe and her husband learned that their own servant, Zilah, was a runaway slave. They helped her to escape to freedom in Canada.

Stowe refused to spare any detail of the degradation of slavery. She focused on its horrors and cruelty, how it destroyed families, and how its injustices debased all Americans, Northern and Southern alike.

"I wrote what I did because as a woman, as a mother, I was oppressed and broken-hearted with the sorrows and injustice I saw, because, as a Christian, I felt the dishonor to Christianity. Because as a lover of my country, I trembled at the coming day of wrath."

The novel was also written in response to Stowe's private grief. In 1849, her 18-month old son, Samuel, died. After *Uncle Tom's Cabin* was published, she wrote to a friend:

"I have been the mother of seven children, the most beautiful and most loved of whom lies buried near my Cincinnati residence.

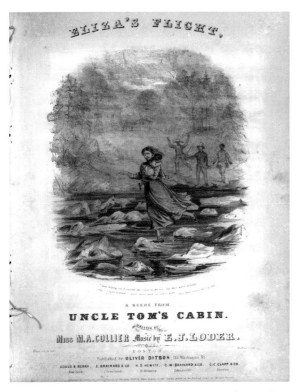

Sheet music cover to "Eliza's Flight," inspired by Uncle Tom's Cabin, *1852.*

It was at his dying bed and at his grave that I learned what a poor slave mother may feel when her child is torn away from her. In those depths of sorrow which seemed to me immeasurable, it was my only prayer to God that such anguish might not be suffered in vain. There were circumstances about his death of such peculiar bitterness, of what seemed almost cruel suffering that I felt I could never be consoled for it unless this crushing of my own heart might enable me to work out some great good to others.

"I allude to this here because I have often felt that much that is in that book had its root in the awful scenes and bitter sorrow of that summer. It has left now, I trust, no trace on my mind except a deep compassion for the sorrowful, especially for mothers who are separated from their children."

A FAMOUS AUTHOR: *Uncle Tom's Cabin* made Stowe a famous author. The work was translated into 60 languages, and her fame spread worldwide. She travelled to Europe to speak to groups about the evils of slavery.

THE IMPACT OF *UNCLE TOM'S CABIN*: In the United States, the book inspired people to confront the issue of slavery. Stowe had succeeded in taking the issue and personalizing it, creating living,

Harriet Beecher Stowe's house in Hartford, Connecticut.

breathing characters whose lives were torn apart by slavery. Her language and her themes were clear and straightforward. It was a call to action.

As the nation moved toward Civil War, *Uncle Tom's Cabin* played a role. Because it had outlined the evils of slavery so clearly, people understood it. For many, it helped define the direction the nation needed to make.

"So you're the little lady who wrote the book that started this great war": In 1861, the South seceded from the Union, and the Civil War began. Legend has it that Abraham Lincoln, on meeting Stowe in 1862, said to her, "So you're the little lady who wrote the book that started this great war." Whether he said that or not, it gives modern readers a glimpse of the novel's power.

OTHER WORKS: Stowe wrote many more novels, including *The Key to Uncle Tom's Cabin*, where she discussed the sources she used to write the work. She wrote another anti-slavery novel, *Dred, A Tale of the Great Dismal Swamp*, and more than 30 other books altogether. But none of them had the impact of *Uncle Tom's Cabin.* Stowe was also an outspoken advocate for women's rights, and one of her sisters, Isabella, helped found the National Women's Suffrage Association with **Susan B. Anthony** and **Elizabeth Cady Stanton.**

LATER YEARS: After the success of *Uncle Tom's Cabin*, Stowe was able to purchase a large home in Hartford, Connecticut, for her family. She also bought a home in Florida, where she and her husband spent the winters in her later years. Harriet Beecher Stowe died in Hartford on July 1, 1896, at the age of 85.

HER LEGACY: *Uncle Tom's Cabin* was one of the most influential books ever written. Its depiction of slavery roused the nation to action, as Stowe hoped it would. Her style was simple but direct. Her novel spoke directly to people in a way that all could understand, and changed the way the nation viewed slavery.

WORLD WIDE WEB SITES

http://digital.library.upenn.edu/women/stowe/StoweHB.html

http://www.greatwomen.org/women/

http://www.harrietbeecherstowecenter.org/

http://utc.iath.virginia.edu/

Mother Teresa

1910-1997
Albanian-Born Religious Leader
Who Served the Poor of India for 50 Years

MOTHER TERESA WAS BORN August 26, 1910, in Skopje (SKAWP-ya), a city in what is now Macedonia, near Greece. Her name when she was born was Agnes Gonxha Bojaxhiu (AGG-nis GONE-yah bow-yahk-YOU). She took the name "Mother Teresa" years later when she became a Catholic nun.

Her parents were Nikola and Dranafile Bojaxhiu. Nikola was a building contractor and Dranafile was a homemaker.

Agnes was the youngest of three children. She had an older sister named Aga and an older brother named Lazar. When she was little, she was called by her middle name, which means "flower bud." Her brother said she was like a "rosebud, plump, round, and tidy."

MOTHER TERESA GREW UP in a large, comfortable house surrounded by her loving family. When she was nine, her father died suddenly. Her mother had to find work and care for the children on her own. Soon, her mother started a business making embroidered cloth, and the family had a regular income again.

MOTHER TERESA WENT TO SCHOOL at the local city schools. Not much is known about her education, but from a very young age she was very religious. She was part of a group of Catholic girls and women who supported missionaries in India. She also helped her mother deliver food and clothing to the poor.

DECIDING TO BECOME A NUN: When she was just 12, Agnes knew she wanted to become a nun. "I had a vocation to help the poor," she remembered. "I wanted to become a missionary. "She knew she would miss her family. Still, she felt a deep need to devote her life to God and the poor.

TRAINING TO BE A NUN: At the age of 18, Agnes decided it was time to begin her training to become a nun. She left her home and her family and traveled to Ireland to study. After one year, she moved to India to continue her training. In 1929, at the age of 19, she took her vows and became a nun. She took the name Sister Teresa, honoring two saints with that name, Teresa of Avila and Therese of Lisieux.

For the next 17 years, she taught at a Catholic girl's school, called a convent. The school, Saint Mary's High School, was in

Calcutta. That is a city in southern India. She taught geography, history, and religion. She was very happy with her work. Then Sister Teresa had an experience that changed her life forever.

A MESSAGE FROM GOD: In 1946, while riding on a train in India, Sister Teresa felt God speak directly to her. "The message was clear," she recalled. "I was to leave the convent and help the poor while living among them. It was an order."

SETTING UP HER MISSION IN INDIA: In 1948, Mother Teresa began her work in Calcutta with some of the poorest people in the world. She started her own "order", or group of nuns, called the Missionaries of Charity. Together they worked to relieve the suffering of "the poorest of the poor." They cared for people who, in Mother Teresa's words, "live in conditions unworthy of human dignity."

Mother Teresa with a young Indian child.

It is hard for Americans to imagine what life in India is like for the poor. Some of the poorest people in the world live in Calcutta. Many of them are homeless and live and die on the streets.

Mother Teresa went into the streets of Calcutta to find the poor, especially those who were sick and dying. She asked the city of Calcutta to provide her with space for a mission. There, she and her nuns cared for the poor and sick. Some would get better and leave the mission. Some died of their illnesses in an atmosphere of care and love.

For Mother Teresa, the ill and dying were like her family. "My community is the poor," she said. "Their heart is my own. My house is the house of the poor—not just of the poor, but of the poorest of the poor." To these people she devoted her life.

The nuns who were part of Mother Teresa's order came from all over the world. The money that kept the mission going came from all over the world, too. In 1969, there was a television special on Mother Teresa that brought contributions and help from everywhere.

Mother Teresa used the money to build schools for poor children, orphanages, and hospitals. She also started missions in other poor nations. Soon there were missions in Africa, South America, Australia, and some U.S. cities.

Mother Teresa was a small woman: she was less than five feet tall. But she was strong and determined to do what she felt she was called to do. She and her nuns lived as their patients lived. Their only possessions were their nun's robes, their sandals, and a bucket for washing. Every day they rose at 4:30 for prayers, then worked for 16 hours. "To be able to love the poor and know the poor we must be poor ourselves," she said.

Mother Teresa receiving the 1979 Nobel Peace Prize.

Mother Teresa described herself this way: "By blood and origin I am Albanian. My citizenship is Indian. I am a Catholic nun. As to my calling, I belong to the work. As to my heart, I belong entirely to the heart of Jesus."

WINNING THE NOBEL PRIZE: In 1979, Mother Teresa received the Nobel Peace Prize. That is one of the most important prizes in the world. She won for her tireless work with the poor. The committee who awards the prize praised her "respect for the individual human being, for his or her dignity and innate value."

When she found out she had won, Mother Teresa said she was not worthy of the award. But she did accept it, she said, "in the name of the hungry, of the homeless, of those who feel unwanted,

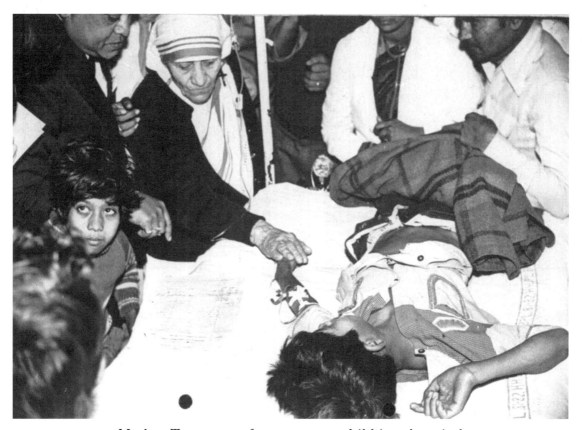

Mother Teresa comforts a young child in a hospital.

uncared for." With the prize money, she was able to build a new care facility in India.

DEATH: Mother Teresa was 87 years old when she died on September 5, 1997. People everywhere expressed their sadness at her passing. Religious leaders from many faiths attended her funeral in Calcutta. In India, most people are followers of the Hindu or Muslim faith. But they had great respect and love for Mother Teresa.

HER LEGACY: Mother Teresa is revered around the world for her devotion to helping the "poorest of the poor." She was a humble woman who lived her life to serve. "In this life we cannot do great things," she said. "We can only do small things with great love."

WORLD WIDE WEB SITE

http://www.motherteresa.org

http://nobelprize.org/nobel-prizes/peace/laureates/1979/teresa/bio.
  html

Valentina Tereshkova

1937–
Russian Cosmonaut and First Woman to Travel in Space

VALENTINA TERESHKOVA WAS BORN on March 6, 1937, in Maslennikovo, Russia. Her mother worked in a clothing factory and her father was a tractor driver. Valentina was the second of three children. She has an older sister and a younger brother.

VALENTINA TERESHKOVA WENT TO SCHOOL at the age of eight. When she was 16, she left school and started working at a textile plant.

GETTING CHOSEN FOR THE SPACE PROGRAM: Tereshkova loved parachute jumping. It was because she was so good at it that she was chosen for the Soviet space program.

THE COLD WAR: When Tereshkova was growing up, Russia was part of the Soviet Union. The Soviet Union and the U.S. were locked in what was called the "Cold War." After World War II, the Soviet Union and the U.S. became the two strongest nations in the world. They represented two very different political systems. The U.S. was a democracy; the Soviet Union was a Communist state. The two "superpowers" also had powerful nuclear weapons. The relationship between the two nations was very important. For more than 40 years, the hostilities between these two nations affected world politics.

***SPUTNIK* AND THE SPACE RACE:** On October 4, 1957, the Soviets launched the very first satellite, *Sputnik 1*. It was the beginning of the Space Age and the Space Race.

Because of its military importance, the Space Race between the U.S. and the Soviet Union was always about much more than exploration. The Space Race was also about domination. Each country was afraid that the other would develop the weapons and technology to dominate them. The U.S. was astonished at the success of *Sputnik*. U.S. military leaders had no idea that the Soviets had the technology to launch a satellite. And the same technology that could launch a satellite could launch a missile. But *Sputnik* wasn't the only tremendous "first" for the Soviet space program.

YURI GAGARIN: On April 12, 1961, the Soviet cosmonaut Yuri Gagarin became the first person to leave Earth and travel in space. Aboard the space capsule *Vostok 1*, he orbited the Earth once. He reached an altitude of 188 miles, traveling at 18,000 miles an hour. His flight lasted 108 minutes. The Soviets had beat the Americans into space. Now they would send the first woman into space.

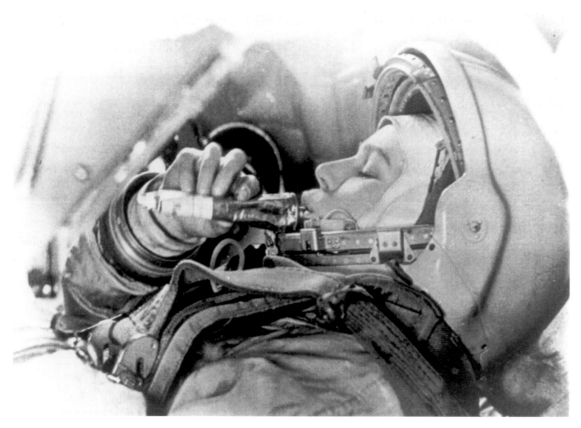

Tereshkova eats food from a tube on her flight into space, June 1963.

TRAINING FOR HER FLIGHT IN SPACE: In 1962, Tereshkova was one of four women chosen to be part of the Soviet space program. She had no piloting experience, so she spent the next year training. She learned to pilot the space capsule. She also trained for the physical demands of space travel, like weightlessness, and the changes in gravity that take place during re-entry.

THE FIRST WOMAN IN SPACE: On June 16, 1963, Valentina Tereshkova entered history as the first women to travel into space. She took off aboard the *Vostok 6*. She spent 71 hours in space (just under three days), orbiting the Earth 48 times.

When she returned, she was greeted as a hero. She recently recalled that her first feeling was that "I had done my duty." She also said she was "convinced that men and women could work in space." After she landed, she was "simply overwhelmed with joy that it was all over and behind."

Tereshkova received many awards and was named a Hero of the Soviet Union. She also accepted the United Nations Gold Medal of Peace.

Tereshkova never flew again. She became active in the Communist Party and spoke all over the Soviet Union. She is now head of the Russian Center for International and Scientific Cooperation. She oversees educational programs for business people and students. One program brings students from all over the world to study in Russia.

VALENTINA TERESHKOVA'S HOME AND FAMILY: Tereshkova married another cosmonaut, Andrian Nikolayev. They had one daughter, Elena. Soviet scientists were interested in Elena, because she was the first child born to two astronauts. She was a perfect-ly normal child, and is now a doctor in Russia. Tereshkova and Nikolayev are now divorced.

HER LEGACY: Tereshkova is remembered as the first woman to travel in space. It took the U.S. 20 years to match that achieve-ment. It wasn't until 1983 that **Sally Ride** became the first American woman to travel in space.

WORLD WIDE WEB SITE

http://starchild.gsfc.nasa.gov/docs/StarChild/whos_who_level2/
  tereshkova.html

Margaret Thatcher

1925-
British Political Leader and First Female
Prime Minister of the United Kingdom
First Woman to Lead a Major Country in the Modern Era

MARGARET THATCHER WAS BORN on October 13, 1925, in Grantham, England. Her name when she was born was Margaret Hilda Roberts. Her parents were Alf and Beatrice Roberts. They ran a grocery store, and the family lived in the apartment above the store. Margaret had one sister, Muriel.

GROWING UP: Margaret grew up at a time when Britain was going through very difficult times. World War I (1914-1918) had taken a terrible toll on Britain. They lost many men, and it took the economy years to recover.

When Margaret was growing up, there were many people who had trouble finding work. Her family helped out when they could, and often gave food away to the poor through their church.

Margaret loved movies when she was a child. She also loved radio, and she and her family would sit around the "wireless," as they called it, every night. They liked to listen to news, music, and comedies.

EDUCATION: Margaret went to the public schools in Grantham, and was an excellent student. She continued her education at Oxford University, where she studied chemistry.

Margaret Thatcher's birthplace, in Grantham, England.

GETTING INTERESTED IN POLITICS: Margaret was also interested in politics. She first ran for political office in college. She ran for president of the Conservative Student Association, and won. It was her first taste of her future career.

FIRST JOBS: After graduating from Oxford, Margaret got a job as a chemist in Dartford, near London. She also continued her political career, running for Parliament (the British legislature) in 1950 and 1951. She didn't win, but it didn't lessen her interest in politics. And, because she was the youngest woman running for political office in the country, newspapers and magazines followed the story of the young politician.

MARRIAGE AND FAMILY: In Dartford, Margaret met Dennis Thatcher. They fell in love and married in 1951. Two years later, in 1953, they had twins, Carol and Mark.

While her children were growing up, Thatcher decided to study law. She became a lawyer in 1954, and specialized in tax law.

RUNNING FOR PARLIAMENT AGAIN: In 1959, Thatcher decided to run for office again. She faced some prejudice from members of her political party, the Conservatives. Some of them didn't believe that a woman with children should run for office.

Margaret Thatcher didn't let that stop her. She ran for Parliament and won. She became an "MP" (Member of Parliament) for Finchley, an area in north London.

Soon, she was actively involved with the government. In 1961, she worked on committees studying retirement pensions and national insurance. From 1964 to 1970, she became a major voice for the Conservative Party in Parliament.

In Great Britain, there are two major political parties, the Labour Party and the Conservative Party. (In the United States the two major parties are the Democrats and the Republicans). During the 1960s in Britain, Labour was generally the party in power.

In 1970, the Conservative Party won the majority of votes in the national election. As part of that victory, Thatcher took on a new role. She became the Education Secretary. In that job, she was responsible for the education system in Britain, from elementary through college level.

In 1974, the Conservatives were voted out, and the Labour Party took control. In 1975, the Conservatives voted for their new leader. They chose Margaret Thatcher. She was the first woman ever to lead a political party in Britain.

Over the next five years, Thatcher helped define the

Margaret Thatcher, elected as Leader of the Opposition in September, 1975.

Conservative Party's political philosophy. At that time, Britain was having difficult economic problems. The Labour and Conservative politicians battled about what changes could be made to improve the economy. In 1979, the country voted again. This time, the Conservatives won. And they chose Margaret Thatcher as their Prime Minister.

PRIME MINISTER: The Prime Minister (PM) of Great Britain is very similar to the President of the United States. The PM is both head of his or her political party, and the government. He or she chooses a Cabinet to run various government offices, like Treasury or Education. The PM also defines the political direction of the country.

Under Thatcher, the government took a very different direction. She believed that to improve the economy, the government should be smaller. That meant fewer services for individuals. It also meant less power for the labor unions in Britain, which up to that point had been very strong.

Falkland Islands: In 1982, Argentina invaded the Falkland Islands. They are a group of islands off the coast of South America that had been under British control for years. Thatcher sent troops to the Falklands and defended them for Britain. She gained a reputation for toughness in handling the crisis.

Re-Election: Thatcher won re-election in 1984. That year, the country was involved in a long labor strike in the mining industry. Many people lost their jobs. Thatcher became very unpopular with some British people. Others thought she had saved the economy through her system of cutbacks.

A Terrorist Attack: In 1984, at the annual Conservative Party meeting in Brighton, England, the Irish Republican Army (IRA), a terrorist group, tried to kill Thatcher and other members of her party. They set off a series of bombs at their hotel, including one in the room next to hers. She wasn't injured, but some of her friends and colleagues were hurt or killed.

"THE IRON LADY": Thatcher refused to be frightened by the experience. She earned the nickname "Iron Lady" for her strength. She was resolved to keep Britain safe, and to follow her own political conscience. In that, she had a good friend in U.S. President Ronald Reagan.

FRIENDSHIP WITH RONALD REAGAN: Ronald Reagan had become President in 1980. Like Thatcher, he was conservative politically. He also believed in smaller government. And, like her, he wanted to see the fall of Communism.

COLD WAR: After World War II (1939-1945), the Soviet Union and the U.S. became the two strongest nations in the world. They represented two very different political systems. The U.S. was a democracy; the Soviet Union was a Communist state. The two "superpowers" also had powerful nuclear weapons. The relationship between the two nations was very important. For more than 40 years, the hostilities between these two nations affected world politics.

Margaret Thatcher at the White House Oval Office with President Ronald Reagan, and Vice-President George H.W. Bush, 1981.

Thatcher and Reagan became colleagues in fighting the power of the Soviet Union. Thatcher supported Reagan when he met with Mikhail Gorbachev to try to end hostilities between the superpowers. They were strong and powerful allies. Their policies toward the Soviet Union helped lead to the collapse of European Communist regimes in the 1990s.

RETIREMENT FROM POLITICS: Thatcher served out her third term as Prime Minister in 1990, and retired from politics. She had been the longest serving Prime Minister since the 1920s, and the first woman. She had made major changes in the government and political direction of the nation.

LATER LIFE: Since her retirement, Thatcher has written several books. She has had health problems and no longer speaks in public. But at the funeral of her old friend Ronald Reagan in 2004, she had prepared a moving speech, which she had someone read for her. She continues to live and write in London.

HER LEGACY: Margaret Thatcher was the first woman Prime Minister of Great Britain, and the first woman elected to lead a major country in the 20th century. The people of Britain still argue about her policies. Some think they were too harsh and harmful to many people. Others argue that she helped the nation out of a difficult economic crisis and brought about needed reforms in government. But all agree that, as the "Iron Lady," she followed her political philosophy with strength and commitment.

WORLD WIDE WEB SITES

http://www.margaretthatcher.org/

http://topics.time.com/margaret-thatcher/index.html

Sojourner Truth
1797(?)–1883
African-American Abolitionist and Activist

SOJOURNER TRUTH WAS BORN around 1797 in Ulster, New York. She was born a slave. Her name when she was born was Isabella Bomefree. (She chose the name "Sojourner Truth" later, when she became an activist.)

Her parents were James and Betsy Bomefree. They were slaves, and belonged to a Dutch immigrant named Hardenbergh. Isabella had 10 to 12 sisters and brothers. Each of them was sold into slavery when they were small. Her earliest memories were of her parents' overwhelming grief over the loss of their children.

The first language Isabella spoke was Dutch. Later, when she learned English, she still spoke with a Dutch accent.

LIFE AS A SLAVE: Over the first 30 years of her life, Isabella was owned by four men. In 1806, when she was only nine, she was taken from her parents and sold to an Englishman named John Nealy. She worked for him for about two years. She was sold again in 1808 to Martinus Schrynver. Two years later, she was sold again, to John Dumont.

Isabella worked for Dumont on his farm in New Paltz, New York, for 17 years. During those years, she married a man named Thomas, who was also a slave. They had five children. To her great horror, her son Peter was illegally sold to an Alabama slaveholder. She was determined to find him.

FREEDOM: The state of New York abolished slavery on July 4, 1827. Dumont promised Isabella that he would free her one year early, in 1826. But he went back on his word. Isabella was furious.

In late 1826, Isabella escaped to freedom. She was only able to take her baby daughter, Sophia, with her. "I did not run off, for I thought that wicked," she later claimed. "I walked off, believing that to be right."

Maria and Isaac Wagener, who lived in nearby Wagondale, took Isabella and Sophia in. She worked for them for several years, as a domestic employee.

Truth presents President Abraham Lincoln with a Bible from the African-Americans of Baltimore, October 29, 1864.

Isabella began to search for Peter. She found him in Alabama, then sued his owner for his return. She became the first black woman in history to sue a white man, and win. Peter was joyfully reunited with his mother. They moved to New York City in 1829.

A WOMAN OF DEEP CHRISTIAN FAITH: Isabella became a devout Christian. She said that God appeared to her in a vision. She remembered being "overwhelmed with the greatness of the Divine presence." She believed she was called to preach the Gospel.

Isabella joined a religious group headed by a man named Elijah Pierson. He believed he was a prophet. Isabella worked for him, and preached with him. Another member of the group was a fiery speaker named Matthias. Matthias believed he was God.

When Pierson died under mysterious circumstances, Matthias was accused of his murder. Though she was innocent, Isabella was also charged. She was cleared of all charges, but she decided to leave New York. She wanted to pursue her calling on her own. She helped Peter find a job on a whaling ship, then became a traveling preacher.

BECOMING SOJOURNER TRUTH: In 1843, at the age of 46, Isabella changed her name to Sojourner Truth. She explained that she received the name from God. "My name was Isabella. But when I left the house of bondage, I left everything behind. I went to the Lord and asked him to give me a new name. And the Lord gave me Sojourner, because I was to travel up and down the land, showing the people their sins, and being a sign unto them."

For the next 40 years, Truth traveled the country as a preacher and activist. She was devoted to the cause of **ABOLITION** and women's rights. Abolitionists wanted to "abolish," or end, slavery in the country. In 1844, she joined a group in Northampton, Massachusetts, called the Northampton Association of Education and Industry. It was a community devoted to abolition. The group supported itself and its mission by raising and selling farm goods.

At Northampton, Sojourner met Frederick Douglass and William Lloyd Garrison. They encouraged her to speak and continue to fight against slavery. She also met Olive Gilbert. Gilbert was devoted to abolition and women's rights, too. Sojourner couldn't read or write.

417

So Gilbert helped her complete her autobiography, *The Narrative of Sojourner Truth: A Northern Slave.* It was first published by William Garrison in 1850. The book provided an income for Truth, and she was able to buy a house in Northampton.

The book helped make Sojourner a well-known and respected speaker. She traveled the country speaking out against slavery and for women's rights. She often spoke of her own life, and listeners were moved by her straightforward, uncompromising vision. One of her speeches is still studied today.

"AIN'T I A WOMAN?" On May 29, 1851, Truth gave her most famous speech at a women's rights convention in Ohio. One speaker claimed that women were too weak to be able to vote. Truth's response has thundered across the ages. "That man over there says women need to be helped into carriages, and lifted over ditches," she said. "Nobody ever helps me into carriages, or over mud-puddles, or gives me any best place! And ain't I a woman? Look at me! I have plowed and planted, and gathered into barns, and no man could head me! And ain't I a woman? I could work as much, and eat as much as a man—when I could get it—and bear the lash as well! And ain't I a woman?"

FREE LECTURE!

SOJOURNER TRUTH,

Who has been a slave in the State of New York, and who has been a Lecturer for the last twenty-three years, whose characteristics have been so vividly portrayed by Mrs. Harriet Beecher Stowe, as the African Nybil, will deliver a lecture upon the present issues of the day,

At   On

And will give her experience as a Slave mother and religious woman. She comes highly recommended as a public speaker, having the approval of many thousands who have heard her earnest appeals, among whom are Wendell Phillips, Wm. Lloyd Garrison, and other distinguished men of the nation.

☞ At the close of her discourse she will offer for sale her photograph and a few of her choice songs.

Newspaper announcement for one of Truth's lectures.

In 1853, Truth met **Harriet Beecher Stowe**. Stowe was the author of *Uncle Tom's Cabin.* That famous novel spelled out the evils of slavery, and inflamed the nation. Stowe wrote about Truth in the *Atlantic Monthly* magazine. Truth's fame continued to grow.

In 1857, Truth moved from Massachusetts to Michigan. She lived with a community of Quakers who worked for abolition, women's rights, and nonviolence. As the country headed toward Civil War, Truth continued to travel and to speak.

When the Civil War began in 1861, Truth rallied African-Americans to join the cause. She spoke to black soldiers and encouraged others to join. She was proud that her grandson James served in the honored 54th Regiment from Massachusetts. That unit was made up of all African-American volunteers. It also included two of Frederick Douglass's sons.

During the war, Truth met with President Abraham Lincoln. She presented him with a Bible from the freed blacks of Baltimore. The scene of their meeting became a famous painting. (See the painting in this entry.)

WORK ON BEHALF OF FREEDMEN AND WOMEN: After the Civil War ended in 1865, Truth worked for the betterment of black Americans. She worked for the Freedman's Relief Association. As part of that group, she helped former slaves to begin lives as free people. She worked in the Freedman's Hospital in Washington, D.C.

Almost 100 years before **Rosa Parks,** Truth filed a lawsuit to desegregate public transportation. She wanted black people to be able to ride on the streetcars of Washington, D.C. She won her case. She also

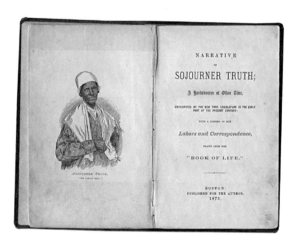

Title page of Truth's autobiography.

spoke before Congress. She wanted the government to grant land to former slaves in the West. They gave her a standing ovation, but didn't approve her proposal.

Truth also continued to travel and speak all over the country. Well into her 80s, she spoke in support of women's rights and **TEMPERANCE** (the banning of alcohol). She tried to vote in the Presidential election of 1872, but wasn't allowed to.

Finally, Truth's health began to fail. She died on November 26, 1883, at her home in Battle Creek, Michigan. She was 86 years old. There is a memorial and institute in Battle Creek that celebrate her many achievements.

SOJOURNER TRUTH'S HOME AND FAMILY: Truth married a man named Thomas while she lived on the Dumont farm. They had five children. Four survived to be adults. Those four were Diana, Peter, Elizabeth, and Sophia. Peter was most likely lost at sea in the 1840s. Diana and Elizabeth and their families lived with their mother in Battle Creek until the end of her life.

HER LEGACY: Sojourner Truth was a woman of strength, determination, and courage. She overcame the horrors of slavery to become a tireless advocate for African-Americans and women. With passion and the promise of freedom for the oppressed, she truly "spoke Truth to Power."

WORLD WIDE WEB SITES
http://www.lkwdpl.org/wihohio/trut-soj.htm
http://www.sojournertruth.org
http://www.sojournertruthmemorial.org

Harriet Tubman

1820? – 1913
African-American Abolitionist and Activist
Conductor of the Underground Railroad

HARRIET TUBMAN WAS BORN around 1820 in Dorchester County, Maryland. She was born a slave. Her name when she was born was Araminta Ross. Her parents were Ben and Harriet Ross. She changed her first name to Harriet in honor of her mother. Her parents were both slaves. Harriet was one of 11 children. Despite their plight as slaves, Ben and Harriet Ross loved and protected their children. They raised them all to have a deep Christian faith.

LIFE AS A SLAVE: When she was about five years old, Harriet began to work as a house slave. Her master hired her out to help another slave owner as a nursemaid. Only a child herself, Harriet was beaten if she fell asleep, or if the baby in her care cried. When she was about 12, she was sent to work in the fields. The work was brutally hard. So was the overseer's treatment of the slaves.

One day Harriet tried to save a fellow slave from a beating by the overseer. The overseer threw a heavy rock, and it struck Harriet. The blow nearly killed her. She suffered from seizures the rest of her life.

In 1844, Harriet married a free black man named John Tubman. She continued to live as a slave. By 1849, Harriet feared she might be sold. She made a decision to run away.

ESCAPING TO FREEDOM: In 1849, Tubman fled Maryland and slavery. Her husband refused to come with her. Guided by the North Star, she made her way to Philadelphia, where she was finally free. "I had crossed the line of which I had so long been dreaming," she said. But she missed her family. She was determined to rescue them from slavery and bring them to the North.

Tubman found work as a cook in Philadelphia. As soon as she had enough money, she arranged to help her sister and her sister's children to escape to freedom. Over the next several years, she brought her entire family to the North, and to freedom.

BECOMING A CONDUCTOR ON THE UNDERGROUND RAILROAD: Through freeing her family members, Tubman met many other slaves who wanted to escape. She joined what was called the Underground Railroad. It was a secret network of roads and safe houses, where slaves could stay on their route to the North. The

This lithograph, entitled "Underground Railroad," depicts African-Americans escaping slavery.

"railroad" led all the way to northern states, including New York and Michigan, and into Canada.

Tubman met William Still, the station master for Philadelphia. He was an important organizer of the Underground Railroad. He helped Tubman learn the system of the "Railroad."

Tubman became a "conductor." That meant that she organized and led groups of slaves to freedom. It was dangerous work, but she was fearless. There were large rewards for her capture, as both a runaway slave and a "conductor."

Tubman insisted that the slaves in her care follow her rules. She carried a rifle at all times. She threatened to use it against any slave who wanted to return to slavery. But she never wavered in her work. And she never lost a single person. "On my Underground Railroad I never ran my train off the track, and I never lost a passenger," she recalled.

"THE MOSES OF HER PEOPLE": Over the span of 16 years, Tubman led over 300 slaves to freedom. As Moses in the Bible led the Israelites from bondage in Egypt, she led her people to freedom. For this, she became known as "The Moses of Her People."

Through her work, she met some of the most important **ABOLITIONISTS** of her time. (Abolitionists wanted to "abolish," or end, slavery in the country.) She met Frederick Douglass and John Brown. Douglass said, "Excepting John Brown, I know of no one who has willingly encountered more perils and hardships to serve our enslaved people than Harriet Tubman."

Another important friend was William H. Seward. He was a prominent abolitionist and Republican from Auburn, New York. Seward championed Tubman, and helped her buy a home in Auburn. He was also Lincoln's Secretary of State as the nation entered the Civil War.

THE ELECTION OF ABRAHAM LINCOLN: Abraham Lincoln was elected President in 1860. He was the candidate of the Republican Party. That party had been formed by people who were opposed to slavery in the new territories. The Southern states knew that a vote for Lincoln was a vote against slavery. Two months after the election, seven Southern states "seceded" from the Union. That means that they chose to no longer be a part of the United States. Instead, they formed their own new country, called the Confederate States of America.

THE CIVIL WAR: The national argument over slavery led the nation to Civil War in 1861. The war lasted four years, and losses on both sides were horrific. Tubman continued to play an important part in her nation's cause. She served as a nurse, a soldier, and a spy for the Union.

NURSE: In 1862, Tubman was sent to Beaufort, South Carolina, to nurse soldiers. She also helped the new black freedman to learn to make a living on their own. But her work in South Carolina included other, more dangerous, assignments.

A SPY FOR THE UNION: Tubman led a group of former slaves on a scouting mission. They prepared reports on the location of Confederate camps for the Union. These aided the invasion of South Carolina led by Colonel James Montgomery. Tubman served as a soldier for Montgomery, too. In 1863, Tubman and 150 black soldiers took part in a gunboat raid in South Carolina.

SETTLING IN AUBURN, NEW YORK: After the war, Tubman moved to Auburn, New York. She married a soldier she'd met in the war, named Nelson Davis. She decided to devote herself to the care of children and the elderly. She also became involved in the fight for women's rights.

WOMEN'S RIGHTS ACTIVIST: Tubman met many of the prominent members of the women's rights movement. **Susan B. Anthony** and **Elizabeth Cady Stanton** became her friends and fellow activists. Tubman was a delegate to the National Federation of Afro-American Women's first meeting in 1896.

BUILDING THE HARRIET TUBMAN HOME: Tubman bought 25 acres of land near her home in Auburn. On that property, she built the Harriet Tubman Home for Aged and Indigent Colored People. It became home to many of the area's poor and elderly blacks.

Portrait of Harriet Tubman taken in 1911.

Although she had been a hero of the abolitionist movement and the Civil War, Tubman didn't receive any money for her services until the 1890s. She died in the home she had built on March 10, 1913, at the age of 93. She was buried in Auburn with military honors.

HARRIET TUBMAN'S HOME AND FAMILY: Tubman was married twice. Her first husband was John Tubman. He and Harriet married in 1844. From 1849 until the Civil War, Harriet helped all of her family escape to the North. When she returned for John, he had married another woman. After the Civil War, Tubman married again. Her second husband was named Nelson Davis.

HER LEGACY: Tubman was a woman of incredible courage and devotion to the cause of freedom. Yet this champion of civil rights rarely received the honors she surely deserved. "I have wrought in the day—you in the night," wrote Frederick Douglass to Tubman. "I have had the applause of the crowd and the satisfaction that comes of being approved by the multitude. The most that you have done has been witnessed by a few trembling, scarred, and footsore bondsmen and women, whose heartfelt "God bless you' has been your only reward."

In recent years, Tubman's achievements have been more widely recognized. Her Auburn home is now a state historical site. In 1995, the U.S. Post Office honored her with a commemorative stamp. And in 2003, the Governor of New York declared March 10th "Harriet Tubman Day."

WORLD WIDE WEB SITES

http://www.americaslibrary.gov/cgi-bin/page.cgi/aa/tubman
http://www.nyhistory.com/harriettubman.life.htm
http://www/pbs.org/wgbh/aia/

Published according to Act of Parliament, Sept. 1.1773 by Arch.d Bell,
Bookseller N.º 8 near the Saracens Head Aldgate.

Phillis Wheatley

1753? – 1784
African-American Poet
First African-American to Publish a Book

PHILLIS WHEATLEY WAS BORN around 1753 in Gambia, Africa. No one is sure of her exact birth date or her original name. When she was around seven years old, she was captured from her African home and sold into slavery. She was brought by a slave ship called *Phillis* to Boston. There, she was bought by John and Susannah Wheatley on July 11, 1761. They named her Phillis Wheatley.

PHILLIS WHEATLEY GREW UP in the Wheatley home. She was supposed to be a servant, but she was often in poor health. She was very intelligent, and learned English very quickly.

LEARNING TO READ AND WRITE: The Wheatleys discovered Phillis writing on a wall with chalk. They encouraged her to devote herself to learning. They taught her to read and write, and she thrived. She learned several languages, including Latin and Greek. She studied theology—the study of religion—and literature. She especially loved poetry.

STARTING TO WRITE POETRY: Soon Phillis began to write poetry of her own. One of her poems was published in 1767, in a Rhode Island newspaper. It was called "On Messrs. Hussey and Coffin."

Wheatley liked to write a form of poetry called an "elegy." An elegy is a poem celebrating the life and works of an individual, usually written at the individual's death. Wheatley showed her deep Christian faith and her admiration for Colonial leaders in these poems. They made her a very popular poet. Some of her work appeared as broadsides and were widely read.

Wheatley attended services at the Old South Church in Boston. When her minister, Joseph Sewall, died in 1769, she wrote an elegy commemorating his life. It was admired by many Bostonians.

In 1770, she published her most famous elegy, "On the Death of Mr. George Whitefield." Whitefield was an English minister who was well known in Colonial America. Wheatley's poem was read and celebrated in Boston and London. It caught the attention of a wealthy English admirer, the Countess of Huntingdon.

A TRIP TO LONDON: Wheatley sailed to England in 1773, hoping to meet the Countess. Although they were unable to meet, the Countess provided the money to publish Wheatley's first book of poetry.

PUBLISHING HER BOOK: Wheatley's first book, *Poems on Various Subjects, Religious and Moral,* was published in 1773. It was the first book ever published by an African-American. And it was only the second book of poetry by an American woman ever published. (The first was by **Anne Bradstreet**, an earlier Colonial American.)

BECOMING A FREE WOMAN: When Phillis returned from England, the Wheatleys freed her. She was a free woman at last.

Wheatley continued to write poems. In 1776, the colonies declared war against England. Wheatley wrote a poem dedicated to General George Washington. He praised her verse and her support of the Revolutionary War. He also invited her to meet him. They met in 1776. Wheatley's poem on Washington was printed and distributed during the war, rallying Americans to the cause.

Wheatley was a strong supporter of the cause of independence, and liberty for all people. She also believed that slavery was a curse that Colonial Americans must confront. In one poem, she states that white people cannot "hope to find/Divine acceptance with th'Almighty mind" when "they disgrace/And hold in bondage Afric's blameless race."

Wheatley's letters also reveal her hatred of slavery. In a letter to a friend, she wrote: "In every human Breast, God has implant-ed a Principle, which we call Love of Freedom. It is impatient of Oppression, and pants for Deliverance."

Wheatley's last known poem was published in 1784, the year of

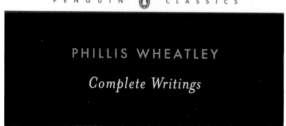

PENGUIN CLASSICS

PHILLIS WHEATLEY

Complete Writings

her death. It was called "Liberty and Peace." In it, she celebrates the victory of the Revolution. She tried to find subscribers to pay for the publication of another collection of her poems, but died before she could find enough supporters. Her final manuscripts were never found.

PHILLIS WHEATLEY'S HOME AND FAMILY: Wheatley married John Peters in 1778. He was a free black man. He had a business, but it failed. The family struggled in poverty for several years. Phillis had to find work as a servant. She had three children, but, tragically, all died. Phillis Wheatley died on December 5, 1784, around the age of 30.

HER LEGACY: Wheatley is honored as the first African-American to publish a book in the U.S. Her poetry was admired for its religious and patriotic themes. She was a woman of great intelligence and poetic gifts. She used those gifts to praise God, and also to promote freedom for all.

WORLD WIDE WEB SITES

http://americanslibrary.gov/cgi-bin/page.cgi/jb/revolut/poetslave_
http://www.pbs.org/wgbh/aia/part2/2p12/html

Babe Didrikson Zaharias

1911-1956
American Golfer and Athlete
One of the Greatest Athletes of the Twentieth Century

BABE DIDRIKSON ZAHARIAS WAS BORN on June 26, 1911, in Port Arthur, Texas. Her name when she was born was Mildred Ella Didrikson. Her parents, Hannah and Ole Didrikson, had moved to the U.S. from Norway. Babe was one of seven children in the family. Her siblings were named Dora, Nancy, Ole, Lillie, Louis, and Arthur.

GROWING UP: Babe lived in Port Arthur until 1915. That year, a hurricane hit the coastal town, and the family moved inland, to Beaumont, Texas.

From an early age, it was clear that Babe was an exceptional athlete. She seemed to be able to excel at any sport she tried. She was great at baseball, basketball, track, golf, tennis, swimming, diving, boxing, volleyball, bowling, skating, and cycling. Once, when asked if there was anything she didn't play, she said, "Yeah, dolls."

Her nickname even came from her sports talent. In her early teens, she was such a great baseball player that her teammates called her "Babe," for the famous Babe Ruth. The name stuck.

Babe was a tough competitor, and she wanted to be the best. "My goal was to be the greatest athlete who ever lived," she said.

EDUCATION: Babe went to the local schools where she was a good student and a great athlete. She started competing in sports in high school, and was a basketball star. She graduated from Beaumont High School in 1929.

FIRST JOBS: After high school, Babe moved to Dallas, where she got a job with Employers Casualty Insurance Company. She was hired as a secretary, but they really wanted her to play on the company's basketball team, the Golden Cyclones.

AAU CHAMPIONSHIPS: While she was working, Babe started to compete in sporting contests sponsored by the Amateur Athletic Association (AAU). In 1930, she won four track and field events at the 1930 AAU Championships, in the javelin throw, hurdles, and high jump.

Zaharias preparing for the 1932 Olympics.

In 1932, Babe once again competed in the AAU championships, which were also that year's U.S. Olympic qualifying trials. At the AAU championships, she competed in eight events in three hours, and won five of them. She set world championship records in three events, and when the championships were over, she had qualified for five Olympic events.

1932 OLYMPICS: At that time, women were limited to competing in only three events, no matter how many they had qualified for. So Babe competed in the javelin throw, the 80-meter hurdles, and the high jump. She won gold medals in the javelin and hurdles, and she tied for gold in the high jump. She wound up getting a silver in that event, a ruling that most commentators thought was wrong, and unfair.

GOLF: In addition to her achievements in track and field, Babe became a golfing powerhouse in the 1930s. She started to compete in 1933, and soon she had conquered the game. She was so good that the U.S. Golf Association said she had to compete as a professional, "for the best interest of the game."

Babe kept playing, and winning, in the sport she loved. She was an incredibly powerful hitter, able to drive the ball over 250 yards. She wasn't very big—just 5 feet 5 inches, and weighing about 145 pounds. When she was asked where she got the power to hit so hard, she said, "You've got to loosen your girdle and let it rip."

MARRIAGE: In 1938, Babe met George Zaharias, a professional wrestler, at the Los Angeles Golf Open. They fell in love and married on December 23, 1938. He became her manager, and she began a string of golf victories that made her a world champion.

Zaharias on the golf course.

A GOLFING PHENOMENON: Babe was able to regain her status as an amateur in 1943, and soon she was dominating golf again. In 1943, she won 17 tournaments in a row. In 1947, she competed in the British Women's Open, one of the most prestigious events in golf. She won, and became the first American to win the tournament.

Babe went on to win an incredible 82 golf tournaments in her career. Between 1940 and 1950, she won every title in women's golf. She beat the field to win the world championship four times, and the U.S. Women's Open three times. She also was the first woman ever to become the pro at a golf club.

To expand the opportunities for women in the sport, Babe helped form the Ladies Professional Golf Association, the LGPA. It is still the major association for women's pro golf. She traveled and played all over the world, an international ambassador for women and sports. She won award upon award. The Associated Press voted her Female Athlete of the Year six times. In 1950, it named her the Female Athlete of the Half-Century.

ILLNESS: Babe was diagnosed with colon cancer in 1953. She continued to play after her cancer treatment, and made an amazing comeback. Just three months after surgery, she competed in a golf tournament. She rejoined the professional women's golf tour, and soon she was winning again.

Babe won her final tournament, the Peach Blossom Open, in 1955. Tragically, her cancer returned, and she became too weak to compete. Babe Didrikson Zaharias died of cancer on September 27, 1956, in Galveston, Texas. She was 45 years old.

HER LEGACY: Babe Didrikson Zaharias was one of the greatest athletes, male or female, the world has ever seen. She never saw herself as a feminist, or a fighter for women's rights. She saw herself as an athlete, who loved to compete, and win.

She was praised by athletes and sports fans around the world. Bobby Jones, one of history's greatest golfers, said she was one of the top 10 golfers of all time. Sportswriter Grantland Rice described her as "the most flawless specimen of muscle harmony, of complete physical coordination, the world of sport has ever seen." In competing in the sports she loved, she brought joy and awe to millions.

The year before she died, she created the Babe Zaharias Trophy to honor outstanding female athletes. It is a lasting legacy of this legendary athlete.

WORLD WIDE WEB SITES

http://espn.go.com/sportscentury/features/00014147.html
http://www.babedidriksonzaharias.org

Photo and Illustration Credits

Every effort has been made to trace copyright for the images used in this volume. Any omissions will be corrected in future editions.

Abigail Adams: Courtesy of the National Park Service and the Library of Congress

Jane Addams: Courtesy of the Library of Congress; Swarthmore College Peace Collection of Jane Addams

Louisa May Alcott: Used by permission of Louisa May Alcott's Orchard House/ Louisa May Alcott Memorial Association; Courtesy of the Library of Congress.

Marian Anderson: Courtesy of the Library of Congress

Susan B. Anthony: Courtesy of the Library of Congress

Aung San Suu Kyi: Courtesy Burma Campaign UK.

Clara Barton: Courtesy of the Library of Congress

Mary McLeod Bethune: Courtesy of the Library of Congress.

Elizabeth Blackwell: Courtesy of the Library of Congress

Nellie Bly: Courtesy of the Library of Congress

Anne Bradstreet: Courtesy of the Library of Congress

Rachel Fuller Brown: Courtesy of the Wadsworth Center, New York Dept. of Health

Pearl S. Buck: Courtesy of the Library of Congress; Courtesy of Pearl S. Buck International

Rachel Carson: Courtesy of NOAA; Lear Center for Special Collections, Connecticut College

Mary Cassatt: Courtesy of the Library of Congress.

Catherine the Great: russianpaintings.net

Cleopatra: Courtesy of the Library of Congress

Hillary Clinton: Courtesy U.S. Department of State

Marie Curie: AIP Emilio Segre Visual Archives, Brittle Books, William G. Meyers, and Fermi Collections

Emily Dickinson: Amherst College Archives and Special Collections by permission of the Trustees of Amherst College; Todd-Bingham Picture Collection, Yale University

Amelia Earhardt: Courtesy of the Library of Congress; Amelia Hearhart Birthplace Museum

Sylvia Earle: Courtesy Dr. Sylvia Earle

Gertrude Elion: Courtesy GlaxoSmithKline

Elizabeth I: Courtesy of the Library of Congress; englishhistory.net

Jane Goodall: Jane Goodall Institute

Hatshepsut/Photos: Keith Schengili-Roberts; © by James G. Howes

Elizabeth Lee Hazen: Courtesy of the Wadsworth Center, New York Dept. of Health

Isabella: Courtesy of the Library of Congress.

Mae Jemison: Courtesy NASA

Joan of Arc: Courtesy of the Library of Congress; copyright © 2001 by Steven G. Johnson.

Glossary
and
Brief Biographies

The Glossary contains terms used in the entries. It includes descriptions and definitions of concepts relating to the history of women's achievement. The "Brief Biographies" section includes short profiles of women who do not have full entries in the volume. Glossary terms are capitalized and bold-faced in the entries.

ABOLITION, ABOLITIONIST: The abolitionist movement began in the 1780s in the United States and Europe. Abolitionists wanted to "abolish," or end, slavery, as well as the slave trade. **Susan B. Anthony, Lucretia Mott, Elizabeth Cady Stanton, Harriet Beecher Stowe, Sojourner Truth,** and **Harriet Tubman** were early and ardent advocates of abolition.

NINETEENTH AMENDMENT: The Nineteenth Amendment guaranteed the right of women to vote. The fight for the right to vote began in the 19th century, and was led by **Susan B. Anthony, Lucretia Mott**, and **Elizabeth Cady Stanton**. The three women had actually written a draft of the amendment in the 1850s, and Anthony and Stanton presented the amendment to the U.S. Congress for the first time in 1878. In 1919, the Nineteenth Amendment passed both houses of Congress. It was ratified on August 26, 1920 and became law.

SENECA FALLS: Seneca Falls, New York, was the home of **Elizabeth Cady Stanton.** In 1848, Stanton and **Lucretia Mott** organized the first women's rights convention at Seneca Falls, where participants signed a "Declaration of Sentiments and Resolutions." That document outlined the beliefs and goals of the new movement for women's rights, especially the right to vote. It was the first of many women's conventions held at Seneca Falls, which is now a national park devoted to the history of women's rights.

TEMPERANCE: The temperance movement was devoted to the prohibition of alcohol in the United States. It was based on the belief that alcohol was a dangerous drug, and that alcoholic men abused their wives and children. Many members of the temperance movement were also active in the fight for women's suffrage, including **Susan B. Anthony, Lucretia Mott, Sojourner Truth,** and **Elizabeth Cady Stanton.**

WOMEN'S SUFFRAGE: The term "women's suffrage" refers to the movement to win women the right to vote. The movement began in the United States and England in the 19th century. The major figures fighting for women's suffrage in the U.S. included **Lucretia Mott, Susan B. Anthony,** and **Elizabeth Cady Stanton.** The fight for women's suffrage ended in 1920, when the **NINETEENTH AMENDMENT**, guaranteeing women the right to vote, was ratified. In England, the movement for women's suffrage was led by **Emmeline Pankhurst,** who worked tirelessly for women's rights. The right of a woman to vote in Great Britain was finally achieved in 1928.

* * *

BRIEF BIOGRAPHIES

ALBRIGHT, MADELEINE (1937-) Albright was the first woman to serve as U.S. Secretary of State. She was born in Prague, in what is now the Czech Republic, and her family fled from the Nazis and settled in Denver. Albright served as a member of President Jimmy Carter's National Security Council from 1978 to 1980. She returned to national office in 1993, when President Bill Clinton named her U.S. Ambassador to the United Nations. In 1996, Clinton named Albright Secretary of State, and she became the first woman ever to hold that office. Albright served as Secretary of State until the end of Clinton's term in 2000. She is now an author and professor of political science.

BLOOMER, AMELIA (1818-1894) Bloomer was an advocate for women's rights, who founded the first newspaper for women, *The Lily*, a **TEMPERANCE** journal which she published from 1849 to 1853. Bloomer is also remembered as the person who introduced **Elizabeth Cady Stanton** and **Susan B. Anthony**. She attended the first **SENECA FALLS** convention, and continued to be interested in women's issues, including dress reform. She is best known today for advocating an outfit for women that included a knee-length dress worn with pants, that became known as "Bloomers," for its most prominent advocate.

CHISHOLM, SHIRLEY (1924-2005) Chisholm was a legislator and teacher who became the first African-American woman elected to the U.S. House of Representatives in 1968. She served seven terms in Congress, from 1969 to 1983. She was known as a tireless advocate for the rights of African-Americans and women. She ran for the presidential nomination in 1972. Chisholm retired from Congress in 1982 and became a college professor.

EDDY, MARY BAKER (1821-1910) Eddy was an American author, teacher, and religious leader, who founded the Church of Christ, Scientist religion, whose members are called Christian Scientists. She based the main tenets of the faith on her study of the Christian Bible and her own theories and study of spirituality and holistic medical practice. She founded the faith in 1875, and in 1879 built the main Church of Christ, Scientist in Boston, Massachusetts. There are now branches and members of the church around the world. Eddy also founded *The Christian Science* newspaper, one of the leading papers in the country.

FERRARO, GERALDINE (1935-2011) Ferraro was the first American woman nominated for the Vice Presidency by a major party. In 1984, Democratic presidential candidate Walter Mondale chose Ferraro as his running mate, and she became the first woman ever nominated for Vice President from a major party. Mondale and Ferraro lost in a landslide to incumbent President Ronald Reagan and his Vice President George H.W. Bush. But Ferraro remained a role model and a champion for many American women and young girls, who saw in her achievement the possibility of political power on the national level.

FRIEDAN, BETTY (1921-2006) Friedan was an American writer and women's rights activist whose writings, especially her nonfiction book *The Feminine Mystique*, helped create and define the women's movement during the second half of the 20th century. In her writings, Friedan advocated for a woman's right to achieve equality with men in education, careers, and politics, including equal opportunity and equal pay. Friedan went on to become a founder of the National Organization of Women (NOW), and, with **Gloria Steinem**, founded the National Women's Political Caucus.

HILDEGARD VON BINGEN (1098-1179) Hildegard was one of the most remarkable people of medieval Europe. She was born in Germany and became a Benedictine nun and later established her own convent. She was an outstanding scholar, whose religious works made her a major thinker of her time. She also was a virtuoso musician, who composed Gregorian chants that are still performed today; in fact, Hildegard is the first known European composer. She was also a playwright, and studied and practiced holistic medical healing.

HOWE, JULIA WARD (1819-1910) Howe was an American poet and advocate for **ABOLITION** and women's rights. She is best known as the author of the poem that, set to music, became "The Battle Hymn of the Republic," the unofficial song of the Union forces during the American Civil War. Her husband, Samuel Gridley Howe, was also a fierce abolitionist. After his death in 1876, Julia Ward Howe continued to advocate for social reforms, including **WOMEN'S SUFFRAGE**, and she helped found the New England Woman Suffrage Association. Howe was also the editor of *Woman's Journal* from 1870 to 1890, and, in 1908, was the first woman elected to the American Academy of Arts and Letters.

JORDAN, BARBARA (1936-1996) Jordan was an African-American legislator, educator, and civil rights advocate. She was the first woman to serve in the Texas legislature and the second black woman to serve in the U.S. House of Representatives. (The first was **SHIRLEY CHISHOLM**). She was a powerful speaker and renowned for her eloquence, intelligence, and deep commitment to the Constitution. She served on the Judiciary Committee that investigated President Richard Nixon during the Watergate scandal in 1974. Jordan retired from Congress in 1977 and began a distinguished teaching career at the University of Texas.

PERKINS, FRANCES (1882-1965) Perkins was the first woman to serve in as a U.S. Cabinet official. She began her career as a social worker and became an advocate of the labor movement as head of the New York Consumers League. When Franklin D. Roosevelt was governor of New York, he chose Perkins to be the state's labor commissioner. When he was elected President, he appointed Perkins as Secretary of Labor, a post she served in from 1933 to 1945. She helped to develop several of the major employment initiatives during Roosevelt's New Deal programs, and advocated for Social Security and minimum wage legislation. She later served as a professor of Industrial Relations at Cornell University.

RANKIN, JEANNETTE (1880-1973) Rankin was an advocate for **WOMEN'S SUFFRAGE** and a confirmed pacifist who was the first American woman elected to the U.S. House of Representatives. She began her career as a social worker, then became involved in the movement to gain women the vote on the state level in Washington. That benchmark was achieved in 1910, and Rankin then moved to Montana, where she helped guide that state's referendum on a woman's right to vote in 1914. In 1916, Rankin ran for and won a seat in the U.S. Congress. Pledging to work for a constitutional amendment granting all women the right to vote on the federal level, Rankin was also a pacifist, and in 1917 voted against the U.S. entering World War I. She served in the Congress until 1919, then left to devote herself to various organizations promoting suffrage and world peace. Rankin ran again for Congress in 1940, and was elected to the House from Montana. Once again, she faced a vote on American involvement in World War; once again, she voted against the war. She did not seek re-election, and spent the remainder of her life advocating for peace and women's rights.

MADAME C. J. WALKER (1867-1919) Walker was an African-American businesswoman who was the first self-made millionaire in the U.S. The daughter of slaves, she began a successful career in the cosmetic industry in the 1890s, creating products for African-American women at a time when business careers were not yet open to blacks or women. She was hugely successful, and shared her expertise with thousands of other African-American women, whom she hired and trained in business, allowing them to achieve financial success and independence.

IDA B. WELLS-BARNETT (1862-1931) Wells-Barnett was an African-American journalist and civil rights activist best known for her fearless crusade against the practice of lynching in the South. As a journalist living in Memphis, Tennessee, Wells-Barnett documented racial discrimination and the horrors of lynching in Memphis in her newspaper, *The Free Speech*. She faced great personal danger, yet continued to publish articles and speak out against racial violence. She moved to Chicago, where she continued to publish and also helped found civil rights organizations for women. Wells-Burnett was also one of the founding members of the NAACP (National Association for the Advancement of Colored People).

Historic Timeline

c. 1478 B.C.   Hatshepsut becomes Pharaoh of Egypt.

c. 1458 B.C.   Hatshepsut dies

69 B.C.   Cleopatra is born.

30 B.C.   Cleopatra dies.

c. 1412   Joan of Arc is born.

1429   Joan of Arc leads French forces to victory in the Battle of Orleans, during the Hundred Years War.

1431   Joan of Arc dies.

1451   Queen Isabella I is born.

1492   Ferdinand and Isabella conquer Granada. Christopher Columbus sails to the New World.

1504   Queen Isabella I dies.

1533   Queen Elizabeth I of England is born.

1559   Elizabeth is crowned Queen of England.

1603   Queen Elizabeth I of England dies.

1607   The first permanent English colony in America is founded at Jamestown, Virgina.

1612   Anne Bradstreet is born.

1630   Anne Bradstreet moves from England to Massachusetts.

1650   A collection of Anne Bradstreet's poems is published in England, making her the first American woman poet ever published.

1672   Anne Bradstreet dies.

1729   Catherine the Great is born.

1744   Abigail Adams is born.

c. 1753   Phillis Wheatley is born.

1762	Catherine the Great becomes empress of Russia.
1776	The United State declares independence from Great Britain
c. 1778	Sacagawea is born.
1781	The American Revolutionary War ends.
1784	Phillis Wheatley dies.
1793	Lucretia Mott is born.
1796	Catherine the Great dies.
1797	Sojourner Truth is born.
1803	The United States purchases the Louisiana Territory from France.
1804–1806	Merriwether Lewis and William Clark lead the Corps of Discovery on an expedition to explore the western U.S. from St. Louis to the Pacific Ocean. They hire a Shoshone guide, Sacagawea, at Fort Mandan, in mondern-day Bismarck, North Dakota.
1811	Harriet Beecher Stowe is born.
1812	Sacagawea dies.
1815	Elizabeth Cady Stanton is born.
1818	Abigail Adams dies.
1819	Clara Schumann is born.
1820	Susan B. Anthony is born. Florence Nightingale is born. Harriet Tubman is born.
1821	Clara Barton is born. Elizabeth Blackwell is born.
1830	Emily Dickinson is born.
1832	Louisa May Alcott is born.
1833	Lucretia Mott helps found the Philadelphia Female Anti-Slavery Society.

1840	Clara and Robert Schumann are married.
1844	Mary Cassatt is born.
1848	Lucretia Mott and Elizabeth Cady Stanton organize the first annual women's rights convention at Seneca Falls, New York.
1849	Elizabeth Blackwell graduates from Geneva Medical College, becoming the first woman to receive a medical degree from an American medical school.
1851	Harriet Beecher Stowe publishes *Uncle Tom's Cabin*.
1854	Florence Nightingale travels to the Turkish city of Scutari to care for the wounded British soldiers during the Crimean War.
1858	Emmeline Pankhurst is born.
1859	Florence Nightingale writes *Notes on Nursing*, an important resource for nursing studies.
1860	Jane Addams is born.
	The Nightingale School and Home for Nurses opens in London.
1861	The American Civil War begins after a Confederate attack on Fort Sumter, South Carolina.
1863	Susan B. Anthony and Elizabeth Cady Stanton begin the Women's National Loyal League, the first national women's association.
1864	Nellie Bly is born. Clara Barton becomes head of the field nurses of the Union Army during the Civil War.
1865	General Robert E. Lee surrenders his Confederate Army to General Ulysses S. Grant, ending the American Civil War.
1867	Marie Curie is born.

1868	*Little Women* by Louisa May Alcott is published. Elizabeth Blackwell opens the first medical school for women, in New York.
1869	Susan B. Anthony begins campaign for a constitutional amendment giving women the right to vote.
1875	Mary McLeod Bethune is born.
1876	Under the leadership of Lucretia Mott, the National Woman Suffrage Association publishes its "Declaration and Protest of the Women of the United States" at their annual convention.
1880	Helen Keller is born. Lucretia Mott dies.
1881	Clara Barton organizes the American Red Cross.
1883	Sojourner Truth dies.
1884	Eleanor Roosevelt is born.
1886	Emily Dickinson dies.
1887	Georgia O'Keeffe is born.
1888	Louisa May Alcott dies.
1889	Jane Addams opens Hull House to serve the poor immigrant population in Chicago, Illinois. Emmeline Pankhurst founds the Women's Franchise League in England.
1892	Pearl S. Buck is born.
1896	Clara Schumann dies. Harriet Beecher Stowe dies.
1897	Marian Anderson is born. Amelia Earhart is born. Margaret Chase Smith is born.
1898	Rachel Fuller Brown is born. Marie and Pierre Curie discover the elements polonium and radium.

1901	Margaret Mead is born.
1902	Barbara McClintock is born. Elizabeth Cady Stanton dies.
1903	Marie and Pierre Curie receive the Nobel Prize in Physics. Helen Keller publishes *The Story of My Life*. Emmeline Pankhurst founds the Women's Social and Political Union.
1904	Mary McLeod Bethune opens her Daytona Normal and Industrial Institute for Negro Girls, in Daytona, Florida.
1906	Susan B. Anthony dies.
1907	Rachel Carson is born.
1910	Elizabeth Blackwell dies. Florence Nightingale dies. Mother Teresa is born.
1911	Babe Didrikson Zaharias is born. Marie Curie wins a second Nobel Prize in Physics. She is the first person to win the award twice.
1912	Clara Barton dies.
1913	Rosa Parks is born. Harriet Tubman dies.
1918	Gertrude Elion is born.
1920	The nineteenth amendment to the U.S. Constitution, guaranteeing a woman's right to vote, is ratified.
1921	Helen Keller helps establish the American Foundation for the Blind.
1922	Nellie Bly dies.
1925	Margaret Thatcher is born.
1926	Mary Cassatt dies.

1927	Coretta Scott King is born.
1928	Emmeline Pankhurst dies.
	Margaret Mead publishes *Coming of Age in Samoa.*
	The British Parliament passes the Representation of the People Act, guaranteeing the right to vote for all women in Great Britain.
1930	Sandra Day O'Connor is born.
1931	Toni Morrison is born.
	Jane Addams becomes the first American woman to win the Nobel Peace Prize.
	Pearl S. Buck publishes *The Good Earth.*
1932	Amelia Earhart becomes the first woman to complete a solo flight across the Atlantic Ocean.
	Babe Didrikson Zaharias wins two gold and one silver Olympic medals.
1934	Marie Curies dies.
	Jane Goodall is born.
	Gloria Steinem is born.
1935	Jane Addams dies.
	Sylvia Earle is born.
	Eleanor Roosevelt begins the popular daily newspaper column, "My Day".
1937	Amelia Earhart dies.
	Valentina Tereshkova is born.
1938	Pearl S. Buck receives the Nobel Prize for Literature, the first American woman to win the award.
1939	Marian Anderson, denied the right to perform at Constitution Hall in Washington DC, gives a performance at the Lincoln Memorial.
1940	Wilma Rudolph is born.
1941	Barbara McClintock begins her genetic research at the

laboratories at Cold Spring Harbor, New York.

1945 Aung San Suu Kyi is born.
Eleanor Roosevelt is appointed the first U.S. delegate to the United Nations, where she helps write the Universal Declaration of Human Rights.

1947 Hillary Rodham Clinton is born.

1948 Margaret Chase Smith becomes the first woman to be elected to the U.S. Senate.
Mother Teresa begins her mission caring for the poor people of Calcutta, India.

1949 Pearl S. Buck founds Welcome House, the first organization to promote interracial adoption.

1951 Sally Ride is born.
Gertrude Elion discovers the chemical "6MP", a breakthrough in treating leukemia.

1954 Condoleezza Rice is born.

1955 Mary McLeod Bethune dies.
Rosa Parks is arrested for refusing to give up her bus seat to a white man, which triggers the Montgomery Bus Boycott, one of the first major demonstrations of the Civil Rights Movement.

1956 Mae Jemison is born.
Babe Didrikson Zaharias dies.

1957 Rachel Fuller Brown and Elizabeth Lee Hazen receive a patent for Nystatin, the first successful anti-fungal antibiotic medicine.

1959 Maya Lin is born.

1960 Wilma Rudolph becomes the first American woman to win three Olympic gold medals in track and field.
Gloria Steinem co-founds *New York* magazine.

1962 Jackie Joyner-Kersee is born.
Eleanor Roosevelt dies.

Rachel Carson publishes *Silent Spring*.

1963 Valentina Tereshkova becomes the first woman in space.

1964 Rachel Carson dies.
The U.S. government enacts the Civil Rights Act.

1968 Helen Keller dies.
Dr. Martin Luther King is assassinated.

1972 Gloria Steinem creates *Ms.* magazine.

1973 Pearl S. Buck dies.

1978 Margaret Mead dies.

1979 Sylvia Earle sets a new record by diving to a depth of 1,250 feet.
Mother Teresa receives the Nobel Peace Prize.
Margaret Thatcher is elected Prime Minister of Great Britain.

1980 Rachel Fuller Brown dies.

1981 Sandra Day O'Connor becomes the first woman Supreme Court Justice.

1983 Barbara McClintock receives the Nobel Prize for Medicine.
Sally Ride becomes the first American women in space.

1986 Georgia O'Keeffe dies.

1987 Toni Morrison publishes *Beloved*.

1988 Gertrude Elion receives the Nobel Prize for Medicine.

1989 Burmese government places political reformer Aung San Suu Kyi under house arrest.

1991 Aung San Suu Kyi is awarded the Nobel Peace Prize.

1992 Barbara McClintock dies.
Mae Jemison becomes the first African-American

woman in space.

1993   Toni Morrison receives the Nobel Prize for Literature. She is the first African-American to be awarded this prize.

1994   Wilma Rudolph dies.

1995   Margaret Chase Smith dies.

1996   Marian Anderson dies.

1997   Mother Teresa dies.

1999   Gertrude Elion dies.

2000   Hillary Rodham Clinton is elected as a Senator for New York.

Condoleezza Rice is appointed as National Security Advisor to President George W. Bush, the first woman to hold this position.

2005   Rosa Parks dies.

Condoleezza Rice becomes the first African-American woman Secretary of State of the United States.

2006   Coretta Scott King dies.

Sandra Day O'Connor retires from the Supreme Court.

2008   Hillary Rodham Clinton is named U.S. Secretary of State.

2010   Aung San Suu Kyi is released from house arrest.

Subject Index

This index contains the names, occupations, and key words relating to the individuals profiled in this volume.